Bibliographia Catholica Americana:

A LIST OF WORKS

WRITTEN BY CATHOLIC AUTHORS, AND PUBLISHED IN THE UNITED STATES.

BY

REV. JOSEPH M. FINOTTI.

PART I.

From 1784 to 1820 inclusive.

NEW YORK:
THE CATHOLIC PUBLICATION HOUSE,
9 WARREN STREET.

1872.

TO

MY HIGHLY ESTEEMED FELLOW-MEMBERS

OF THE

New England Historical and Genealogical Society,

THIS HUMBLE WORK ON KINDRED PURSUITS

IS CORDIALLY INSCRIBED.

BROOKLINE, MASS., September, 1871.

Si quel' un a commis quelque crime odieux,
S' il a tué son père, ou blasphémé les dieux,
Qu' il fasse un lexicon! S' il est supplice au monde
Qui le punisse mieux, je veux que l' on me tonde.

By way of

PREFACE,

I beg the reader to observe that I now publish only the *first* part of a work, the idea whereof suggested itself to my mind whilst I was cataloguing my private library. But, indeed, as the work was growing in my hands, I felt that

Quem Jupiter oderit Pædagogum fecit!

which words, 'tis true, apply in a direct sense to him of the ferula; yet, when I read them first, they were applied to himself by a lexicographer, who had labored under difficulties very much akin to that of my *cataloguing*.

Be that as it may, I intend—*adeste superi!*—to publish a list of works written by Catholics and published in these United States. I divide my list in five parts, as follows:

I. Works written by Catholics, and published previous to 1820 *incl.*

II. " Original, } from 1821 to 1873 *incl.*
III. " Translated, } from 1821 to 1873 *incl.*
IV. " Republications, } from 1821 to 1873 *incl.*

V. Addenda.

To this work I have allotted all *subsecivas horas* for some years, while it has also happened that at times I could not copy one single title for months. Duties too sacred to be neglected kept me busy at something else. The most favorable time for work was when an old-fashioned N. E. rheumatism (envious friends most perversely call it *podagra!*—my physician assures me *on oath* 'tis a slander) would at stated times confine me to an *otium cum dignitate,* days, weeks, and months, on a venerable armchair in my library. Fortunately, whilst the underpins of the animal fabric were all ablaze, the upper story was cool and free, ready to take in storage day and night. In sooth, it has been my harvest time. It has reminded me forcibly of the ancient saw, to wit: "'Tis an ill wind," etc.

I am under profound obligations to the Rt. Rev. Prelates who never tired with my importune demands for information, although they had often to search old records and write lengthy epistles. Many clergymen have also furnished me with valuable items. Among my correspondence I treasure letters from eminent laymen of all denominations. In only three instances have I been disappointed. But I can find a very satisfactory excuse for not receiving a reply: my letters were most assuredly miscarried. In only one instance a friend wrote "not to bother him any more." Amenities of literature!

Most earnestly do I beg of all who may feel an interest in the work to favor me, either by letter to my publisher or to myself, or through the press, with any correction, suggestion, or addition. I shall most gratefully make use of, and *acknowledge* them in the *Addenda*—for "blessed be the mending hand!"

The greatest pleasure I have found in the irksome work was when I discovered historical or biographical items which, I flatter myself, may one day prove useful to a competent historian of the Catholic Church in America—a work the sooner commenced, the better.

In one element my list is deficient: I mean the German element. My knowledge of the German language being rather inadequate for the task of examining books written in it, and some applications I have made having failed of their aim, I have had very little chance of adding the titles of German authors to my list. Should my work fall under the eye of some scholar who feels an interest in the matter, it will afford me great pleasure to place such titles as may be sent to me or to my publisher among the *Addenda*, faithfully crediting the contributors.

This seems to me the best fitting place to give some account of Bernard Dornin, to whom the place of honor will most assuredly be given amongst the earliest Catholic publishers in this country. Mathew Carey has done a great deal; but Mr. Carey devoted his energy and his talents and his money to every kind of publications. Mr. Dornin was the first *exclusively* Catholic publisher. For the following, alas! very scanty information I am indebted to Commodore Thomas Aloysius Dornin, U.S.N., of Baltimore. The gallant and veteran officer,* in a courteous reply to my enquiries, says: "My limited knowledge of my deceased father's career may be attributed to my having entered very early in my life into the navy as a midshipman, and, in fact, fresh from school, and having been kept very actively employed abroad, ... I was thus cut off from much family chat and family history." Then he informs me that Mr. Bernard Dornin removed to this country from Dublin in 1803. He left Ireland in consequence of his

* At p. 14 of the *Register . . . . of the Navy of the U. S.*, to January 1, 1866, I read the following entry: "COMMODORES. *Retired List.* T. ALOYSIUS DORNIN. Waiting orders. *Born in* Ireland; *appointed from* Maryland; *resided in* Maryland; *entered the service*, May 2, 1815; *date of present commission*, July 16, 1862; *in the service*, 50 *years* 8 *months*.

political opinions. He enjoyed the warm friendship of the Emmetts, Dr. McNeven, and Counsellor Samson, some of whom afterwards resided in New York. Soon after settling in New York, he set up an establishment in Newburg, N. Y., and another in Edenton [?], N. C., book-selling and stationery. Mr. Dornin enjoyed the warm friendship of Archbishop Carroll and of his successors, including Dr. Kenrick. He was esteemed an excellent writer, highly educated, gifted with a fine memory, which happily told in literary and social circles. At last he withdrew from business, and went to Ohio, to reside near his daughters, and died in 1836, aged 75 years. Mr. Dornin's name as a bookseller I find as early as 1805 in the "*New Testament.* Brooklyn: Printed by T. Kirk for Campbell & Mitchell. . . . . D. Smith & B. DORNIN, Booksellers. New York, 1805" (*O'Callaghan's Bibles,* p. 80, ad an. No. 3). From the titles of "Mumford," and "Fletcher," and "Elevation of the Soul," we learn that he was in New York in 1808, in Baltimore in 1809, whence he removed to Philadelphia in 1817. A little pamphlet (*Charity School, v. infra*) was published by B. D. in Baltimore, and bears the date 1807; but probably it refers to the establishment of the school, not to the date of printing. Laffan, the talented New York correspondent of the Boston *Pilot*, wrote once of Bernard Dornin :

"We believe that Mr. Bernard Dornin was the first *distinctively* Catholic publisher of the United States. He is certainly the first of whom we can find any trace in our notes. He was in business in 1820, if not earlier. Our friend, Mr. Eugene Cummiskey, of Philadelphia, was the next in order of time. He was the most eminent Catholic publisher in the country for the twenty years from 1820 to 1840. Our lamented friend, John Doyle, formerly of New York, and more recently of San Francisco, was a Catholic publisher and bookseller of distinction, from 1830 to 1849 or 1850. He had a wonderful partiality for the pro-Catholic writings of William Cobbett, most of which he stereotyped. His plates are now worked by the Messrs. Sadlier of New York."

In conclusion, I send forth the little work with many misgivings; nor would I publish it but for the urgent request of my friends.* In a work of

* "Rev. and Dear Sir :

"Since my return home I have thought over the matter, and am more and more convinced of the soundness of the advice which I gave you, to publish immediately your most interesting and valuable Bibliographia Catholica Americana.

"If you wait until such a work is perfect, you will never publish it.

"You have collected a great amount of curious Bibliographical and Biographical matter, which should not be allowed to pass into oblivion.

"The publication of your work will excite an interest on the subject, and will bring out additional information, which will enable you to perfect it in a second edition.

"It is a great mistake to suppose that such works are only curious or this kind, written amidst many interruptions, and unable as I have been to visit many public and private libraries, mistakes must have crept in. Let, then, this *Bibliographia* go forth as a pioneer. Scholars of keener scent and larger erudition, I hope, will follow me, and try to fix the landmarks of Catholic literature, and do justice, although a tardy one, to those great and good men who, amidst so many difficulties, have so earnestly, aye, successfully, worked in the cause of religion.

JOSEPH M. FINOTTI.

BROOKLINE, Mass.

interesting—they are most useful; and one of the best signs that the Catholic Church has taken root, and is growing up vigorously in this country, will be an increased interest among our people about everything connected with the planting and spread of our Faith in this part of the world.

"Bibliography is a sort of antiquarianism in which every one takes an interest.

"You may put me down as a subscriber for twenty copies if you publish it.

"Yours, with sincere regards,

"✠ J. ROSEVELT BAYLEY,

"*Bishop of Newark.*"

ABBREVIATIONS.

[ ]—Notes by the compiler.

V.—*vide;* cfr. *confer.*

B.B.—Library of the Bishop of Boston.

G. T. C.—Library of the College at Georgetown, D. C.

S. S.—Library of the Seminary under the Sulpitians, Baltimore, Md.

A. B.—Library of the Archbishop of Baltimore.

H. ✠ C.—Library of the College of Holy Cross, near Worcester, Mass.

F.—Library of Rev. J. M. Finotti, Brookline, Mass.

B. P. L.—Boston Public Library.

R. H. C.—Richard H. Clarke, Titles of M. Carey's Pamphlets.

Ath.—Athenæum Library, Boston.

J. G. S.—John Gilmary Shea, New York. Some titles I have copied from his list of "The First Catholic Books Printed in this Country" (Baltim. *Cath. Mirror*, June 2, 1860). It gives *sixty-eight* titles, down to 1820 *excl.* This particular reference is marked "J. G. S.—B. M." Not being certain, however, whether the list is made up from ocular inspection of the works quoted or only from *advertisements*, we can depend on it only *usquequo.*

R.—G. W. Richards, Esq., of Philadelphia, than whom a more prolific, accommodating, and interesting correspondent to aid me in my work I have not had. Alas! on the eve of my sending this copy to the printer, I receive (Sept. 10, 1871) the melancholy news of Mr. Richards's death. "He died at Burlington, N. J., on the 9th of last July, and is there interred at St. Paul's Church." He crowned his many years of courteous correspondence (I never knew him personally) by bequeathing unto me a selection from his valuable library. R. I. P. Mr. R. was an elegant writer. The titles of some of his works will be given in the Second Part of this *Bibliography.*

Earliest Records of Catholic Literature

IN

THE COLONIES.

A learned writer on *Catholic Literature in the United States* in the *Metropolitan* (Baltimore, 1854, vol. ii. pp. 69, 133, 198) remarks: "When the Pilgrims were yet in Holland, a Peruvian wrote, in Florida, the first of its historical books; Ulloa, the first Spanish Governor of Louisiana, is a well-known name in literature; Lescarbot, on the coast of Maine, composed his *Muses de la Nouvelle France* . . . ; Jogues, in the office of the Dutch commandant at Albany, wrote in Latin . . . the narrative of his sufferings, which Rome and Austria reprinted at length." *

1592. In Mr. Shea's *History of the Catholic Mis-*

* Louis de Oré, *Historia de los Martires de Florida*, 1604; Ulloa, *Histor. Relation of a Voyage to South America*, etc.; Lescarbot, 1615. [Carli, v. *infra*, wrote a continuation to Ulloa's work.]

sions among the Indian Tribes of the United States (New York, 1857), we read at p. 66: "More Franciscans were invited (to Florida) in 1592. . . . Meanwhile, the Mexican father, Francis Pareja, drew up, in the language of the Yamassees, his *Abridgment of Christian Doctrine,* the first work in any of our Indian languages that issued from the press." In the *Metropolitan* (Balt., 1856, iv. p. 662) we read, in an article on St. Augustine, Fla., "that the old Franciscan Convent is now the U. S. Barracks," and "here labored Pareja, compiling for the converts those works on Témuquana which are the oldest books in any of our Indian languages, and are now so rare that no price can be deemed extravagant."

1750. Some of Fénelon's works printed this year were sold in New York during 1870. I missed them, and have mislaid the *Memo.* (*v.* Fénelon).

1781. Chastelleux, *Travels in N. A.*, Dec. 7, 1782, v. ii. p. 305: "Mr. Beard . . . . an Irishman . . . . had long lived as a merchant in New York, and even *sold books.*" [Was he a Catholic?]

Before the Revolution, a few Catholic books were quietly printed in Philadelphia, such as *The Garden of the Soul, Following of Christ,* etc., and some Catholic books were apparently kept on sale near old St. Joseph's. A gentleman of one of our older Catholic families has a copy of *Bossuet's Exposition*, printed at London in 1735, in which his great-grandfather had written, "Obtain'd in Philadel., Nov. 28, 1766, this book." [Appendix IX. to *History of Catholic Church in New York*, by Rev. J. R. Bayley, 2d ed., Cath. Pub. Soc'y, 1870. I have in my library a copy of *Fr. Da Ponte's* (of Puente) *Meditations*, at St. Omer's, Anno Domini 1619, which had been in the Carroll family for many years previous to the War of Independence. Was not some Catholic book printed in N. Y. before the war, during the existence of a Catholic school there (*v.* Bayley's *History of the Catholic Church in N. Y.*, p. 31, N. Y. Cath. Pub. Soc'y, 1870)? The Catholics in the Colonies were put to great straits for Catholic books. A Jesuit missionary (Frambach?) copied the whole *Missal*, preserved, I think, in Georgetown College.

Two of the following titles are copied from Dr. O'Callaghan's work, *v. infra:*

1770–1774.

The | *Garden of the Soul:* | or, a | Manual | of | Spiritual Exercises | and | Instructions | for | Christians, who | living in the World | aspire to devotion. | The seventh edition, corrected. |

London: Printed. | Philadelphia: reprinted, | by Joseph Crukshank, in Market | Street, between Second and Third Street. | n. d. 18.

36 pp.; wood-cut Crucifixion facing title, pp. 14-20; Bible texts; p. 104, Benedicite, Dan. iii; p. 105, Ps. xciv; p. 106, Ps. xcix; p. 107, Ps. cii; p. 109, Ps. cxvi, cxxxvii; p. 110, Ps. cxlviii; p. 111, Ps. cl; Benedictus, Luke, p. 124–136, Vespers (Latin and English); p. 144–150, Complin English; p. 157–167, Seven Penitential Psalms. This is said to be the *first* Catholic Prayer printed in this country.—J. G. S.

[*V. Garden of the Soul, infra.*

Manual, A—of Catholic Prayers. "In the multitude of thy mercy, I will come into thy house: I will worship towards thy holy temple in thy fear."—Ps. v. 8. Philadelphia: Printed for the Subscribers, by Robert Bell, Bookseller, in Third Street. MDCCLXXIV. G. T. C.

Facing title-page, the *Crucifixion;* ante, three leaves, one having the title-page: *Proposals for Publishing by Subscription The Catholic Christian Instructed, etc.* By R—— C——. Same date as above. Another leaf contains Table of Contents, and the remainder gives a sample of the work. I am indebted to Rev. Fr. John Sumner, of Georgetown College, for this title. Such another early date must have been unknown.]

1784.

The | *History* | *of the* | *Old and New* | *Testaments,* | interspersed with | moral and instructive | reflections | chiefly taken from | the Holy Fathers. | From the French. | By J. Reeve. |

The Third Edition. | Philadelphia: | Printed by M. Steiner, in Race Street, | for C. Talbot, late of Dublin, Printer and Bookseller. | 1784. | 8vo. F.

Title and Preface, pp. i.–vi.; Subscribers' names, 2 pp.; Text, pp. 1–536 (*rectius* 436).

The | *History* | *of the* | *New Testament*, | interspersed with | instructive and moral | reflections, | chiefly taken from the Holy Fathers. | From the French. | By J. Reeve. | Philadelphia: | Printed for C. Talbot, late of Dublin, Printer and Bookseller. | p. 295; *verso*, blank. J. G. S.

["This is in my opinion the first book issued in this country by a Catholic bookseller. Of Talbot of Dublin I know no more, nor have I met another book with his imprint. T. Lloyd (*v.* Challoner, Unerring Authority, etc.) seems to have followed; then Carey and Dornin."—J. G. S.]

ABRIDGMENT *of Christian Doctrine; v.* Catechisms.

ACCOUNT, *A Short—of the Establishment of the New See of Baltimore, Md.*, and of Consecrating the Rev. Dr. John Carroll, first Bishop thereof, on the Feast of the Assumption, 1790. With a Discourse delivered on that Occasion, and the Authority for Consecrating the Bishop and Erecting and Administering the said See. London: Printed. Philadelphia: Reprinted by Carey, Stewart & Co. 1791. pp. 20. 12mo. B. B.

[Fr. Charles Plowden, S.J., is the author of both the

Account and the *Discourse;* b. at Plowden Hall, Salop, May 1, 1743, d. suddenly at Jougné, in France, June 13, 1821. He was on his way back from the General Congregation held in Rome by the Fathers of the Company of Jesus. The English lay-brother who accompanied him, unable to express himself in French, repeated so often the word *general* in connection with the father having attended the General Congregation in Rome, that the functionaries came to the conclusion that the deceased Englishman must have been a general, and he was accordingly buried with military honors. Fr. Plowden was Abp. Carroll's intimate friend and adviser through life; *v.* Allibone, ad n.]

ALEXANDRIA, *The—Controversy;* or, A Series of Letters between M. B. and Quæro, on the Tenets of Catholicity, which appeared in the Alexandria Newspapers. With Notes. Georgetown, D. C.: Printed by W. Duffy, Bookseller and Stationer. 1817. pp. viii.–266. 12mo. F.

[The controversy was carried on from May 9 to Dec. 1, 1817, between Rev. Roger Baxter, S.J., and Rev. Mr. Wilmer (who seems to have provoked it), an Episcopal minister of St. Paul's Church, Alexandria, Va. The *Alexandria Gazette*, Snowden, editor, published Baxter's letters, and the *Herald* his opponent's. I am told, on very good authority, that the controversy "made *one* convert to the Church, and he turned out badly"; *v. infra* Baxter. Next year appeared the following:

The Controversy between M. B. and Quæro, which appeared in the Alexandria Newspapers in the year 1817, on some Points of Roman Catholicism: to which is added an Appendix, containing a Brief

Notice of Luther . . . . of Indulgences . . . . of the Inquisition . . . . and of the Order of the Jesuits. By a Protestant. | Quot. Jude 3; St. Augustine de Un. Eccl., c. 16, Vinc. Lirin. | Alexandria: Printed by Samuel Snowden. 1818. pp. viii. and 236. 8vo. F.

[A much larger work, evidently taking advantage of the woman's privilege "to have the last word." This edition is scarce. I knew of it only after my work was in the printer's hands. The Rev. F. J. Sumner, S.J., who, on receiving my circular, most kindly searched the library of G. T. C., and sent me a list of titles, whereof some had been forgotten by me, adds to the Georgetown ed. of 1817 the following: "And the notes by G. Ironside, formerly an Episcopal minister of N. Y., now a Catholic layman."]

ALMANAC, The Catholic—*The Catholic Laity's Directory to the Church Service*: with an Almanac for the Year 1817. Price 25 cents. Contents: Abstract of the Directory; Explanation; Calendar; Explanatory Preface; St. Francis de Sales's Exhortation to attend Vespers; Suitable behavior in Church; Gother on Cleanliness; Extraordinary High Mass; New Year's Gift; Litany for a Happy Death; Obituary; Miraculous Events in Italy; Anecdote of St. Simon Stock; Dr. Milner's Account of an extraordinary Miracle; Reflections on Miracles; Churches, Colleges, Seminaries, Convents, and Benevolent In-

stitutions; O'Leary's Apology for Catholic Servants refusing to go to a Protestant Church; Particulars of a Prophetic Sermon lately published in England; The Thirty Days' Prayer; Ward's Errata—his Life, etc.; Spouse of Christ; Catalogue; Litany for the Dead; Catholic Magazine. New York: Published and sold by M. Field, 177 Bowery. pp. 68. 32mo.
F.

Two blank pages; next page, *Address to the Catholic Public*, soliciting communications. The paging begins with a title-page, as follows:

By permission of the Right Rev. Bishop Connolly: To be published annually, *The Laity's Directory to the Church Service*, for the Year of our Lord 1817. Being the first after Leap Year, and forty-first of the Independence of the United States of America. To which are added an Obituary, Biography, and an account of the Catholic Churches, Colleges, Seminaries, Benevolent Institutions, etc., etc., in the United States and Canada. Also, A New Year's Gift, and a variety of edifying and interesting information. With an *Almanac*, exclusive of all useless matter. New York: Published and sold by M. Field, at his Library, 177 Bowery, within a few doors of Delancey Street. . . . 1817.

[Daniel Fanshaw, 241 Pearl Street, was the printer of this work. The four pages unnumbered were perhaps intended as a circular or manifesto; pp. 64 68 contain the catalogue of a library well stocked, for the times, with Catholic books for sale. The *Directory* was not continued. The copy before me, faulty as it is, manifests a great deal of enterprise in Mr. Field, who announces also a *Catholic Magazine*, saying that "a periodical of this kind . . . . is in a state of preparation for publication," etc., etc., etc. Was it ever started? A printed prospectus of it was circulated.

Matthew Field was an Irishman by descent, b. in England; his family, intensely Catholic, left Ireland during the Rebellion: and resided in Stockport, England, in order to avoid prosecution. A brother or brother-in-law of M. F. was kidnapped for singing a rebel song, and was never heard from afterwards. The family came to America in '15 or thereabout. Matthew Field died of cholera in Baltimore (1832?). His son, Joseph M., was six years old when he came to this country, became a prolific and brilliant writer, a contributor to many magazines, a writer of fine plays, but died suddenly of asthma, in Mobile, 1856. He made no profession of religion, although he was baptized in the Catholic Church, and had also served as a clerk at the altar. He often wrote for the press under the pseudonym of "Straws." His talented daughter, Kate Field, baptized a Catholic, professes no determined religion, and has written valuable contributions to magazines and newspapers, often signing herself "Straws, Jr." Amongst her ancestors she reckons Nathaniel Field, a member of the "Shakespeare's Company," and author of *Woman as a Weathercock*. Allibone speaks of a Matthew C. Field, but his items do not square with our *family* information.]

ANDREWS, John—*An Attempt to Explain and Vindicate the Doctrine and Worship of the Roman Catholic Church.* By J. A., of Norfolk, Virginia. Norfolk: Printed by Shields, Charlton & Co. 1818. pp. 46. 8vo. Abp. B. & G. T. C.

[I have written more letters courting information on this

author than on any one else, but so far all my efforts have been fruitless. "The man with a library" in Va. never heard of him (April 6, 1870). But as I was preparing these pages for the printer, a friend at my elbow whispered another source of information—Dr. Thos. Andrews (Apr. 24, 1871). Letter written, but returned through the Dead Letter Office. Allibone seems to have never heard of him.]

APPLETON, Rev. Jas.—*Pious Lectures, Explanatory of the Principles, Obligations and Resources of the Catholic Religion.* Translated from *La Doctrine Chrétienne par Lhomond.* 1st American from the 8th Engl. Ed. Phila.: Printed for B. Dornin, at his Catholic Bookstore, corner of Walnut and 3d Sts. 1817. F.

Pp. xii. and 388; six pp. unnumbered Subscribers' names, and 12 pp. a catalogue of books, Prospectus of a Library, etc.

[This work can hardly be called a translation. Mr. A., at p. viii., calls it "a work taken from the French of" etc. Unknown to Allibone.]

ASSOCIATION.—*A Brief Account of the Female Humane* [Catholic] *Charity School, of the City of Baltimore.* Baltimore: Printed by Warner & Hanna. 1803. pp. 23. 12mo. Abp. B.

[Bishop Carroll, President. It was started in 1798 by some ladies from pity for the sufferings of poor women in winter. Then the charity was extended to poor girls also. A Catholic institution in its origin, it made no distinction of creeds.]

AUTHORITY, *The Unerring—of the Catholic Church in Matters of Faith*, maintained against the Exceptions of a late author in his answer to a *Letter on the Subject of Infallibility;* or, A Theological Dissertation, in which the Infallibility of the Church of Christ is demonstrated from innumerable Texts of Scripture, from the Creed, from the Fathers, and perpetual Tradition. To which are prefixed, Eight preliminaries by way of introduction to the True Church of Christ. "Seek, and you shall find."—Matt. vii. 7. London: Printed. Philadelphia: Re Printed for T. Lloyd. MDCCLXXXIX. pp. 208. 12mo. F.

[At the end, four pp. unnumbered Subscribers' names. Although published anonymously, it is the work of Dr. Challoner, Bp. of Debra and Vic. Ap. of London, b. Sept. 29, 1691, d. a. 1781, æt. 91. He became a Catholic when twenty years old; *v. Challoner and his Life*, by James Barnard, Lond., 1784.]

BADIN, REV. STEPHEN THEODORE—*Carmen Sacrum.* A Latin Poem, composed on occasion of Bishop Flaget's Arrival in Kentucky in June, 1811.

[Mr. Kean O'Hara, of Frankfort, translated it into English; *v.* Abp. Spalding's *Sketches of Kentucky*, Appendix No. I.]

—— *Epicedium.* A Latin Poem, written on the occasion of the Death of Col. Joe Daviess, at the Battle of Tippecanoe, Nov. 7, 1811.

[Dr. Mitchell, of New York, made a translation of it; *v.* A. S. *Sketches*, Appendix No. II.]

—— *The Real Principles of Roman Catholics in Reference to God and the Country.* A New Edition, carefully revised and elucidated with Notes. Dedicated to all Lovers of Truth. By a French Clergyman. "Sanctify the Lord Jesus Christ in your hearts, being always ready to satisfy every one that asketh you a reason of that hope which is in you." —1 Peter iii. 2. Bardstown (Ky.): Printed by F. Peniston. 1805. pp. iv.–96. 32mo. F.

[Is there an edition of 1803 at G. T. C.?]

[He signs his name in full at the end of the *Introduction*, dated "Bardstown, Aug. 24, 1805." On last page, after *Contents*, is written, "N. B.—A copyright shall be procured."]

"His Latin poetry, in praise of Perry's glorious victory over Britain's flag on Lake Erie, was, at the time, extensively circulated and admired."—*Cincinnati Catholic Telegraph*, April, 1833; reported also in the *Metropolitan Magazine*, Baltimore, 1853, p. 273.

[S. T. B., b. at Orleans, France, July 27, 1768; arrived at Baltimore on March 28, 1792; became *Proto sacerdos, i. e.*, the first priest ordained in the United States. Dr. Carroll ordained him in the old Cathedral of St. Peter's, Baltimore, May 25, 1793. Fr. Badin died in Cincinnati, O., April 19, 1853, æt. 85, within a few days of his sixtieth year of priesthood. The late V. R. Mr. Collins told me that after he had administered the sacrament of Extreme Unction to the glorious veteran, the latter remarked, "Poor Protestants! they have none of this." Fr.

Badin preserved his national vivacity to the end, always "on the go" for some holy purpose. When his portrait, a very fine one, was taken, a friend remarked, "Lo! the first time I see him still." It is unpardonable that the lives of men like Fr. Badin, Nerinckx, Richard, and such other pioneers of the Catholic Church should not have been written *in extenso*. The generation of Catholic priests connecting those heroes with us is fast passing away, and thus the sweet odor of their great virtues will vapor away from the memory of mankind. In the *Sketches of the Early Catholic Missions in Kentucky*, by M. J. Spalding, D.D. (the late venerated Archbishop of Baltimore), Bardstown, 1844, at p. 125, we read the following note: "A volume of considerable size might be made of the various writings of M. Badin, which are well worth preserving in this form. We have reason to hope that something of the kind will be hereafter published." Hereafter! . . . . Badin's name is not in Allibone, yet he was an American patriot, scholar, and writer.]

BAKER, Rev. P., O.S.F.—*The Devout Communicant;* or, Spiritual Entertainments for Three Days before and Three Days after Communion. With a Devout Method of Visiting the Blessed Sacrament, and some Pious Hymns, Fervent Prayers, Aspirations, Soliloquies, etc.; to which is added an Appendix, containing Spiritual Regulations, extracted from the Writings of St. Francis of Sales and the Rev. F. Valois, for the Use of People of every State of Life who aspire to Christian Perfection, etc. The whole Revised and Enlarged, by the Rev. William Gahan, O.S.A. The First American Edition, in which is inserted the Holy Mass, the Evening Office of the Church, etc., etc. Philadelphia: Published by Bernard Dornin, at the Catholic Bookstore, corner of Third and Walnut Streets. 1818. pp. xvi.–335. 18mo. F.

Verso of title, *Lydia R. Bailey, Printer*, pp. ii.-xi.; Preface, by Mr. Gahan, who mentions the author's name; pp. xii.–xvi., Contents. Eleven pp. taken up at the end with Subscribers' names; last page, advertisements of Catholic books.

[V. GAHAN *infra.*—Rev. Pacific Baker, O.S.F., is called by Dr. Oliver an eminent *spiritualist* (*i. e.*, ascetic). He wrote many ascetic works, among the rest *The Lenten Monitor*, and a controversial work on *Scripture Antiquity.*—Was Lydia R. Bailey a Catholic? She has printed books for B. Dornin; but she afterwards printed many of the anti-Catholic pamphlets in the Hogan controversy. A Francis Bailey printed a N. T. in 1780, Philadelphia, Market Street; and another was printed for J. Cruikshank, F. BAILEY, Young, by Stewart, M'Cullock, and J. Dobson, 1786. I. Thomas says that one Francis Bailey was a printer in Lancaster, A.D. 1772, and moved to Philadelphia after the war; but he there printed a N. T., 1780, v. O'C., p. 30, Thomas adds that he again returned to Lancaster, where, in 1797, J. Bailey and W. & R. Dickson printed a N. T.]

BARRUEL.—*The History of the Clergy during the French Revolution.* In Three Parts. By the Abbé Barruel, Almoner to her Serene Highness the Princess of Conti. Third Edition—First American. Burlington: Printed by I. Neale & H. Kammerer, June, MDCCXXIV. pp. xii.–423. 12mo. F.

[I am sure it is not Burlington of Vermont, but I have not been able to ascertain whether it is the Burlington of New Jersey. In my copy, pages ii.–xiii. (v.–viii. missing) contain *Preface to the English Edition,* which is a translation of the first French edition (1793); then no pages 1 and 2, but the *Dedication to the British Nation* begins at p. 3 in *italics,* and breaks off at p. 6. . . . . At p. 11 it takes up a continuation of *Preface to the First Edition.* This American edition is evidently printed on the *second* (first in the English language) *edition,* printed in Dublin by H. Fitzpatrick, 1794. It contains at p. xiv. *Dedication to the British Nation,* dated "London, where I write under the protection of the English nation. May 10, 1793. BARRUEL."—*Preface to the First Edition.* —*Preface to the English Edition.* Text, pp. 39. 12mo.]

—— *Memoirs, Illustrating the History of Jacobinism.* A Translation from the French of the Abbé Barruel. 8vo. F.

I. Part I. *The Anti-Christian Conspiracy.* Hartford: Printed by Hudson & Goodwin for Cornelius Davis, No. 94 Water Street, New York. 1799. pp. xviii.–226.

II. Part II. *The Anti-Monarchical Controversy.* Id. 16 pp.; iii.–v., Translator's Preface; vii. viii., Contents; i.–v., Preliminary Discourse; text, 264.

III. Part III. *The Anti-Social Conspiracy.* New York: Printed by Isaac Collins for Cornelius Davis, No. 94 Water Street. 1799. pp. xii.–256; p. 41, mystical alphabets.

—— *The Anti-Christian and Anti-Social Conspiracy,* an Extract from the French of the Abbé Barruel. To which is annexed *Jachin and Boaz;* or,

An Authentic Key to the Door of FREEMASONRY, Ancient and Modern. Lancaster: Printed by Joseph Ehrenfried. 1812. pp. viii. and 438. 8vo. F.

[A French edition (Londres, 1797–8), 4 vols. 8vo. B. P. L. For a notice of this excellent Jesuit, d. 1820, æt. 80, among his former confrères in France, *v. De Feller Dict. Hist.* and *L'Ami de la Religion et du Roi*, vol. xxv., pp. 401–11.]

BAUDRAN.—*The Elevation of the Soul to God, by Means of Spiritual Considerations and Affections.* Translated from the French of l'Abbé B. By R. P. First American from the Third London Edition. Two volumes in one. Philadelphia: Printed for Bernard Dornin. 1817. 12mo. F.

I. pp. iii.–v. Preface (by the translator?); vii.–ix., Contents; text, pp. 13–186. II. pp. 187–357; *verso* of last page the following:

BERNARD DORNIN RESPECTFULLY informs his friends that he has taken up his residence in the City of Philadelphia, conceiving it the most central part of the Union, and from which he means to continue disseminating religious instruction foı the edification of his Catholic brethren in the United States.

He has opened store at the CORNER OF WALNUT AND THIRD STREETS, Exactly opposite the *Establishment of Mr. Caldcleugh*, where he humbly solicits their kind patronage.

Seven unnumbered pages are taken up with subscribers' names.

[The above work is a translation from the French *L'Ame*

élevée à Dieu, par Baudran, 2-12mo, by Fr. Robert Plowden, S.J. First edition, 2-12mo, Exeter, n. d. Fr. Bartholomew Baudran, S.J., b. in Vienne (Dauphiné), d. July 3, 1787. An edition of all his works (16 vols. 12mo) was first published in Besançon, 1829.]

BAXTER, Rev. Roger—S.J. *Most Important Tenets of the Roman Catholic Church, fairly explained. "Quod ubique, quod semper, quod ab omnibus creditum est."* Vinc. Lir. Washington: Printed by Davis & Force, Publishers of the *National Calender.* 1820. pp. 76. 24mo. F.

[The work is dedicated to Abp. Maréchal, of Baltimore, from Richmond, Va., September 20, 1819. Roger Baxter, b. in Lancashire, finished his studies at Stonyhurst, came to the United States—as Rev. A. Elder, S.S., informed me—a deacon (with Rev. Mr. Fairclough, who, being ordained in Baltimore, was appointed, a secular priest, to St. Mary's, Alexandria, Va.), d. in Philadelphia, Pa., May 24, 1827, æt. 34. A marble monument stands over his grave. He was the author also of *Remarks on Le Mesurier's Sermon on the Invocation of Saints.* Perhaps it is the sermon on St. Aloysius, a copy whereof is preserved, I think, in G. T. C.; *v. supra, Alexandria Controversy.* In latter years he published *Meditations, etc.*, in connection with which some interesting items will be given in Part II. of this Bibliography.]

BAZELEY, C. W.—*Arithmetical Rules and Tables of Money, Weights, etc., etc.* Third Edition. Philadelphia: Printed for the Author, and sold at the house of the late P. Byrne. William Fry, Printer. 1816. pp. 48. 12mo.

[To which is added, in *uniform printing* but distinct paging—

—— *A Catechism;* or, Short Abridgment of Christian Doctrine. Newly Revised for the Use of the Catholic Church in the United States of America. To which is prefixed *A Short Daily Exercise.* Published with the approbation of the Rt. Rev. Clergy. Philadelphia: Printed for the Publisher. William Fry, Printer. 1816. pp. 48. 12mo. Abp. B.

[In the last chapter, *Catechism of Scripture Names, etc.*, are some not orthodox expressions. C. W. Bazeley acted as chairman in a pro-Hogan committee; *v. Hoganiana*, ad an. 1821, April. Not in Allibone.]

BENEVOLENT SOCIETY, *Rules and Orders to be Observed by the Baltimore* [Catholic]—established in order to raise a Fund for the Mutual Relief of the Members thereof in case of Sickness or Infirmity, and for any other Charitable Purposes to which the Members of said Society may hereafter agree. Baltimore: Printed by Samuel Sower. M,DCC,XCVI. pp. 15. 12mo. Abp. B.

[The Sowers (formerly *Souer?*) are an honored name among printers. Christopher was a printer in Germantown, 1735, and d. July, 1799 (?) in Baltimore, where Samuel was also a printer in

1796, and Brock in 1810, and B. W. in 1822. There exists now the firm of Sower, Barnes & Potts, Booksellers, 500 Market Street, Philadelphia.]

BIBLES.—*Old and New Testament.*

[In the collection of the following titles I have freely used the great work of my venerable friend, Dr. E. B. O'Callaghan, to wit: *A List of Editions of the Holy Scriptures and Parts thereof*, printed in America previous to 1860. With Introduction and Bibliographical Notes. Albany: Munsell & Rowland. 1861. For what regards the publication of the Catholic text in this country, I refer my reader to pp. xxiv.–xxviii. of the *Introduction* to Dr. O'Callaghan's work. John Gilmary Shea (than whom none has more laboriously worked for the preservation of the monuments of Catholic history in this country, and the list of whose works, original or edited, will form a very large contribution to the pages of my catalogue) published in 1859, by the Cramoisy Press, in New York, *A Bibliographical Account of Catholic Bibles, Testaments, and other Portions of Scripture Translated from the Latin Vulgate, and Printed in the United States.* pp. 48. 12mo. Mr. Shea, with great courtesy, placed the corrected copy of his work at my disposal (for any use I may need to make of it). I have returned it since,]

1787. *Selectæ e Veteri Testamento Historiæ.* Ad usum eorum que [qui ?] Latinæ Linguæ Rudimentis imbuuntur. Nova Editio, Prioribus multo emendatior. Philadelphia: Excuderunt Prichard et Hall, vico vulgariter dicto Market Street, et J. James, vico Chestnut Street. M.DCC.LXXXVII. (New York State Library.)

"This work was originally composed by a former professor of the University of Paris, at the suggestion of Mr. Rollin. It contains extracts of some of the historical parts of the Old Testament, and the Histories of Joseph and Tobias entire."—*Preface* (*v.* O'Callaghan, page 33, and "1804 *Selectæ*, and 1814 *Epitome*").

[This *is* a Catholic work, and we are much mistaken if it was not published under the direction of the Jesuit Fathers; *v.* Lhomond.]

1790. *The Holy Bible,* translated from the Latin Vulgate: diligently compared with the Hebrew, Greek, and other Editions in Divers Languages; and first published by the English College at Doway, Anno 1609. Newly revised and corrected, according to the Clementine edition of the Scriptures. With Annotations for elucidating the principal difficulties of Holy Writ. "Haurietis aquas in gaudio de fontibus salvatoris."—Isaiæ xii. 3. Philadelphia: Printed and sold by Carey, Stewart & Co. M.DCC.XC. 4. J. G. S. & Abp. B.

Two vols. bound in one; subscribers' names, pp. v.–viii.; at foot of page 284—

"N. B.—The third and fourth book of Machabees, as also the third and fourth book of Esdras (which some call the first and second of Esdras), and the prayer of Manasses, are here omitted, because they have never been received by the Church." This is the first American edition of the Douay and Rheims versions of the Scriptures, and is supposed to be the first *quarto* Bible published in English in the United States. It was originally advertised to be issued in forty-eight weekly numbers, the first of which appeared December 19, 1789. About twenty sheets were issued in that form, when the plan seems to have been abandoned, and the work was finally published on December 1, 1790. The types for the work were cast in the foundry of John Baine, Philadelphia. The text is reprinted from Challoner's second edition of the Bible, 1763–4, 5 vols. 12mo. The annotations are at the foot of the pages.

" In the following year," says Mr. Shea, page 10, " Dr. Troy's Bible—that is, the Rev. Mr. M'Mahon's revision of Bishop Challoner's translation, made under the direction of the Most Rev. Dr. Troy, Abp. of Dublin—appeared, and as the modifications met with general acceptance, Mr. Carey some years later issued a reprint of this also." (*v.* 1805.)

[We copy the following as a suggestion :

1797. St. Matthew, chapters v. 1–20, vi. 19–34, vii. 1–12 ; St. Paul's Epistle to the Romans, chapter xii. ; to the Colossians, chapter iii. ; St. James's Epistle, chapter i. (N. Y. Hist. Soc.) 8.

" These portions of the New Testament are contained in a volume entitled *Catholic Liturgy, or Forms of Prayer*, printed in Boston, by Isaiah Thomas, 1797."—O'C., page 54.

Might not this be one of the Catholic books published by Dr. Cheverus, as we mention *infra ?* However, considering that Isaiah Thomas has been very careful to omit the name of every Catholic printer in his work, even of Mathew Carey (although Thomas's work was published in 1810), we scarcely believe he would print a Catholic book unless under the pressure of *auri sacra fames.*

Since writing the above, we have been favored with the following title: "*A Catholic Liturgy, or Form of Prayer.* Christians of all Denominations may unite in these Prayers, as they allude to no Doctrines but such as are universally professed by all who call themselves Christians. Printed by Samuel Hall, No. 53 Cornhill, Boston, 1797."

Was it an Episcopalian dish served up, with some manipulation, for the benefit of the Unitarians? A copy of the work is to be found in the New York Historical Library.]

1804. *Selectæ e Veteri Testamento Historiæ.* Philadelphia: 1804. (Brown University.) 12mo.

V. 1787, *Selectæ*, and 1814, *Epitome.*

1805. *The* | *Holy Bible.* | Translated from the | Latin Vulgat: | Diligently compared | with the Hebrew, Greek, and other editions | in Divers Languages. | The | Old Testament, | first published by | the English College at Doway, A.D. 1609. | And the New Testament, | first published by | the English College at Rhemes, A.D. 1582. | With | Annotations, References, and an Historical and Chronological Index. | First American from the Fifth Dublin Edition. | Newly Revised and Corrected according to the Clementin edition of the Scriptures. | Philadelphia: | Published by Mathew Carey, | No. 122 Market Street. | Oct. 15, M.DCCC.V. | 4to.

Abp. New York and F.

Title, 1 f.; *verso*, blank; subscribers' names, 2 pp.; . . . . Hist. and Chronol. Index to the Old Test. (within rules) . . . . on *verso* of last leaf, "The Order of the Books of the O. T., and List of Plates in this Bible." This list is pasted over "The Directions for Placing the Plates," mentioned on next edition. Text: Gen. to 2 Mac., pp. 1–384; then 385*, 386*, 387*, 388*, 385, 568, 573–772. . . . .

The | *New Testament* | *of* | *our Lord and Saviour* | *Jesus Christ.* | Translated from the | Latin Vulgat: | Diligently compared with the Original Greek: | and first published by | the English College at Rhemes, A.D. 1582. | With | Annotations, References, and an Historical and Chronological Index. | First American from the Fifth Dublin Edition. | Newly Revised and Corrected according to the Clementin edition of the Scriptures. | Philadelphia: | Published by Mathew Carey, | No. 118 Market Street. | 1805.

Title, 1 p.; *verso*, blank; "Admonition," "Letter of Pope Pius the Sixth" and "A Prayer," 1 p.; "Decree of the Council of Trent" and "Order of the Books of the New Testament," 1 p.; Text, Matt. to Apocal., pp. 1–40*, 41–48*, 41–57, *verso* of 57 marked 70, then 71–214 . . . ; "Hist. and Chronol. Index to New Test. . . . ;" "Table of References," "Table of Epist. and Gosp. . . ."

The plates are:

1. Scheme of the Life of the Patriarchs.
2. Samuel anointing David. . . . . . *Tanner.*

3. Judgment of Solomon.

4. The Angel appearing to Elijah.

5. Map of Syria and Assyria.

6. The Shepherd in the Stable with our Saviour (marked, Page 46. Front to N. T.).

7. Land of Moriah. . . . . *Bower.*

8. Last Supper. . . . . *Tanner.*

9. Our Saviour in the Temple. . . . . *Tiebout.*

10. Miracle of Bethesda. . . . . . . *Tiebout.*

11. Travels of the Apostles. . . . . *Bower.*

My copy of this edition has no "Hist. and Chron. Index," nor the "Order of the Books in the O. T.," nor "List of Plates," as in Abp. N. Y., yet it does not appear that the leaves are torn off. No plates in the O. T., but in the N. T. as follows:

1. The Land of Moriah (front to N. T..)

2. The Evangelist St. Matthew (marked Page 1). *C. Tiebout, sc.*

3. St. John in the Wilderness (marked, Engraved for M. Carey, Philadelphia. . . . . 1805. Page 2).

4. Christ and the Centurion (marked, Page 6. Engraved for M. Carey, Philadelphia). . . . . . . *C. Tiebout.*

5. The Evangelist St. Mark (marked, Page 28. Engraved for M. Carey, Philadelphia). . . . . . . *C. Tiebout.*

6. The Evangelist St. Luke (marked, Page 44. Engraved for M. Carey, Philadelphia). . . . . . . *Tiebout.*

7. Jesus and the Lepers (marked, Engraved for M. Carey, Philadelphia. 1805. Page 54). . . . . . *Tiebout.*

8. The Evangelist St. John (marked, Page 75. Engraved for M. Carey, Philadelphia). . . . . . . *C. Tiebout.*

9. Jesus Washing the Apostles' Feet (marked, Page 88. Engraved for M. Carey Philadelphia). . . . *Tiebout.*

10. Map of the Travels of the Apostles (facing Chap. i. Acts). [One-half cut off.]

11. St. Peter healing the Cripple (marked, Page 98. Engraved, etc.) . . . . *C. Tiebout.*

[Every plate facing the page marked. On the left side corner, at the bottom and within the line, plates 2, 5, 7, 8, 9, 11, are marked with dots, varying from five to eight. Plate 3 has them at the right, where the engraver's name is usually signed.]

Another copy of the N. T. in my possession, otherwise corresponding exactly with the one described, contains a plate of the "Nativity of our Lord," front of title-page (marked Page 46. . . . *C. Tiebout, Sc.*), and one page with ornamental borders, "Family Record—Births . . . Deaths" (marked, 679); *verso*, "Family Record—Deaths . . . Deaths" (marked, 670); and the fragment of another leaf. Fronting the Gospel of St. Matthew a plate has evidently been cut off. This copy is printed on exceedingly bad, dark paper. It formerly belonged to St. Inigoes, Md.

1805. *Holy Bible.* Translated from the Latin Vulgat, etc. (as in the preceding title). Philadelphia: Published by Mathew Carey, No. 122 Market Street. Oct. 15, MDCCCV. 4to.

G.T.C., Sem. S.S.

The plates accompanying this edition are the same as those above described in my edition of the N. T., with the addition of "Map of Palestine" (front. to O. T.) and "Shepherds visiting the Infant Jesus and his Mother."

[J. G. Shea, l. c. p. 11, remarks: "The expression, 'First American from the Fifth Dublin Edition,' meaning only the first American edition of Dr. Troy's Bible, has led many to suppose this the first American Catholic Bible, and it is so mentioned in Dr. Cotton's *Rheims and Doway* and in Bohn's edition of Lowndes' *Bibliographer's Manual.*"]

The New Testament, etc. 4to.

"This is the N. T. described in connection with Carey's Doway Bible of this year (*v. supra*). It was, however, issued previously to the Bible."—O'C., p. 80.

1806. *New Testament.* Tenth Philadelphia Edition. Philadelphia: Printed for Mathew Carey. 1806.

v. Bible of 1805.

1807. *The | General History | of the Christian Church,* | from her Birth | to her | Final Triumphant State in Heaven: | Chiefly deduced from the Apocalypse of St. John, | the Apostle and Evangelist. | The Fourth Edition. | With a few Additional Remarks and Elucidations, | by the Author, | Sig. Pastorini. | Apocal. i. 3. | New York: | Printed by Hopkins and Seymour | for Bernard Dornin, Bookseller, | 136 Pearl Street. | 1807. | 12mo.

F.

Title, 1 f.; *verso,* blank; Editor's Address, pp. iii.–viii.; Introd., pp. ix.–xxii.; Table of Contents, pp. xxiii., xxiv.; Text, pp. 1–418;

the Apocalypse, pp. 419–456; Subscribers' names, pp. i.–viii.; *verso* of viii., Announcement of New Works, dated Dec., 1807. The Apocalypse in this edition is according to Challoner's text, 1749 (J. G. S.). Dr. Charles Walmesly, afterwards Vicar Apostolic of the Western District of England and Titular Bishop of Rama, was the author of this work. It appeared originally in 1771, and has been published in French, Latin, German, and Italian. O'C.

[A second American edition was published in New York by Doyle, 1834; *v. infra,* Pastorini. The preface states that it appeared originally in 1776. Dr. Walmesly, b. 1721, d. in Bath, 1797, 40th year of his episcopate, much esteemed for his great learning and sanctity of life. He aided in the correction of the Old Style, 1752, and contributed to the Philosophical Transactions. His manuscripts were unfortunately destroyed by fire.]

1810. *Le Nouveau* | *Testament* | *de Notre* | *Seigneur Jésus Christ,* | en Français, | sur la Vulgate. | Traduction de L. M. de Sacy. | Revue sur les meilleurs éditions. | Vol. I. (or II.) | Boston: | De l'Imprimerie de J. T. Buckingham. | 1810. | 2 vols. 8vo. 1st, pp. vii.–403; 2d, pp. 236. F.

The following is a copy of the approbation (at the end of second vol.):

"J'ai lu attentivement, et comparé avec la Vulgate cette nouvelle édition du Nouveau Testament, imprimée à Boston, par J. T. Buckingham. Elle est fidèle; le langage en est pur;

et elle ne contient rien qui ne soit entièrement conforme à la foi Catholique, Apostolique et Romaine.

✠ JEAN, Evêque de Boston.

"BOSTON, 22 Décembre, 1810."

The Text is in paragraphs, without notes, but with an introduction to each book concluding with a pious aspiration.

The version of the New Testament by Le Maistre de Sacy (b. in Paris, 1613, Director of Port Royal, d. 1684) and others appeared at Mons in 1667, but was condemned (by Clement IX., April 20, 1668, and *ed. Bruxellis* 1675, *sive aliis in locis*, Decr. Sep. 19, 1679, Innocent XI.) as made to favor Jansenism. A corrected edition accordingly appeared the same year [?], and subsequent editions omitting or correcting the censured portions were well received. Le Maistre de Sacy, in 1672–95, published a version of the whole Bible (or only the Old Testament (?), composed during three years' confinement in the Bastille), which was modified subsequently by [Carrières ?] Calmet and others. His edition of the New Testament, published at Paris in 1759, with approbation, has been taken as a standard, and was probably followed in this edition, although we cannot say so positively. Having been compared by Bishop Cheverus with the Vulgate and approved by him, 'tis to be presumed that it is after the standard edition.—See further, *Dictionnaire de Bibliographie Catholique*, ch. xi. and xii.

[Since writing the above, I found among my papers a letter of Dr. Cheverus to Mr. Thomas Walley, of Brookline, from which I copy:

"BOSTON, September 24, 1810.

"Dear Sir: I believe you have our 16th volume of *La Bible de Vence.* Be so kind as to send it by the bearer. The part of the New Testament which this volume contains is on the point of going to the press, and we cannot do without this book. . .

"I received yesterday a letter from the worthy Archbishop Carroll. I expect to leave this town for Baltimore either the 8th or the 15th of October. . . . The consecration will take place either on the Festival of All Saints or the Sunday within the Octave.

"With sincere and respectful friendship, yours,

"J. CHEVERUS."

The holy life of the distinguished first Bishop of N. E. has been described by able hands, but I fear my account of the divers sources of information will prove insufficient. The *Biographie Catholique* (Paris, MDCCCXLIV.) says: "On à publié dernièrement une excellente *Vie de M. Cheverus*, en 8vo et 12mo, 3me édition, . . . par M. l'Abbé J. Huen-Dubourg. L'Académie française, en couronnant cet ouvrage, s'est honorée."

Then we have *The Life of Card. C., Abp. of Bordeaux*, and formerly Bishop of Boston, in Massachusetts, by J. Huen-Dubourg, . . . translated from the French by E. Stewart. Boston: James Munroe & Co. 1839. F.

pp. iii–x, Translator's Preface (worth reading as to identity of the French biographer, p. iv); pp. xi–xxvii, Author's Preface and Contents of each page in the Text, of pp. 369, 12mo. pp. 372–389 contain an Appendix of Notes explanatory of the Text and refuting adverse remarks of Protestant papers made at the appearance of the Life. Mr. E. Stewart was a Protestant, according to the Preface of the French edition of '58.

Then, again: *Life of the Cardinal de C., Abp. of Bordeaux.* By the Rev. J. Huen-Doubourg, . . . translated by Robert M. Walsh. Philadelphia: Hooker & Caxton. 1839. F.

It is dedicated to Rev. J. J. Chance, then President of St. Mary's College, Baltimore, by the author, who calls himself *his pupil*, ix–xii, Preface of Translator; Text, pp. 13–265; pp. 267–280 contain Notes different from the Stewart edition, and the texts, although bearing similarity to each other, give evidence of two different hands. Of this Philadelphia edition, a distinguished American Catholic historian writes: "The real author is the Rev. Mr. Hamon, a Sulpitian." And Mr. Hamon is styled the biographer of Cheverus by other writers. (Hamon's *Treatise on Catechism.* Cincinnati: Walsh. 1861.) This puzzle is rendered more intricate by the following title:

Vie du Card. de Cheverus, Archevêque de Bordeaux. Par M. le Curé de Saint-Sulpice, Auteur de la *Vie de Saint François de Sales.* Cinquième édition. Paris: Lecoffre. 1858. F.

In the Preface, pp. 1–5, allusion is made to Mr. Stewart's translation. The Text, pp. 7–410, is more or less the original followed both in the Boston and Philadelphia translations. pp. 410–435, augmented; pp. 437–460, *pièces justicatives,* table, etc. The work is a neat French 8vo edition.

NOTE.—R. M. Walsh published also: *Sketches of Conspicuous Living Characters of France.* Translated by R. M. Walsh. Philadelphia: Lea & Blanchard. 1841. pp. 332. 12mo. F.

It contains sketches, among the rest, of Thiers, Chateaubriand, Lamartine, De La Mennais, Broglie, etc. It is a book both interesting and useful. Allibone mentions another edition of Cheverus's Life, by Mr. Walsh, of 1841. I have failed to secure it. Were the library of the Bishop of Boston *examinable,* I might glean some items of the earliest French editions of Cheverus's Life, but, in consequence of a temporary change of residence, the library may be considered boxed up. We hope to obtain a great deal of light from the forthcoming *History of the Catholic Church in N. E.,* by Rev. James Fitton. Boston: P. Donahoe.

Mr. R. H. Clarke has published a Memoir of Bishop Cheverus in the Baltimore *Metropolitan*, vol. iv., p. 457 ; *v.* also *U. S. Catholic Magazine*, vol. iv., 1845, p. 261.

Whilst correcting these proofs, I receive my much-esteemed friend Clarke's *Lives of the Deceased Bishops of the Catholic Church in the U. S., etc.* New York : P. O'Shea. 1872. It is a noble work, of great merit, written with a true appreciation of historical and biographical worth, and genuine fervor of Catholic feeling.]

1811. *New Testament.* Translated out of the Latin Vulgate. Philadelphia: Printed by Mathew Carey, No. 122 Market Street. 1811. 11 plates. 4to. J. G. S.

1812. *Epistles and Gospels in French and English.* Detroit: T. Mettez. 1812. *v. infra* Fleury.

1814. *Epitome Historiæ Sacræ.* Auctore L'Homond. Editio Nova. Quam Prosodiæ Signis, Novaque Vocum Omnium Interpretatione, adornavit Georgius Ironside, A.M. Novi Eboraci: Impensis Eastburn, Kirk & Co. Typis N. Van Riper (printer, Greenwich cor. Vesey). 1814. pp. iv. and 3–349. 18mo. F.

The Preface or Advertisement says: "The utility of the following Epitome has been already so far tested by experience, not only in France, where it was first produced, but in this country, that it stands in need of no eulogium. It has justly superseded the *Selectæ e Veteri Testamento* (*v. supra*, 1787 and 1804) of M. Rollin in its easiness and classical [God save the mark!] Latinity, and its neatness, brevity, and perspicuity atone for the prolixity of the other."

[It is not in O'Callaghan's list.]

Text, 3–101; p. 103, "A Dictionary of all the Words used in this Work, with their Signification, Derivation, and Prosodial Quantity"; *v. infra*, Ironside.

1814. *The* | *History* | *of the Holy Bible.* | Interspersed with | Moral and Instructive Reflections | chiefly from the | Holy Fathers. | From the French. | By J. Reeve. | In two volumes. | Vol. I. | New York: | Printed by J. Seymour, No. 49 John Street. | 1814. | 12mo. F.

Title, 1 f.; *verso*, blank; Contents, pp. iii, iv; Preface, dated Exeter, 1780, pp. v–viii; Text, pp. 13–220. Vol. II., Title (as above, except Vol. II.), 1 page; *verso*, blank; Contents, 1 page; *verso*, blank; Text, pp. 13–159; *verso*, blank; Subscribers' Names, pp. 161–163.

[J. G. S., in the Baltimore *Mirror*, quotes an edition by Seymour, 1812.]

—— *The* | *History* | *of the* | *New Testament.* | Interspersed with Instructive and Moral Reflections | chiefly taken from the | Holy Fathers. | From the French, by J. Reeve. | New York: Printed by J.

Seymour, No. 49 John Street. | 1814. 12mo. [In O'C.'s List.]

Contents, 2 pp.; Text, pp. 13–272; Subscribers' Names, pp. 173–175.

[Is not there a copy of 1802 in G. T. C.? J. R., as well as his two brothers, Richard and Thomas, were English Jesuits. J. R., b. A.D. 1733, d. May 2, 1820, æt. 87, at Ugbrooke, where he had resided, "the model of pastors," the last fifty-three years of his life. In Exeter, 1780, he published the *History of the Bible*, 2 vols. 12mo, which is wrongfully styled from the French, because, although it was at first a free translation of the *Abrégé de Royaumont*, he afterwards remoulded the whole work, as can be well proven by a collation of texts (see De Feller's *Dict. Biogr.*). Royaumont is a pseudonym assumed by Louis Isaac le Maistre de Sacy (*v. supra*), who is the real author, although by others it is ascribed to Nicholas Fontaine, who had been De Sacy's companion in prison. Says the preface to the Exeter edition, 1780: "The translator had not far advanced in his undertaking before he perceived that the author's intended brevity had made his performance, in many parts, defective and obscure; and that, to convey any tolerably clear and connected account of the sacred history, the rules of translation were to be set aside, and the text itself more closely attended to. It likewise appeared, upon a nearer examination, that the compiler, in some of his reflections, had not less studiously flattered his friends of Port-Royal than he had been partially severe, in others, upon the dignitaries of the Church, and in many of his passages had given such a turn to the thought and expression of the fathers, as was more calculated to support an enthusiastic system of theology than to promote the interests of true piety."]

1816. *New Testament.* Translated from the

Latin Vulgate. Philadelphia: M. Carey, No. 122 Chestnut Street. 4to.

It contains the same number of plates as one of the issues of 1805.—*Carey's Advertisement.* O'C.

1817. *The New Testament of our Lord and Saviour Jesus Christ.* Translated from the Latin Vulgate: Diligently compared with the Original Greek: and first published by the English College of Rhemes, ANNO 1582. With Annotations. Newly Revised and Corrected according to the Clementin Edition of the Scriptures. Georgetown, D. C.: Printed by W. Duffy, Bookseller and Stationer. 1817. pp. 516. 12mo. F.

[Page 3, Admonition; 4, Letter of Pope Pius VI. to A. Martini, approving of his translation into Italian, 1778; 5, Approbation in Latin of the Universities of Rhemes and Doway. 6, Approbation of the Theological Faculty, given A.D. 1748, and the following:

GEORGETOWN, February 20, 1817.

Having had this edition of the *New Testament*—printed in Georgetown, by William Duffy—examined, it has been found strictly conformable to the Dublin edition of the same work, printed 1811, and also that printed 1814. Hence I permit it to be published,

LEONARD, Archbishop of Baltimore.

Text, pp. 1–507; page 507, *verso:* N. B.—In the following Table, the titles of the books and the order of the Psalms are quoted, as they are set down in the Protestant Bible; pp. 509–

513, "A Table of Controversies"; pp. 114–116, "A Table of Epistles and Gospels for all the Sundays and Holidays throughout the Year; six pp., unnumbered, of Subscribers' Names. (One Joseph Idley, of New York, subscribes to five hundred, and Carey, of Philadelphia, to two hundred and fifty.

In title copied by Dr. O'C.: "*Verso* of seventh page, Catalogue of Books for sale by William Duffy, and the following notice: 'W. Duffy has now in the press a splendid edition of the Douway Bible, in quarto, illustrated with plates by the first artists in America, which will be delivered to subscribers at $10, elegantly bound.' There are brief headings to the chapters, and notes at foot of pages. The projected edition of the Bible mentioned above was, we are informed, never published."

Rev. W. Taylor concludes a preface to the *Christian Monitor*, A.D. 1819 (*v. infra*), thus: "I beg leave to announce to the Roman Catholics of this country my intention of causing to be published in this city an edition of the Douay translation of the Scriptures with approved notes selected and translated from unexceptionable commentators and expositors. I reckon on the co-operation of the prelates and of my brother clergymen in the United States. A Prospectus in a few days will be circulated to obtain a sufficient number of subscribers, etc. W. T." "But," remarks Mr. Shea, "how far he proceeded in his attempt I have not learned" (p. 12, l. c., *v. infra*, Taylor). For a notice of Abp. L. Neale *v. Catholic Almanac*, Baltimore, 1835, p. 37, and Creagh's *Laity's Directory*, New York, 1822, p. 131, and Clarke's *Lives of Bishops*, i. 116.

Bernard Dornin, at page 357 (*verso*) of his *Elevation of the Soul*, Philadelphia, 1817, advertises: "In a few days he (B. D.) will submit to his reverend friends a prospectus for publishing an edition of the *Doway Bible and Testament*, in royal octavo, price about five dollars." It was not published.

NOTE.—I herewith subjoin a list of names, connected with printing, publishing, or selling of Protestant Bibles, which generally belong to Catholic families:

Boston, - - -	B. Larkin, - - -	1794.
New Haven, - -	Edw. O'Brien, - -	1797.
Baltimore, - - -	Butler (a), - - -	1801.
" - - -	Butler, - - - -	1802.
Northampton, - -	W. Butler, - - -	1802.
New York, - - -	M'Dermot, - - -	1803.
Boston, - - -	E. Larkin, - - -	1803.
Baltimore, - - -	Butler, - - - -	1803.
Northampton, - -	W. Butler, - - -	1803.
Philadelphia, - -	Rob. Carr, - - -	1804.
New York, - -	C. Flanagan, - - -	1805.
Greenfield, Mass., -	John Macgowan, - -	1805.
New York, - -	B. Dornin, - - -	1805.
" - -	Rob. M'Dermut, - -	1806.
Hartford, - - -	Gleason, - - -	1806–7.
Boston, - - -	E. Larkin, - - -	1809.
Baltimore, - - -	John Hagerty, - -	1810.
Philadelphia, - -	Sweeny, - - -	1811.
Baltimore, - - -	John Hagerty, - -	1811.
Middlebury, Vt., -	J. Cunningham, - -	1812.
Boston, - - -	E. Larkin, - - -	1813.
Philadelphia, - -	E. Foley, - - -	1813.
" - -	Hogan, - - - -	1816.
Albany, - - -	E. F. Backus, - - -	1816.

It is remarkable that according as the Catholics became more numerous, such names disappear from the titles of Protestant publications. However much the list I have made out may seem superfluous, I think it may yet elicit remarks and investigations that will illustrate a particular page of American Catholic bibliography.

(*a*.) From 1803 to 1809 inclusive, one John Butler was the printer of the *Ordo* in Baltimore. From 1790 to 1820 exclusive, Mathew Carey, of Philadelphia, published different editions of the Bible, as follows:

H. B., HOLY BIBLE; N. T., NEW TESTAMENT; c., CATHOLIC; p., PROTESTANT.

1790, H. B., c.; 1801, 2 H. B., p.; 1802, H. B., p.; 1803, 4 H. B., p.; 1805, 1 H. B., c., 2 H. B., p., 1 N. T., c.; 1806, 2 H. B., 1 N. T., p.; 1807, 1 H. B., 1 N. T., p.; 1808, 2 H. B., p.; 1809, 3 H. B., p.; 1810, 2 H. B., p.; 1811, 2 H. B., 1 N. T., p.; 1812, 1 H. B., 1 N. T., p.; 1813, 1 H. B., p.; 1814, 2 H. B., p.; 1815, 3 H. B., p.; 1816, 2 H. B., p., 18 different advertisements, 1 N. T., c., 1 N. T., p.; 1817, 2 H. B., p.; 1818, 2 H. B., p.; 1819, 1 H. B., p.

Protestant, 59; Catholic, 4. Total, 63.

BICHAT, MARIE FRANCOIS XAVIER.—*Physiological Researches upon Life and Death.* Translated by J. Watkins. 1st American Edition. 1809.
B. P. L.

—— *Treatise on the Membranes.* New Edition, with Life, by Husson. Translated by J. G. Goffin. Boston. 1813. B. P. L.

[Bichat, the greatest anatomist of his day, was born at the Jura, November, 1771. Of him writes Bishop Bruté in his journal: "1801, 3 *Thermidor* (July 22, 1802).—Xavier Bichat died this morning at four o'clock, 31 years of age, enjoying the very highest reputation in his profession, and giving the greatest promise for the future. All his pupils [Bruté one of them] loved him. His father and mother were excellent people, very pious, and brought him up in the most Christian manner. When he first came to Paris, he lived with his aunt, Madame Bouisson, and was very regular in the practice of his Christian duties, but afterwards, when he went to live with Dessant, he became careless. Dessant's widow, with whom he still lodged when attacked by his last sickness, watched with the greatest care to keep him from seeing a priest; but yesterday evening the Abbé Pinlibert, his former confessor (and who had been so zealous in assisting the persons guillotined during the Reign of Terror), made out to go to his bedside, and gave him absolution *in extremis.* Bichat, however, never gave in to the reigning impiety, and was unimpeachable in his morals; but he was led away by his love of science and reputation. Let us pray to God for the repose of his soul."—*Bp. Bruté's Life,* by Bp. Bayley. New York: J. G. Shea. 1870. 2d edition. pp. 211. Other works of Bichat, published in the U. S. previous to 1820, I have seen lately advertised for sale at public auctions in N. Y., but, alas! the *marsupium* might be used for a foot-ball!]

BLYTH.—*Apology for the Conversion of Steph. Cleveland* ——. New York: Desnoues. 1815. pp. 64. 12mo. B. B.

[Steph. Cl. B., b. in Salem, Mass., Jan. 20, 1771, after trying many sects, Mohammedanism included, received the first impression of faith in reading Massillon, and was received in the Church by Bp. Cheverus, Whitsunday, 1809. In connection with Mr. Blyth's authorship, I have *A Letter to Mr. S. C. B. occasioned by the Recent Publication of the Narrative of his Conversion to the Romish Faith.* In four parts. By a Catholic Christian. Montreal: Printed by Nahum Mower. 1822. pp. iv and 288. 12mo. This latter work was written in response to a second edition of Blyth's. For some notice of Desnoues, *v. infra,* O'Conor.]

BONAPARTE, Lucien.—*Charlemagne; or, The Church Delivered.* An Epic Poem, in twenty-four Books. By Lucien Bonaparte, of the Institute of France, etc. Translated by the Rev. S. Butler, D.D., and the Rev. Francis Hodgson, A.M. Philadelphia: Published by John Conrad & Co. J. Maxwell, Printer. 1815. 2 vols. 18mo. F.

I. p. v, To His Holiness, Pope Pius VII, signed, "Your Holiness' Most Faithful and Devoted Son in Jesus Christ, Lucien Bonaparte. Rome, May, 1814." Prefaces, etc., pp. vii–xxii; Text, pp. 23–285. II. pp. 287.

B. born 1775, in Ajaccio, d. at his Principality of Canino, near Viterbo, June 29, 1840, æt. 65. Pope Pius VII. had great regard for him. Lucien always opposed his brother Napoleon's measures against the Sovereign Pontiff, and also refused to accept a throne from him. Other works of his have been published in America, I believe. Allibone does not mention this work in connection with Butler, head-master of Shrewsbury School, 1798, Bp. of Lichfield, 1836. For Butler and Hodgson, see *Lond. Gent. Mag.*, Apr., 1853, and Feb., 1840.

——, Louis.—*Maria; or, The Hollanders.* By Louis Buonaparte. Boston: Published by John Eliot & Cumming, and Hilliard. 1815. 2–18mo. F.

I. iii–x, Preface, signed E. A. K., Feb. 6, 1814; pp. 11–216. II. pp. 215.

[L. B., b. September 2, 1778, in Ajaccio; d. at Leghorn, July 25, 1846. He was the father of the late Emperor L. N.; he was a man of excellent qualities of heart and mind.]

BORDALOUE. *v.* Massillon.

BOSSUET, J. BENIGNE.—*An Exposition of the Doctrine of the Catholic Church in Matters of Controversy, and a Letter on the Adoration of the Cross.* Translated from the French by the Rt. Rev. W. Coppinger. The third edition. Published by and with the Authority of the Rt. Rev. Bp. Carroll. Price 50 cents. New York: Printed for B. Dornin. Hopkins, printer. 1808. 12mo.
G. T. C.

—— *Sermons, Select and Funeral Orations.* Translated from the French of B., Bp. of Meaux. To which is prefixed an Essay, considerably augmented, on *The Eloquence of the Pulpit in England.* 1st American edition. Boston: Printed by David Carslile for J. Nancrede, No. 49 Marlborough Street. 1803.

["Adapted for the use of Protestants."—J. G. S.]

BOTTA, Charles Jos. William.—*History of the War of the Independence of the U. S. of America.* Translated from the Italian by George Alexander Otis. Philadelphia: Printed for the Translator. J. Maxwell, printer. 1820–21. 3–8vo. F.

[In subsequent editions valuable additions have been made. B. wrote his history and published it in Paris in Italian. 1809. —F. Is there not an American copy of 1810 at Saint Sulpice, Baltimore? B. was the first historian of our Independence war. Objections have been made against my reckoning Botta among *Catholic* authors. Yet he was born and reared a Catholic, and died in full communion with the Church. If the Index has condemned some of his other works, it was *donec corrigantur.*]

BRADY and EDELEN.—*Correspondence* between the Rev. M. B. [Prot.], Rector in St. Mary's County, Md., and Rev. L. E. [Cath.], Pastor in Newtown, same county. Washington: Davis & Force. 1819. pp. 43. 8vo. F.

[The correspondence was occasioned by a report that Rev. L. Edelen had burnt a Protestant Bible. To Rev. Joseph E. Keller, Provincial Superior of the Jesuit Province of Maryland, I am indebted for the following: "Rev. Leonard Edelen was born in St. Mary's Co., Md., A.D. 1783. Received into the Company of Jesus, by Fr. Robert Molineux, Oct. 10, 1806; professed in Georgetown, Oct. 10, 1808. Bishop L. Neale gave him Tonsure and minor orders, June 8, 1808, in Trinity Church,

Georgetown; Subdeaconship, June 8; Deaconship, June 10; Priesthood, June 11. On Feb. 2, 1821, he was admitted to the profession of Spiritual Coadjutor in the same church, Rev. A. Kohlman officiating. d. at Newtown, St. Mary's Co., Md., Dec. 21, 1823, æt. 40. He was in Philadelphia in 1809, was sent to Newtown, Md., in 1811, and remained there to his death. Fr. Edelen is remembered as an excellent, worthy man."]

BROSIUS, Rev. F. X.—*A New and Concise Method of Finding the Latitude by Double Latitudes of the Sun.* Dedicated to the Boston Marine Society. Cambridge: Hilliard & Metcalf. 1815. pp. 51. 8vo. Bost. Athen.

["With regard to Fr. Brosius, I understood from Rev. Mr. Gallitzin's own lips that he was deputed by his venerable mother to accompany her son to America from Munster in Germany. After a few years in the U. S., he returned to Germany. The Rev. Prince told me that Rev. Brosius wrote to him from Germany, urgently advising him to return, 'that no doubt they would make him a bishop'—little did they know his humility! I have a traditionary knowledge that Fr. Brosius was principal of a college near Philadelphia, called Mount Airy. Rev. Mr. Gallitzin always praised him as 'a pious and learned priest.'"—Letter of V. Rev. T. Heyden, Bedford, Pa.

Mr. Brosius left the Diocese of Boston shortly after his arrival there, 1816 or 1817; *v. Catholicity in N. E.*, in *Boston Catholic Observer*, May 29, 1847. I am indebted to Rev. J. B. Purcell, of the Boston Cathedral, for the following: "The first record of Dr. Brosius (in the *Book of Baptism*) I find April 14, 1816, and the last one June 28, 1816." Rev. Mr. Brosius' name will be found among the subscribers to *Turberville's Manual*, Philadelphia, 1806.

v. Cavallo, *infra ; v.* also conclusion of *Livingston's Conversion.* Brosius not in Allibone, yet he wrote in English and in America.]

BRUTE, Rt. Rev. Simon Gabriel.

[There is no need of my sketching the life of this eminent prelate of the Catholic Church in the U. S. after the works, a list whereof I give below. But Mr. Bruté is said to be the author of the *Seminary of St. Sulpice ; v. infra*, cfr. *Baltimore Cath. Alm.*, 1843, p. 36, *seq.*; where the biographer, whimsically enough, it seems, insists on spelling the prelate's name *Bru-te :* why ?—Bishop Bayley, of Newark, N. J., has published *Memoirs of the Rt. Rev. Simon W. Gabriel Bruté, First Bishop of Vincennes, etc., etc.* New York : D. & J. Sadlier & Co. 1861. But—a puzzle to us—a previous edition on large paper was issued : New York : John Gilmary Shea. MDCCCLX. Unfortunately, '61 copies all the mistakes of '60, and '60 all those of '61. And Lady Herbert, lacking the grace and discretion of consulting the author, makes a compendium of the Life for the benefit of the *Foreign Missionary Series* (London : Burns, Oates & Co., n. d.) in 1870 (?), and stereotypes again all the mistakes of the original American blundering printers. But, was another edition, 1865, published by P. O'Shea (?), all from the same plates ! cfr. Clarke.]

BURKE, Ædanus.—*Address to the Freemen of South Carolina.* By Cassius. Philadelphia: R. Bell. 1783. pp. 33, 8vo.

[This must be the address made for the purpose of having a system of lenity adopted towards American tories, since hostilities had ceased.

b. 1747, in Galway, Ireland, Burke emigrated to America, became Chief-Justice of S. C. and M.C. He had studied at St. Omer's for the priesthood. He died in 1803.]

☞ Adv't: Now selling at Bell's Bookstore, near St. Paul's Church, in Third Street, Philadelphia. Price one-sixth of a dollar:

Considerations | *on the* | *Society or Order* | *of* | *Cincinnati;* | Lately Instituted | by the Major-Generals, Brigadier-Generals, and | other Officers of the American Army. | Proving that it Creates | A RACE OF HEREDITARY PATRICIANS, | or | NOBILITY. | Interspersed with Remarks | on its Consequences to the Freedom | and Happiness of the Republic. | Addressed to the People of South- | CAROLINA and their REPRESENTATIVES. | By Cassius. | Supposed to be written by ÆDANUS BURKE, Esquire, | one of the Chief-Justices of the State of South-Carolina. | 'Blow ye the trumpet in Zion."—*The Bible.*

Here is the title of Mirabeau's translation: *Considérations sur l'Ordre de Cincinnatus;* ou, Imitation d'un Pamphlet Anglo-Américain. Par le Comte de Mirabeau. Suivies de plusieurs Pièces relatives à cette Institution; d'une Lettre signée du Général Washington: accompagnée de Remarques par l'Auteur *François;* Et d'une Lettre de feu monsieur Turgot, Ministre d'Etat en France, au Docteur Price, sur les Legislations *Américaines.* "The glory of soldiers cannot be completed without acting well the part of citizens." La gloire des Guerrieres ne sauroit être complète, que lors qu'il savent remplir les devoirs des Citoyens. *Lettre circulaire au Société d'Etat de l'Ordre des Cincinnati, signée du Général* Washington. A Londres: chez J. Johnson, St. Paul's Churchyard. M.DCC.LXXXIV. pp. xij and 203. 12mo. F.

Burke's pamphlet called forth the *Observations on a Late Pamphlet entitled "Considerations upon the Society or Order of the Cincinnati,"* clearly evincing the Innocence and Propriety of that Honourable and Respectable Institution. In answer to Vague Conjectures, False Insinuations, and Ill-founded Objections. By an Obscure Individual. (Quot. from Thompson and Junius.) Philadelphia: Printed and sold by Robert Bell, in Third Street. Price one-fourth of a dollar. M.DCC.LXXXIII. pp. 28. 8vo. F.

[Was it not by Brig.-Gen. Moylan?

"Burke's pamphlet on the Society of the Cincinnati produced a sensation at the time of its publication. Judge Burke accused the Society of aiming at the establishment of an hereditary order in the State, and denounced it vehemently as an utterly unrepublican association. Randall, in his *Life of Jefferson,* affirms that the appearance of this pamphlet was the signal for a general onslaught on the society. 'The Governor of South Carolina condemned it in an address. The Legislatures of at least three States (Massachusetts, Pennsylvania, and Rhode Island) passed resolutions of censure. Our plenipotentiaries in Europe wrote home, expressing mortified regrets that all our previous doctrines of government were thus repudiated. The friends of popular freedom in Europe generally, who had sympathized with the cause in America, joined in these mortifications and regrets. Four out of five, probably, of the entire population of the United States took the same view of the subject.' (*Life of Jefferson,* by Hon. Henry S. Randall, vol. i. pp. 406, 407.) Alexander Johnston, in his eulogistic *Account of the Society of the Cincinnati,* admits that the pamphlet of Ædanus Burke, an eccentric Irishman (was he or was he not a citizen, and, consequently, an American?) who held a seat on the Supreme Bench of South Carolina, 'was ably written, and caused no little sensation.' He mentions the confirmatory action of several States through their legislatures, and adds that: 'The consternation crosses the Atlantic. The celebrated Mirabeau, . . . then an exile in London, . . . edited a French version of Burke's pamphlet, with copious annotations, in which he was assisted by his friend and faithful adherent, Nicholas Chamfort.' (*Memoirs of the Historical Society of Pennsylvania*, vol. vi. pp. 27, 28.) Judge Burke's elevation to the Bench of South Carolina dated back to the year 1778. (Ramsay's South Carolina edition of 1858, vol. ii. p. 87.)"—*Laffan* (*M. Hennessey*), *N. Y. correspondent Boston Pilot*, April, 1868.

The following notice of an eminent Irish Catholic, a founder of the Order of Cincinnati, from the same pen, will be read with interest:

"Colonel Stephen Moylan's Cavalry was the regiment known as the 4th Light Dragoons in the Continental service. The regiment was organized early in 1777, and all through the war for Independence it did noble work against the 'hereditary enemy.' At the close of that war, its commander ranked as a full brigadier-general, and in the subsequent years of his life he was always called General Moylan. *He was one of the founders of the Society of the Cincinnati.* He died in Philadelphia, on the 11th of April, 1811 (which was a fast-day in Pennsylvania), and was interred in the burial-ground of St. Mary's Church, South Fourth Street. . . . Gen. Moylan was the first and last president of the Society of the Friendly Sons of St. Patrick, Philadelphia, of the history of which we have already given a sketch in our *Records*. . . . He was a brother of the Right Rev. Francis Moylan, Roman Catholic Bishop of Cork, Ireland, from 1787 to 1815, and the intimate friend of the Right Rev. Daniel Delany, Roman Catholic Bishop of Kildare from 1787 to 1814, of whom Mr. Fitzpatrick (in his deeply interesting

Life, Times, and Correspondence of the Right Rev. Dr. Doyle, as published by Mr. Donahoe, six years ago) makes quaint mention. 'Dr. Moylan idolized Dr. Delany, and the Bishop of Kildare was often for three months on a visit with his Right Rev. brother of Cork.' (*Life, etc., of Dr. Doyle,* vol. i, p. 132.) . . . Three other brothers of Gen. Stephen Moylan, namely, Jasper, James, and John Moylan, all took an active part in the establishment of the independence of the United States. They were, of course, all Roman Catholics. Jasper was an able, though not brilliant, member of the Bar of Philadelphia. His practice was extensive. In 1797, his office was at No. 95 Walnut Street. His only child was the wife of an eminent Catholic Irish-American, Robert Walsh, Esq., the celebrated editor and reviewer of the author of the *Appeal of the United States from the Judgments of Great Britain; Diadactics; etc.,* who died in Paris, some years ago." [*v. infra.*]

"In 1799, Col. A. Burr fought his first duel. It arose from scandals connected with the Holland Land Company. One John B. Church had spoken with so much freedom respecting the rumor, as to elicit from the slandered legislator (A. B.) a challenge to mortal combat. At Hoboken, September 2, the parties met. A ridiculous incident . . . furnished a byword for many a day. Before leaving home, Col. Burr had been particular to explain to his second, Judge Burke, of South Carolina, that the balls were cast too small for his pistols, and that the chamois-leather, cut to the proper size, must be greased and put around them to make them fit. Leather and grease were placed in the case with the pistols. After the principals had been placed, Burr noticed Judge Burke vainly endeavoring to drive in the ramrod with a stone, and at once suspected that the grease had been forgotten. A moment after, the pistol was handed to him. With that singular coolness which he was wont to exhibit at critical moments, he drew the ramrod, felt of the ball, and told the Judge it was not home.

"'I know it,' replied the second, wiping the perspiration from his face. 'I forgot to grease the leather; but, you see, your man is ready; don't keep him waiting. Just take a crack as it is, and I'll grease the next.'

"Shots were exchanged without effect. Mr. Church then made the requisite apology, and the parties returned to the city in the highest good-humor."—*Parton's Life of A. Burr.*

BUTLER'S *Lives of the Saints.* A Selection of thé most Edifying, Useful, and Instructive Lives of the Saints, taken from the Excellent Work of the Rev. Alban Butler. To which are prefixed: I. *The Life of Our Lord Jesus Christ*, from the *History of the Bible*, of the Rev. Joseph Reeve. II. *The Life of Blessed Virgin Mary*, chiefly compiled from the Rev. Alban Butler's Discourses on her Various Festivals. First American Edition. Compiled by a Rev. Catholic Clergyman of Baltimore. Vol. I. "Let us praise men of renown," etc.—Eccl. xlix. Baltimore: Published by Bernard Dornin, and sold at his Catholic Library, 30 Baltimore Street. C. Dobbin & Murphy, printers. 1811. F.

P. iii., Advertisement of the American editor; *verso*, blank; pp. 6–9, Preface; Text, pp. 13–216. 12mo.

[In my copy, the *Life of Christ* ends at p. 116. Then follows the *Life of Bl. Virgin Mary,* to p. 152; *St. Joseph's,* to p. 158; *The Holy Innocents,* to p. 163; *St. Peter's,* to p. 192; *St. Paul's,* to p. 216, ending with an unfinished sentence. In 1812, Dornin advertises, "*The Lives of the Saints* are now publishing in numbers, the first, second, and third of which are printed. 25 cents each." Were any more issued? In 1810, D. advertised that the work would be published in four vols., one every month, 500 pages each, to subscribers, $1 50 per vol.]

BUTLER, CHARLES.—*Horæ Juridicæ Subsecivæ.* Being a Connected Series of Notes concerning Geography, Chronology, and Literary History of the Principal Codes and Original Documents of the Grecian, Roman, Feudal, and Canon Law. Philadelphia. 1808. [Same as 2d London edition, 1807.] 8vo. B. P. L.

—— *Horæ Biblicæ.*

[Literary Researches on the Bible. Was not an American edition published in Boston by Munroe & Co.? The first edition, pp. 109, 12mo, dedicated to J. C. Throckmorton, from Lincoln's Inn, 1797, was printed only for circulation among friends. F.]

—— *The Life of Fénelon, Abp. of Cambray.* Quotations from Cic. pro Archia and D'Aguesseau. Philadelphia: Published by A. Finley. Also, by P. H. Nicklin & Co., Baltimore; D. W. Farrand & Green, Albany; E. Sargeant, New York; D. Mallory & Co., Boston; Lyman Hall & Co., Portland; Swift & Chipman, Middlebury, Vermont. 1811. pp. 236. 12mo. F.

[Portrait of Fénelon by Jones. Book printed by R. & W. Carr, No. 51 Sansom Street. Dedicated to Henry Lord (Prot.), Bishop of Norwich. Some interesting items about Dr. Bathurst will be found in the *Life of Bishop Doyle,* by W. J. Fitzpatrick, vol. i. p. 177, and vol. ii. pp. 207, 283. Boston edition. 1862. P. Donahoe.

Charles Butler is a familiar name with the Catholics who are well acquainted with the *Lives of the Saints* written by his uncle, the Rev. Alban Butler, whose very interesting biography, by Charles, is prefixed to the American editions of the work. Allibone, in his *Dictionary of Authors,* gives for once a pretty good account of the literary habits and persevering labors of this Catholic author. Yet, my readers should know that Charles Butler had the misfortune of trespassing on Catholic questions, for which discussions he was not qualified. For, in the language of the able historian of the *Church of England,* "Butler's successful pursuits as a great conveyancer left him but few intervals for the study of history. How much he is at a loss in this extensive field of study is obvious at a glance. . . . His *Memoirs,* useful as they really are, yet abound with inaccuracy. . . . To rectify some of his errors, Dr. Milner wrote, perhaps too warmly, his excellent Supplementary Memoir." Canon Flanagan, *History of England,* v. ii. ch. xxvii. B. was b. in London, Aug. 14, 1750; was educated at Douay; d. June 2, 1832, æt. 82. His numerous works have gone through many editions.]

BYRNE, Patrick, *Trial of—for Mutiny,* before a General Court Martial, held at Fort Columbus on the 22d of May, 1813. Sentence, DEATH! Published at the request of the numerous friends of the deceased in the City of New York. New York: Printed by Edward Gillespy, No. 24 William Street. 1813. pp. 12. 12mo. F.

CALMET.—"*Taylor's Edition of Calmet's Great Edition of the Holy Bible,*" *etc.* Charlestown: Printed and sold by Samuel Etheridge. June, 1812. 4 vols. 4to. Double col. F.

I. p. v., "To the Reader;" pp. vii.–xiv., "Introduction to the Second London Edition; sig. 1–81, A–IZR.

II. 1813. "Faith," fronting title-page; 3 pp., "Preface to this American Edition," signed, "Charlestown, March 13, 1813;" "Preface to the Second Volume of the London Edition, Jan. 1, 1801;" sig. 1–110, K–Y; last 4 pp., "Errata."

[Vols. i. and ii. have in the title-page "Revised, Corrected, and Augmented, with an entirely new set of Plates, Explanatory, Illustrative, and Ornamental, under the direction of C. Taylor." This announcement is left out in vols. iii. and iv., which latter volumes are not Calmet's. In fact, even the first and second are maimed and mangled, and, of course, the Bible quotations changed from the Vulgate to King James I. The English editor does not disguise the fact that he has Protestantized the work (vol. i., pp. xii., xiii.), inasmuch as the author had mingled in his remarks sentiments which Protestants in general *justly reject*, etc. Charles Taylor, an engraver, of London, b. 1756, d. 1821 or '23 (*v.* Allibone). Dom. Augustine Calmet, O.S.B., b. in Mesnil-la-Horgue, Feb. 26, 1672, d. Oct. 25, 1757.

The illustrious Abbot of Senones is a grand ornament of both the Church and of his order. His life was divided between prayer and study. Profoundly humble, he seemed unaware of the honors bestowed upon his works by all nations and all denominations. He indited his own epitaph :

Frater · Augustinus · Calmet
Natione · Gallus · Religione · Catholico-Romanus
Professione · Monachus · Nomine · Abbas
Multum · Legit · Scripsit · Oravit
Utinam · Bene !

"Brother Augustin Calmet; Frenchman by birth; Roman Catholic in religion; by profession a monk, in name an abbot. He read much, wrote, prayed. God grant it was all well done !"]

CANISIUS, VEN. P., S.J.—*Catolich Catechism*, wherein Catholic Doctrines, according to the Chapters of Ven. P. Canisius, are explained and compiled by Adam Britt, Pastor of the Catholic Church of Holy Trinity, Philadelphia. With approbation. Philadelphia: Conrad Zentler. 1810. pp. 180. 18mo. F.

[German.]

CANTIQUES FRANCAISES *à l'usage du Catéchisme de l'Eglise de Saint Patrice de Baltimore.* A Baltimore: De l'Imprimerie de Jean Hayes, pour le compte de Jacques Rice et Comp. M,DCC,XCVIII. pp. 108. 8vo. F.

—— *Recueil de—à l'Usage de la Congregation établie parmi les élèves du Collège de Ste Marie sous le nom de Société de la Ste Famille.* A Baltimore: De l'Imprimerie G. Dobbin & Murphy, 4 Harrison St. 1811. pp. 154. 64mo. S.S.B.

[Dobbin & Murphy appear very often among the early publishers of Catholic works in Baltimore. Judge Dobbin, a son of the printer, has kindly furnished the following:

"BALTIMORE, Dec. 30, 1871.

"*Dear Sir:* I greatly regret that I can give you so meagre an account of the publishing firm of 'G. Dobbin & Murphy,' which existed in Baltimore from about the year 1804 or 1805 (it may be a year earlier) till 1811 or 1812. The members of the firm were George Dobbin, born in County Armagh, Ireland, and Thomas Murphy, born in the City of Cork, Ireland. Mr. Dobbin fled from Ireland in the troubles of 1798, in the exciting transactions of which he took an active part as a United Irishman.

"Mr. Murphy came to this country in his boyhood. Both gentlemen were Presbyterians, . . . in which communion Mr. Dobbin died. In the latter part of his life, Mr. Murphy belonged to the Protestant Episcopal Church. . . .

"I am, very truly, yours,

"GEORGE W. DOBBIN."

My excellent friend, J. Murphy, Esq., of Baltimore, to whom I am indebted for the above, and many other favors, adds:

"I knew Mr. Murphy very well; he was a remarkably clever and truly good man. Very few men in Baltimore commanded more respect, and few, if any, were most justly entitled to it, than Thomas Murphy. He died a bachelor about ten years ago."—*Baltimore, Nov.* 28, 1871.

I. Thomas, in his *History of Printing in the United States*, makes no mention of Dobbin & Murphy.]

CAREY, MATHEW.—*v.* Appendix E.

[So many new titles of Carey's publications are daily added to my manuscript that I have determined to devote a whole chapter to his name in the *Appendix*, else the printer will not get this copy for several months to come.]

CARLI, LE COMTE J. R.—*Lettres Americains, Dans lesquelles on examine l'Origine . . . . des Anciens Habitans de l'Amérique ; les grandes Epoques de la Nature, l'Ancienne Communication des deux Hémisphères et la dernière Revolution qui a fait disparoître l'Atlantide : pour servir de suite aux Memoires de D. Ulloa . . . . Avec des Observations et Additions du Traducteur.* A Boston, et se trouve à Paris. . . . . M.DC.LXXXVIII. 2 vols. 12mo. F.

I. pp. xxii. and 520 ; three maps. II. pp. 536.

[G. R. Carli, b. at Capo d'Istria, April, 1720, d. in Milan, Feb. 22, 1795. Of him says the celebrated Andres : " Era certamente l'erudito, che unisse più universalità con maggiore profondità di quanti viventi in Italia, e pochi eguali n'avrà avuto anche fuori d'Italia." The above title is actually of a Paris edition, translated from the Italian by Lefabure de Villebrune. The work is intended as a confutation of Pau, and the writer finds traces of Catholicity in the religion of the old Peruvians and Mexicans; *v. supra, Earliest Records of Catholic Authors in America.*]

CARROLL, Most Rev. John.—*An Address to the Roman Catholics of the United States of America.* By a Catholic Clergymen. Annapolis: Printed by Frederick Green. M.DCC.LXXXIV. F.

[This is the first Catholic work written by an American Catholic published in the United States. It was called for by the apostasy of the ex-Jesuit Wharton, a Marylander of some note, and a relative of the writer.

I thought, *operæ pretium,* to give here a list of works connected with this lamentable affair. The list will also form a link of reference to obtain the historical information of the case.]

A.—*A Letter to the Roman Catholics of the City of Worcester* [England], from the Chaplain of said Society, stating the Motives which induced him to relinquish their Communion and become a Member of the Protestant Church. . . . . Philadelphia: Robert Aitken, at the sign of the Pope's Head, in Market Street, near the Coffee-House. M.DCC.LXXXIV. pp. 40. 8vo.

—— do., with name "Mr. C. H. Wharton" between *Society* and *stating.* New York: Republished by David Longworth. No. 11 Park. Clayton & Kingsland, Printers. 1817.

CARROLL & WHARTON.—*A Concise View of the Principal Points of Controversy between the Protestant and Roman Churches.* I. "A Letter to the Roman Catholics of Worcester in England;" pp. 40. II. "A Reply to the above Address, by the late Abp. Carroll;" pp. 120. III. "An Answer to the late Abp. Carroll's Reply;" pp. 96. IV. "A Short Answer to the Appendix to *The Catholic Question* [*v. infra* Sampson] decided in New York, 1813;" pp. 130. V. "A few Short Remarks on Dr. Gallagher's Reply to the above *Answer;*" pp. 72. By the Rev. Charles H. Wharton, D.D., Rector of St. Mary's Church, Burlington, N. J., etc., etc. New York: D. Longworth. Clayton & Kingsland, Printers. 1817. 8vo. F.

1 vol. 8vo. All separate pamphlets, uniformly printed and bound. The Preface contains an affectionate letter from Bp. Bruté, and a *rude* answer to it.

B.—*Dr. Carroll's Address. Ut supra.*

A London edition of Dr. Carroll's *Address,* with Preface and Postscript, appeared, whereupon Rev. A. O'Leary, O.S.F., published:

A Review of the important Controversy between Dr. Carroll and the Rev. Messrs. Wharton and Hawkins; including a Defence of the Pope Clement XIV. (Ganganelli) in suppressing a late Religious Order. In a Letter to a Gentleman. London: Printed for and sold by the Editor, P. Keating, No. 4 Air Street, Piccadilly. MDCCLXXXVI. (*v.* American edition of O'Leary's Works. Boston: P. Donahoe. 1868. Edited by J. M. F.) F.

To remedy the evil done by this interpolated London edition, another was immediately issued, contemporaneously in America and England:

An Address to the Roman Catholics of the United States of America. By a Catholic Clergyman. Annapolis: Printed by Frederick Green. And Worcester: Reprinted by J. Tymbs, at the Cross. MDCCLXXXV. pp. 120. 8vo. F.

In a short preface is remarked: "A spurious and subreptitious edition of *Mr. Carroll's Address to Mr. Wharton* having been lately smuggled into the world in a clandestine manner, at London," etc. Indeed, Fr. O'Leary was rather hasty, and his services officious. This called forth:

C.—*A Reply to an Address to the Roman Catholics of the United States of America.* By the author of *A Letter to the Roman Catholics of the*

City of Worcester. To which are annexed a few Observations on a late Pamphlet entitled *An Essay on Matter*, in a Letter to a Friend. Philadelphia: Printed by Charles Cist, at the corner of Fourth and Arch Streets. 1785. F.

Pp. 97. 12mo. Then follows advertisement, p. unnumbered, on the *Essay on Matter*; pp. 1–9, Letter: "February 20, 1785. My Amiable Friend." Signed, "Madam, Your most obedient, humble servant, C. H. W. Miss V——g, W——n." Last p. unnumbered, some additions and corrections to previous pamphlet.

[Charles Cist, b. in St. Petersburg, Russia, brought up a druggist, studied "physic," and came to America in 1769, and engaged with Henry Miller, a German editor and publisher in Philadelphia, as a translator of English into German. In 1775, he entered into partnership under the firm of Styner & Cist, Second Street, corner Coat's Alley. He died in Bethlehem, Pa., December 1, 1805.

Green, F., son of Jonas and Anne Catherine, succeeded his mother (d. March 23, 1775, æt. 42) as printer to the Colony of Maryland. The firm still continues. They are the fifth generation of a regular descent of printers in this country. Their great-great-grandfather began printing at Cambridge, Mass., 1649. I. Thomas, *History, etc.*, A.D. 1810. Does B. Green, publisher, in Boston, of Brownson's *Quarterly Review*, belong to the clan?]

D.—*A Few Remarks on an Address to the Roman Catholics of the United States of America, occasioned by A Letter Addressed to the Catholics of Worcester* by Mr. Wharton, their late Chaplain. By the Right Rev. Dr. Carroll. By a Fair Inquirer [John Hawkins, apost. priest]. Worcester: Printed for the Author. Sold by J. Tymbs, and most of the booksellers in town and country. pp. 24. 12mo. F.

Page 1, "To the Reader," signed "Barborne Lodge, Saturday, July 9." At p. 24, before *Finis*, signed J. H. I remember to have seen the date 1796 connected with this production. Certainly the writer speaks of Dr. Carroll as a bishop (he was elected May, 1789); unless he mistakes for a bishopric the faculties of a Vicar Apostolic, bestowed by Pius VI. on Dr. C., June 9, 1784. J. H. apostatized in 1782-4, *v.* Milner's *Supp. Memoirs.*

John Hawkins, in the short preface above mentioned, remarks, "A work has long since been under the press in reply to a late *Caveat*, and which will be given to the public with all convenient speed." To wit:

E.—*A Caveat addressed to the Catholics of Worcester against the Insinuating Letter of Mr. Wharton.* By William Pilling [O.S.F.]. Quotation from Epis. of John, c. ii., vs. 18, 19, Protestant translation, and "St. Cyprian De Unitate Ecclesiæ." London: Printed by J. P. Coghlan, in Duke Street, near Grosvenor Square. MDCCCLXXXV. pp. incomplete. 12mo. F.

The late Abp. Spalding, of Baltimore, had a complete copy of it, and to his Grace I am indebted for my copy. His Grace seemed never tired of answering my many importunate questions. Fr. W. Pilling "was a well-read scholar, a clear-headed theologian, and an exemplary missionary."—*Dr. Oliver: English Franciscan Writers.*

Hawkins' endeavor to defend himself in the person of his fellow-apostate Wharton, drew upon him Rev. Dr. Berington's

F.—*Reflections Addressed to Hawkins.* By Joseph Berington. 1775. Intended as an answer to *Hawkins's Appeal. Cfr.* Flanagan's *History,* v. ii. p. 385, *ad calcem.*

G.—*An Essay on the Law of Celibacy Imposed on the Clergy of the Roman Catholic Church,* and observed in all the Religious Orders Abroad: in which are delineated its Rise and Progress from the most early ages of its existence down to our present times; and the impropriety of this Ecclesiastical Constitution is Shown, whether it be considered in a moral, a physical, or a political light; as also, A summary account is given of the Origin of the MONASTIC Life, of the prejudices which chiefly contributed to introduce it, and in what manner these have been perpetuated, etc. interspersed with various remarks upon several other observances of the Roman Catholic Discipline. *Quotations:* August. lib. 1, De Trinit.; *Idem* Epis. 238 Ad Pascent.; John 5, 39. Worcester:

Printed and sold by M. Lewis, in High Street; sold also by J. F. & C. Rivington, No. 62 St. Paul's Church-yard, and J. Bew, Paternoster-Row, London; Fletcher, Oxford; Pearson & Rollason, Birmingham; Pugh, Hereford; and Evans, Gloucester. pp. 195. 12mo. F.

John Hawkins is the author. Like all apostate priests, he turns back to throw mud at his mother: Protestant ministers after becoming Catholics do not turn around to vilify their former associations—a fact worth recording.

Elsewhere will be found in this *Bibliographia* the title of the famous *Catholic Question* in 1813 (*v.* Sampson). Dr. Wharton improved the opportunity to have another fling at the Church, and published:

A Short Answer to "A True Exposition of the Doctrine of the Catholic Church touching the Sacrament of Penance, with The Grounds on which this doctrine is founded," Contained in an Appendix to the *Catholic Question* (*v. infra* Sampson) decided in the City of New York, in July, 1813. By Charles H. Wharton, D.D., Rector of St. Mary's Church, Burlington, N. J. (Some texts.) Philadelphia: Published by Moses Thomas. J. Maxwell, printer. 1814. pp. 130. 12mo. F.

It is dedicated "To the Rt. Rev. the Bishops, etc. etc., by their affectionate humble Servant and Brother, etc." It called forth:

A Brief Reply to A Short Answer to a True Exposition of the Doctrine of the Catholic Church touching the Sacrament of Penance, etc. New York: Printed for the Author, by Sherman & Pudney, No. 30 Nassau Street. 1815. pp. 178. 8vo. F.

The author, Rev. Fr. S. F. O'Callaghan, O.S.F., of Charleston, S. C., dedicates the work, over his own name, to the Hon. Maj.-Gen. Ch. C. Pinkney. Wharton replied to it. *v. supra* A.

Cfr. Canon Flanagan's *History of the Church of England,* vol. ii. p. 388. London: 1857. B. Campbell's *Memoirs of Life and Times of Abp. Carroll. U. S. Catholic Magazine,* vol. iii., A.D. 1844, pp. 662, *et seq. Biographical Sketch of the Most. Rev. J. Carroll, First Abp. of Baltimore.* By John Carroll Brent. Baltimore: J. Murphy. MDCCCXLIII. Dr. Oliver's *Biographies of Irish, English, Scotch Jesuits.* London: Dolman. 1845. *Remains of C. H. Wharton, with a Memoir,* by G. W. Doane. Philadelphia: W. Stavely, Geo. Latimer & Co. New York: Swords, Sanford & Co. 1834. 2 vols. 12mo. An interesting *Memoir,* by R. H. Clarke, in the *Baltimore Metropolitan,* iv. p. 265, and *Lives of Deceased Bishops.*]

—— *An | Address | from the | Roman Catholics | of America | to | George Washington, Esq., | President | of the | United States.* | London: | Printed by J. P. Coughlan, Duke Street, Grosvenor Square; and sold by | Messrs. Robinsons, Pater-Noster Row. | M.DCC.XC. | Price, sixpence. F.

Pp. 12, folio; fac-simile republished in New York, 1866, by

John Gilmary Shea, Esq., with Portraits of Gen. Washington and Bp. Carroll. The *Address* is signed, "John Carroll, in behalf of the Roman Catholic clergy. Charles Carroll, of Carrolltown, Daniel Carroll, Dominick Lynch, Thomas Fitzimmons, in behalf of the Roman Catholic laity;" pp. 9–11 contain Historical Notes on the Signers of the *Address*, by J. G. S.

[This address was copied from the *American News.* Whilst the copy by Coughlan cost sixpence, in 1790, the fac-simile cost ten dollars in 1869.]

—— *A Discourse on General Washington*, Delivered in the Catholic Church of St. Peter, in Baltimore, Feb. 22d, 1800. By the Right Rev. Bishop Carroll. Baltimore: Printed by Warner & Hanna. pp. 24. 12mo. F.

[This copy contains the usual portrait by J. P. de C., an autograph letter of the Bishop (Nov. 26, 1806) to Felix Dougherty, Esq., at his office, East Street; also an Engraving of the Washington monument, Baltimore; also an extremely rare profile portrait of Washington, similar to the one on the "Manly Medal." The plate is said to be owned in New York.]

—— —— Another copy, containing same portrait of Dr. Carroll, and a beautifully engraved portrait (by Tanner) of the General (by Savage). F.

—— *Pastoral Letter to the Catholics of Trinity*

Church, Philadelphia [dated], Baltimore, Feb. 22, 1799. Printed by J. Hayes. pp. 8. 4to. F.

[Neither John nor Charles Carroll mentioned in Allibone.]

—— AND MARECHAL.—*Pastoral Letters of Abp. Carroll to the Congregation of Trinity Church, Philadelphia*, 1797, *and of Abp. Marechal to that of Norfolk*, 1819. 2d Edition. Baltimore: Printed by John Robinson. Circulating Library, 94 Market Street, corner Belvidere St. 1820. pp. 85. 8vo. F.

[The schisms of Philadelphia and Norfolk were so alike in their origin and tendencies, that it was thought proper to publish the two *Pastorals* together; *v. infra* Marechal.]

—— An interesting communication from "John, Bishop of Baltimore, November 21, 1792," was addressed by Dr. Carroll to a Baltimore paper, as *An Answer to Strictures on an Extraordinary Signature, i.e.*, to his signing himself "Bishop of Baltimore." It can be found in the *Metropolitan* for May, 1830, p. 181 (Baltimore: P. Blenkinsop), and in the *Catholic Expositor*, by Pise & Varela, N. Y., ii. 123. Other writings by the grand old Bishop may be seen in John Carroll Brent's excellent *Biographical Sketch.* A sermon by the Archbishop is preserved in the *Expositor*, iii. 49.

[What an interesting volume might be written on the life of Bishop-Archbishop Carroll ! *Exoriare aliquis !* See *Laity's Directory.* New York : Creagh. 1822. p. 127. When this was written, the work of R. H. Clarke on the *Deceased Bishops* had not appeared.]

CARROLL, Charles, of Carrollton.

It is useless to give here a sketch of his life. Of his famous *Journal*, published in 1845, by Murphy, of Baltimore, of which I have a costly copy, with nineteen illustrations and C. Carroll's autograph, I will speak in the second part of the *Bibliographia.*

But Mr. Carroll was an early Catholic writer. As early as 1765 (twenty-one years before his reverend cousin's *Address, v. supra*), when he returned from Europe, "a finished scholar and an accomplished gentleman," he engaged in public controversy in vindication of the colonists during the excitement of the Stamp Act. The *Maryland Gazette* was his organ. He was only twenty-seven years old. The *Gazette* was in so much demand, that Mr. Galloway, Speaker of the Pennsylvania Assembly, copied it with his own hand, in order to send it to Benjamin Franklin. Afterwards, Charles Carroll wrote over the signature of "The First Citizen." In 1765, the *Gazette* (it had existed since 1727) was discontinued on account of the Stamp Act, but occasionally its printers issued a paper called *The Opposition of the Maryland Gazette*, "which is not dead, but sleepeth" (Kenny, p. 110). Most probably Charles Carroll contributed to, if he was not the instigator of, these papers. He wrote also, says Clarigny, many articles for the *Pennsylvania Gazette.* See N. Dwight's *The Lives of the Signers of the Declaration of Independence.* New York : A. S. Barnes & Burr, 51 and 52 John Street. 1860.

I have in my possession a bronze medal, rare, and of which no specimen is to be found in the collection at the Mint.

Device—The bust of Charles Carroll, facing to the left (Gobrecht).

Legend—CHARLES CARROLL OF CARROLLTON.

Reverse—A wreath, fastened by a scroll and pen, enclosing the words "The Surviving Signer of the Declaration of the Independence after the 50th Anniversary."

Legend—Upon entering his 90th year.

Exergue—Sept. XX. MDCCCXXIV.

J. Colburn, Esq., of the N. E. Historico-Genealogical Society, informs me that the die was made at the expense of the family, and now belongs to them. Why not have it restruck by the Catholics on the Centennial Anniversary of the Independence of America? Charles Carroll, of Carrollton, died November 14, 1832, in his ninety-sixth year; *v. Memoir*, by R. H. Clarke, in Baltimore *Metropolitan*, iv. p. 329, and *Catholic Expositor*, vol. v., 1843, p. 208, by J. H., and *Eulogy on Charles Carroll of Carrollton.* Delivered at the request of the Select and Common Councils of the City of Philadelphia, December 31, 1832. By John Sergeant, LL.D. Philadelphia: Printed by Lydia R. Bailey, No. 26 North Fifth Street. 1833. *v.* Allibone, *ad n.* "John Sergeant, LL.D." Also "*Eulogy on Charles Carroll of Carrollton.* Delivered before the Academus Society of Mt. St. Mary's College, December 20, 1832. By Rev. John McCaffrey, A.M., Professor of Rhetorick. Baltimore: Published by William R. Lucas. Lucas & Deaver, Printers. 1832.

CATECHISM *of the Foundations of the Christian Faith.* For the use of both the Young and the Old. Followed by *The Celebrated Conversation of Mr. de Fénelon with Mr. de Ramsay*, and by several Extracts on the Existence of God, and on the Worship which is due to Him, from the Letters of the

Illustrious Archbishop of Cambray, M. de Fénelon. Printed with the approbation of the Most Rev. John Carroll, Archbishop of Baltimore. Printed at the Office of the Economical School, No. 59 Church Street, New York. 1811. 1 vol. 12mo. F.

Pp. 3, 4, Notice concerning this new edition; pp. 1–113, "Catechism on the Principles of the Christian Faith;" p. 113, *verso* blank; pp. 1–31, "Extracts on the Existence of God;" pp. 31–2, "Advice on the Life of Mr. Ramsay;" pp. 33–35, "The Conversation," etc., given by Ramsay himself; p. 56, cont.

[Is this *Catechism* by Fénelon or Legris-Duval? In 1869 a finely printed octavo translation of *The Conversation* (private circulation?) was published in New York by A. E. Silliman, who, however, falls into an historical blunder in the preface. Q. What and where was the Economical School?]

——? Translated by Charles Butler. Philadelphia: Finley. 1811. G. T. C.

—— Baltimore: Dornin. 1809.
J. G. S., B. M.

Catechism, A—or, Short Abridgment of Christian Doctrine. Newly Revised for the use of the Catholic Church in the United States. Published with the approbation of the Most Rev. Abp. Carroll, and ornamented by an appropriate Engraving.

Dornin's advertisement, 1810 and 1812. Six cents.

—— (Hay's?) *A Short Abridgment of Christian Doctrine.* Newly Revised for the use of the Catholic Church in the United States of America. To which is added *A Short Daily Exercise.* The Fourteenth Edition. With approbation. Baltimore: Printed by Michael Duffey. M.DCC.XCVIII. pp. 51. Square 18mo. F.

Pp. 41–46, "Daily Exercise;" pp. 47–51, "A Fuller Instruction concerning the Holy Eucharist and Communion," translated from the French Catechism of John Joseph l'Anguet, formerly Archbishop of Sens.

—— do. Title-page torn. F.

The same as the above as regards the matter, but forty pages unnumbered, and an older edition, as it bears the following record on last page: "Benjamin Leslie Corry's Catechism Book, bought of Mr. Flaw, 2d Sunday, September the 14th, 1794.

[Was Mr. Flaw a bookseller? or a printer also?]

—— do. pp. 48. 18mo. F.

Title-page torn. Same as above as far as Chapter VII., to which it adds one question, and then has additional Chapters VIII. and IX. It omits the "Daily Exercise" and "L'Anguet's Instruction," but gives the "Acts" and some prayers. Probably Dornin's edition of 1808 or 1810.

—— do. After the word "Exercise," *With Hymns before and after Catechism.* n. d. *ad calcem*

Published with the approbation of the Most Rev. Archbishop Carroll. pp. 48. 24mo. F.

[It does not seem to be of the Dornin style of printing.]

J. Gilmary Shea has favored me with the following title:

A Short Abridgment of Christian Doctrine. Newly Revised. To which is added *A Short Daily Exercise.* The Twelfth Edition. With approbation. Albany: Printed by Charles R. & George Webster, at their book-store in the White House, corner of State and Pearl Streets. MDCCCI. pp. 36.

A Catechism; or, A Short Abridgment of Christian Doctrine. Newly Revised for the use of the Catholic Church in the United States of America. To which is prefixed *A Short Daily Exercise, with Hymns before and after Catechism.* | A Vignette. | Published with the approbation of the Most Rev. Archbishop Carroll. n. d. pp. 48. 24mo. F.

Catechisme, ou Abrégé de la Foi Catholique. Publié par odre de Mgr. l'Archevêque de Paris, pour les Fidèles de son Diocèse, et enseigné dans les Missions de RR. PP. Capucins aux isles sous le Vent de l'Amerique. Baltimore: de l'Imprimerie de S.

6

Sower, Rue de Fayette, pas loin de la Rue de Haoard. 1796. pp. 113. 24mo. S. S. B.

With twelve distinct pages of French Canticles.

—— *ou Abrégé de la Doctrine Chrétienne.* Précédé de l'Exercice du Chrétien pour le Matin et le Soir; et terminé par quelques instructions sur le Scapulaire, le Rosaire, et quelques autres pratiques de pieté. Seconde Edition de Baltimore. Faite par l'approbation de Mgr. L'Evêque dans laquelle on a changé quelques questions, partagé quelques réponses qui ont paru trop longues, et ajouté quelques articles, qui manquaient dans la Prémière Edition. A Baltimore: Imprimé par Jean W. Butler. 1807. pp. 249. 32mo. Abp. B.

—— *ou Abrégé de la Doctrine Chrétienne* suivi de la Prière du Matin et du Soir, des Prières pour la Ste. Messe. Pour la Confession et la Communion; et de quelque Cantiques Spirituels. Troisième Edition. Avec l'approbation de Mgr. L'Evêque. A Baltimore: Imprimé pour Bernard Dornin, et Vendre par le même a son Office de Libraire Catholique Romain, No. 30 Rue du Marché, à Baltimore. 1809. pp. 276. 24mo. F.

—— *Et Prières, ou Abrégé de la Doctrine Chré-*

tienne. Précedé de l'Exercice du Chrétien, des prières pour la Ste. Messe, la Confession et la Communion, et suivi d'instructions familières sur toutes les fêtes de l'année, des Vespres du Dimanche, etc. De litanies pieuses, et de plusieurs cantiques choisis, pour être chantés avant et aprez le Catechisme. Cinquième Edition. Revüe et corrigée, et considerablement augmentée. Permissu Superiorum. A Baltimore: Imprimé pour F. Lucas, Libraire, par J. Robinson, Imprimeur. 1818. pp. 448. 24mo. F.

[The text of the *Catechism* in this is the same as in previous three editions, even to the forms and number of pages. It is one of the earliest Catholic books printed by Lucas, of Baltimore; *v.* O'Neill.]

—— *Contenant les Eléments de la Foi Catholique Romaine,* avec les Prières du Matin ed du Soir, les Litanies du S. Nom de Jésus, Celles de la S. Vièrge, etc. Et le Cantique de M. de Fénélon, sur la Passion de N.S.J.C. A Philadelphie, de l'Imprimerie de T. et G. Palmer. Et se trouve chez Mathieu Carey, Rue de Marché, No. 122. pp. 85. 12mo. S. S. B.

CAVALLO, Tiberius, F.R.S., etc.—*The Elements of Natural or Experimental Philosophy.*

First American Edition, With Additional Notes, selected from Various Authors, by F. X. Brosius. Philadelphia: Published by Thomas Dobson, at the Stone House, No. 41 South Second Street. William Fry, printer. 1813. 2 vols. 8vo. With plates. F.

1st, pp. xxvi. and 472. 2d, pp. ii. and 551.

[Lots 20427, 8, 9, 30, of Gowan's sale (May 22, 1871), are the titles of new editions published in Philadelphia, 1819, '25, '29, '32. *v.* Brosius. T. C. b. in Naples, March, 1749; d. in London, 1809. The first (?) edition of the *Elements* was published in London, 1803, 4 vols. 8vo. He was the author of many valuable works.]

CAVEAT *against the Methodists.* Printed for the Publishers. Mount Vernon [Ohio]: Printed by John P. McArdle. A.D. 1817. G. T. C.

[Title furnished by the ever-obliging Mr. Sumner.]

CHALLONER, Rt. Rev. Richard.

[*v. supra, Authority, Unerring* —.]

—— 1789. *The True Principles of a Catholic.* By Bishop Chalenor [sic]. To which is added, *An Exposition of the Commandments.* Philadelphia: Mathew Carey. M.DCC.LXXXIX. (Price threepence, or 2*s.* per dozen.) pp. 12. 12mo. F.

[*v. infra, Garden of the Soul.*]

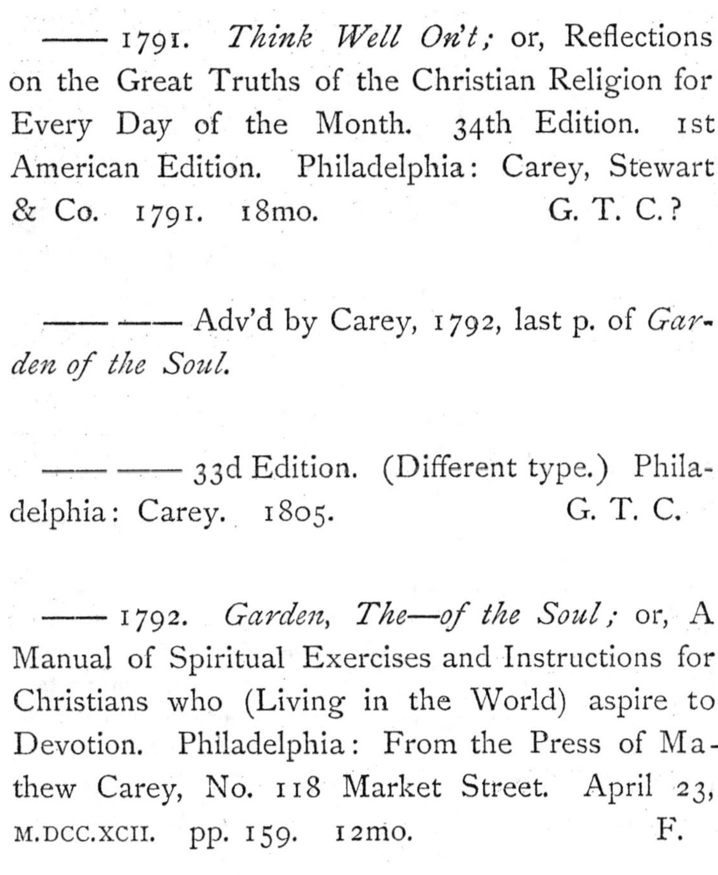

—— 1791. *Think Well On't;* or, Reflections on the Great Truths of the Christian Religion for Every Day of the Month. 34th Edition. 1st American Edition. Philadelphia: Carey, Stewart & Co. 1791. 18mo. G. T. C.?

—— —— Adv'd by Carey, 1792, last p. of *Garden of the Soul.*

—— —— 33d Edition. (Different type.) Philadelphia: Carey. 1805. G. T. C.

—— 1792. *Garden, The—of the Soul;* or, A Manual of Spiritual Exercises and Instructions for Christians who (Living in the World) aspire to Devotion. Philadelphia: From the Press of Mathew Carey, No. 118 Market Street. April 23, M.DCC.XCII. pp. 159. 12mo. F.

—— —— Baltimore. 1814. J. G. S., B. M.

—— 1809. *Christian, The Catholic—Instructed in the Sacraments, Sacrifices, Ceremonies, and Observances of the Church, by way of Question and*

Answer. By the Rt. Rev. R. Challoner, D.D. Containing, by way of Introduction, his Celebrated Answer to Dr. Conger Middleton's *Letter from Rome.* Baltimore: Printed by J. Dobbin & Murphy for Bernard Dornin, Roman Catholic Library, No. 30 Baltimore Street. 1809. [Copy formerly belonging to Mrs. Patterson of Baltimore.] pp. xxiv.–285. F.

After p. 285, the Contents, pp. i., ii., iii.; eight pages unnumbered, Subscribers' Names; two do., Advertisements of books already printed.

[The first edition appeared in England, 1737. It so provoked Middleton and his friends that they endeavored to procure Challoner's arrest under pretence of his being disaffected to the Government. He therefore withdrew to the Continent. Become a convert in 1704, was consecrated Coadj. Bp. of Dr. Petra, Vic. Ap. of London, January 29, 1741. Of him wrote a Protestant minister: "January 12, 1781. Buried Dr. Challoner, popish priest, titulary Bp. of Debra, London, and Salisbury (?), Vic. Ap. for the Roman Church in England, a very good, very pious, very learned man, one of extraordinary qualities." During his administration the Church suffered terribly, perhaps no less than under Queen Elizabeth.]

—— 1813. *History, Short—of the First Beginning and Progress of the Protestant Religion,* Gathered out of the Best Protestant Writers, by way of Question and Answer. By the late Venerable and Rt. Rev. Dr. Richard Challoner. The twelfth edition. "A good tree cannot bring forth evil fruit: neither can a corrupt tree bring forth good fruit."—St. Matt. vii. 18. Baltimore: Published by B. Dornin, No. 29 Saratoga Street. Gamble, printer. 1813. pp. 108. 32mo.

R. and G. T. C.

—— 1814. *Grounds, The—of the Old Religion;* or, Some General Arguments in Favor of the Catholic Apostolic Roman Communion. Collected from both Ancient and Modern Controvertists. By a Convert. "Thus saith the Lord, Stand ye in the ways, and see, and ask for the old paths, where is the good way, and walk therein, and ye shall find rest for your souls."—Jerem. vi. 16. Philadelphia: Printed and published by Augustine Fagan, No. 133 South Front Street. 1814. pp. vi.–198. 12mo. F.

[Pp. 199–204, Subscribers' Names. I have *doubtingly* ascribed the above work to Dr. Challoner on the authority of De Feller, who, *ad nom.*, gives amongst the list of the Doctor's works *Les Fondements de la Doctrine Catholique.* For a notice of A. Fagan, *v.* Appendix C.]

—— 1815. *Touchstone, The—of the New Religion;* or, Sixty Assertions of Protestants Tried by their Own Rule of Scripture Alone, and Condemned by Clear and Express Texts of their Own Bible. To which is added, *A Roman Catholic's Reasons Why he Cannot Conform to the Protestant Religion.* "To the Law and to the Testimony: if they speak not according to this Word, it is because there is no light in them."—Isaiah viii. 20. Philadelphia: Published by Daniel Dougherty. A. Fagan, printer. 1815. pp. 87. 24mo. G. T. C.

CHARITY SCHOOL.—*A Brief Statement of the Proceedings and Present Condition of the Female Humane Association.* April 21, 1807. Baltimore: Printed by George Dobbin & Murphy, No. 10 Baltimore Street. pp. 8. 18mo.

Abp. Balt.

CHATEAUBRIAND'S American editions, re corded chronologically, as far as I know of them:

1812. *The Martyrs;* or, The Triumph of the Christian Religion. From the original French. . . . With Notes. In three volumes. New York: Published by Whiting & Watson. John Forbes, printer. 1812. 12mo. V. I., pp. xxviii. and 292. II. pp. 267. III. pp. 260. F.

[The Messrs. Sadlier republished, 1863, Wight's translation of 1849, same paging; it differs from the translation of 1812.

In 1827, appeared *Los Martires*, etc. Traducido del Frances por D. L. G. P. (?) Nueva York: Los Publican Behr y Kahl. 1827. 2 vols. 12mo. I. pp. xvi. and 277. II. pp. 303. F.

B. & K. printed Catholic devotional works as well as Voltaire's.]

1813. *Travels in Greece, Palestine, Egypt, and Barbary, during the Years* 1806 *and* 1807. Translated from the French by Frederic Shoberl. Philadelphia: Published by Moses Thomas. No. 52 Chestnut Street. James Maxwell, printer. 1813. pp. vi and 542. 8vo. F.

An advertisement, pp. iii., iv., signed "F. Shoberl, London, October 3, 1811."

1814. Same title to word *Shoberl,* then: Embellished with a map and four [six] wood engravings. New York: Published by Van Winkle and Wiley, corner of Wall and New Streets. T. C. Fay, printer. 1814. pp. 441, and Appendix, pp. 1–36; Index, 37–46. 8vo. F.

—— *Portrait of Bonaparte;* being a View of his Administration. Together with an Ode to Napoleon. New York: Published by Eastburn, Kirk &

Co., at the Literary Rooms, corner of Wall and Nassau Streets. 1814. pp. 37. 24mo. F.

[10,000 copies were sold at once of the first edition. Chateaubriand issued a second and revised edition. The Ode is by Lord Byron.]

1815. *The Beauties of Christianity. . . .* Translated from the French by Frederic Shoberl. With a Preface and Notes by the Rev. Henry Kett, B.D., Fellow of Trinity College, Oxford. Philadelphia: Printed for and Published by M. Carey. 1815. pp. xiv. and 524. 8vo. F.

[Mr. Kett says: "To render the work more palatable to the Protestant reader, a few chapters and paragraphs (!) . . . are omitted, and a few (!) expressions softened; yet some descriptions of the Catholic ceremonies are so beautiful, that it is presumed no reader of taste, whatever may be his religious opinions, will pronounce they had better been left out. A few long notes have been omitted, . . . some short ones are introduced in order to confirm the statements of the author, . . . and to do justice to the Protestant cause, etc." And Carey published this garbled work of an author yet living!]

1816. *Recollections of Italy, England, and America.* With Essays on Various Subjects in Morals and Literature. Philadelphia: Published by M. Carey. F.

Title-page; *verso*, Geo. Phillips, Printer, Carlisle; iii., iv., Contents; v.–xiii., Editor's Preface; 364 pp. Text.

[For this work as well as for Eustace, *v. infra*, I am indebted to the kindness of my old and highly esteemed friend, John Murphy, of Baltimore.

A note worth being carefully read: "Fr. de Ravignan—his zeal redoubled at the sight of death approaching his friend (Chateaubriand)—by his presence and his words gave comfort and courage to the veteran politician and writer now standing on the brink of the grave; beyond the fading poetry of life, beyond the shades of death, now almost seeming to lose their darkness, he pointed out the bright, all-important reality, Hope, the daughter of Faith, and that better immortality which is not of this world. The great writer, brought face to face with eternity, with faculties yet unimpaired, resolved to cut out of his works every page which his conscience rejected. The happiness he felt in tearing them up was some compensation for his grief in having written them. On his death-bed, he dictated the following memorandum to his nephew, who put it in our hands:

"'I declare, before God, that I retract every passage in my writings opposed to the Faith, to good morals, or to sound principles in general.

"'Signed in behalf of my uncle, Francis de Chateaubriand, who is unable to hold the pen, and agreeably to his request.

"'GEOFFROY-LOUIS DE CHATEAUBRIAND.'

"When this declaration had been put in writing, the dying man caused it to be read to him, insisted even on reading it with his own eyes, then, with peace in his soul, . . . he passed without a struggle to that God, etc.

"This last will has hitherto (1860) remained without effect. But the literary heritage of the author of the *Memoirs from Beyond the Tomb* no longer belongs to his family."—From *De Ravignan's Life*, by De Ponlevoy. Paris. 1860. Madame Récamier deserves much credit also in bringing about this reconciliation of the Viscount's soul with his God. An interesting biography of Chateaubriand is given in the *Baltimore Metropolitan*, iii. 78, 201.]

? CLARKE, JOHN.—Formerly Master of Public Grammar School in Hull. His Latin classics were published in N. Y. about 1804, 5, or 6.

CLAVIGERO.—*The History of Mexico.* Collected from Spanish and Mexican Historians, from Manuscripts and Ancient Paintings of the Indians. Illustrated by Charts and other Copper-plates. To which are added *Critical Dissertations on the Land, Animals, and Inhabitants of Mexico.* By Abbé D. Francesco Saverio Clavigero. Translated from the original Italian by Charles Cullen, Esq. In three volumes. Richmond, Virginia: Published by William Prichard. 1806. 3–8vo. F.

I. pp. iii.–vi. Contents (map torn off); vii., viii. Translator's Preface; ix.–xiv. Preface; xv.–xxxviii. "Account of Writers on Ancient Mexico"; xxxix. Advertisement; 1–378, Text; nine plates.

II. Map, front; iii.–viii. Contents; 1–444, Text; eighteen plates.

III. iii., iv. Contents; 1–485, Text.

—— Same title; after the word *Indians:* "Together with the Conquest of Mexico by the

Spaniards, Illustrated by engravings, with Critical," etc. Philadelphia: Published by Thomas Dobson, at the Stone House, No. 41 South Second Street. 1817. 3–8vo. F.

I. Map, front; *verso*, blank and unnumbered; ii. Directions for placing the Plates; the rest, same plates and types as above.

II. Same as above, better preserved.

III. do.

[Clavigero was a Jesuit. B. in Mexico, A.D. 1720, he followed the fate of his brethren after the mysterious edict of Charles IV., a Bourbon of Spain, who banished them from all Spanish dominions. He settled in Cesena, Papal States, where he died in 1793. There he published (1780, '81, 4 vols. 8vo) in Italian the great history whereof we have given the title, and also a *History of California*, a posthumous work published in Italian, Venice, 1789, 2 vols. 8vo. The Mexican history was translated into English by C. Cullen (not mentioned in Allibone), and published in London, 1787, 2 vols. 4to. There also exists a German abridged translation and a Spanish. His Mexican history was the result of thirty-six years uninterrupted travel over that country.]

CLERY.—*A Journal of the Occurrences in the Tower of the Temple during the Confinement of Louis* XVI., *King of France.* Animus meminisse horret. . . . Virg. By M. Cléry, the King's Valet-de-Chambre. Translated from the Original Manuscript, by R. C. Dallas, Esq., Author of *Miscella-*

neous Writings, etc. Boston: Printed by Manning & Loring for David West, No. 56 Cornhill. 1799. pp. 154. 12mo. F.

CLORIVIERE.—*Further Documents Showing the Causes of the Distressed State of the Roman Catholic Congregation in the City of Charleston.* By J. P. De Clorivière. Charleston: Moff. 1818. pp. 37. 8vo. B. B.

[*v.* in Bishop England's Works, iii. 253, a notice of Rev. Joseph Peter Picot de Clorivière, from the *National Intelligencer*—the *Baltimore Metropolitan*, 1855, iii. 654. I am indebted to the Mother Superior, Academy B. V. M., Georgetown, D. C., for the following: "Mr. Clorivière took charge of the Sisterhood, whose pecuniary embarrassments he greatly relieved, January 19, 1819, and remained until his death, September 29, 1826. His remains repose in the chapel of the convent."]

CONFIRMATION.—*v. Instruction.*

CORET, Jacques, S.J.—*L'Ange Conducteur dans la Devotion Chrétienne,* Reduite en Practique en Faveur des Ames Devotes. Philadelphia. 1811. 18mo. F.

Advertised by M. Carey, 1816, as printed for him.

[Coret's name is still highly honored in Liège, where he d. December 6, 1721.]

CORNARO.—*Sure and Certain Methods of Attaining a Long and Healthy Life*, with Means of Correcting a Bad Constitution. Written by Lewis Cornaro, an Italian Nobleman, when he was near an Hundred Years of Age. With a Recommendatory Preface, by the Hon. Joseph Addison, Esq. The First American Edition. Philadelphia: Reprinted for the Rev. M. L. Weems by Parry Hall, Chesnut Street. M.DCC.XCIII. pp. xvii.–156. 18mo.
F.

[Mr. Carey advertised in June, 1816, *The Immortal Mentor*; or, Man's Unerring Guide to a Healthy, Wealthy, and Happy Life. In Three Parts. By Lewis Cornaro, Dr. Franklin, and Dr. Scott. 12mo. One dollar.

An interesting parallel:—

The late Amos Lawrence, of Boston, was a rigid observer of Cornaro's system. "His extreme sensitiveness . . . led him to adopt a system . . . which limited him to the use of certain kinds of food. . . . It was of the most simple kind, and was taken in small quantities, after being weighed in a balance, which always stood before him," etc. See more interesting details at pp. 123, 4, and 326 in his *Life*, by his son, W. R. Lawrence, M.D. Boston: Gould & Lincoln. 1855.]

CREVECOEUR, HECTOR ST. JOHN DE.—*Lettres d'un Cultivateur Americain.* Ecrites a W. S., Ecuyer, depuis l'Anné 1770, jusqu'à 1781. Traduites de l'Anglois par * * * A Paris: Chez

Cuchet, Libraire, Rue & Hotel Serpente. M.DCC.LXXXIV. 2 vols. 12mo. F.

Vol. I., pp. iii.–vj., "A Mr. de la Fayette, . . . l'Auteur et Traducteur. New-Yorck, 24 Sept., 1781"; pp. vij.–xxiv., two "Lettres d'Introduction by Lacretelle, Sr., | 1751–1824;" | Text, 422. First letter date, Carlisle County, 18 Août, 1770.

II. pp. iv. and 400. W. S., *i.e.*, William Seton, father-in-law of Elizabeth Seton, foundress of Sisters of Charity in the United States. The French is far more copious than the English.

—— *Lettres . . . . Adressées à Wm. S . . . on, Esq., depuis l'a* 1770 *jusqu'en* 1786. Par M. St. John de Creve Coeur, traduites de l'Anglois. "Keen feelings inspire resistless thoughts." A Paris: Chez Cuchet, Libraire, Rue et Hôtel Serpent. 1787. 8vo. F.

Vol. I. *Verso* title-page, engraving of "A Happy Family," Indian and European; motto, "Ubi Panis et Libertas, ibi Patria;" title-page, vignette: Monument to Warren, Montgomery, Wooster, Mercer; "O Manes Heroum Vestra Libera est Patria;" pp. j.–xiv., dedication to Lafayette, Lacretelle's Lettres; xv.–xxxij., an article from the *Mercure*, 1775; Map U. S.; Text, 478.

Vol. II. A larger Map of several States and Canada; Text, 438; at p. 99, Map of Nantucket; 147, Martha's Vineyard.

Vol. III. pp. 592; p. 413, "Rivière du Grand Castor et Muskinghum;" p. 517, Plan of the Bridge over the Shétucket (Thames), near Norwich, Conn. The engravings are uncommonly skilful, and this edition is even larger than that of '84.

—— *Letters from an American Farmer*, Describing certain Provincial Situations, Manners, and Customs, and Conveying some Idea of the State of the People of North America. Written to a Friend in England, by J. Hector St. John, a Farmer in Pennsylvania. Philadelphia: From the Press of Mathew Carey. March 4, M.DCC.XCIII. pp. viii–240. 12mo. F.

Pp. iii., iv., "To the Abbé Raynal, F.R.S. J. Hector St. John, Carlisle, in Pennsylvania." pp. v., vi., Advertisement to the first London edition; pp. vii., viii., Contents; 9–240, Text.

[For items of H. St. John Crevecoeur, *v. History of Catholic Church in the United States*, by De Courcy & Shea. Dunigan. 1856. p. 353. Also, *Duyckinck's Cyclopædia of American Literature*, vol. i., 172. The latter says that these *Letters* were first written in English, and made their first appearance in London, 1782, 8vo. (A copy sold at Rice's sale, New York, March, 1870, and another London, of 1783, 8vo, sold at Stevens's sale, Boston, April, 1870. I have seen a 12mo edition, Belfast, 1783.) The author then translated them into French. *Vide* also Continuation of De Feller.]

De Crevecoeur wrote also:

Voyage dans la Haute Pensylvanie et dans l'Etat de New-York. Par un Membre Adoptif de la Nation Onéida. Traduit et publié par l'Auteur des *Lettres d'un Cultivateur Américan.* 3 vols. 8vo.

De l'Imprimerie de Crapelet. A Paris : Chez Maradan, Libraire, Rue Pavée S. André-des-Arcs, No. 16. An ix., 1801. F.

Vol. I. pp. ii.–xiv., Avant-propos du Traducteur; "The translation is an affectation, purporting to be from a manuscript cast ashore from a wreck on the Elbe;" xv.–xvii., "A S. E. Geo. Washington;" pp. 427, Text; facing title-page, profile laurelled Portrait of George Washington, né en Virginie le 11 Février, 1732, | gravé d'après le Camée peint par Madame de Brehan à New York, 1789. Gravé par Roger. Dirigé par P. F. Tardieu. | Page 115, portrait of Késkétomah, Ancient Sachem de la Nation Onondaga. Bonfils delineavit—Tardieu—Roger. (Very fine engraving.) Page 233, "L'Aigle à tête chauve enlevant la proie de l'Aigle Pêcheur." At the close of the volume, "Carte de la Partie Septentrionale des E.–U."

Vol. II. pp. xiv. and 434. Maps : Niagara ; Eastern Fall do. ; another view do. ; Southern parts of United States. (Excellent engraving.)

Vol. III. pp. xii. and 409. Maps : Canals, finished or projected ; Ancient Fortifications at the junction of the Muskingum with the Ohio, by Captain Hart, U. S. A. ; and fortifications by the Indians, by A. Steiner.

[This work has been translated into German by Tiedemann, 8vo, Berlin, 1802. The history of Crevecoeur's life is both interesting and painful ; the references I have given above supply abundantly the circumstances. C. b. at Caen, France, 1731 ; d. at Sarcelles, 1813. While in New York, he took a prominent part in the affairs of St. Peter's Church.]

DAPONTE, Lorenzo.

[Born in Ceneda, Venetian States, March 10, 1749, d. New York, August 17, 1838. Formerly a Catholic priest, he afterwards married. Came to New York in 1805; introduced the Italian opera here, as J. G. Shea informs me, and was appointed Professor of Italian Literature in Columbia College at the age of 80. He was reconciled with the Catholic Church on his deathbed. "Besides various dramas, he is the author of *Memoirs* of his own life, of a number of sonnets, and of translations of Byron's *Prophecy of Dante*, and of Dodsley's *Economy of Human Life*, all printed in New York."—*Appleton's Cyclopædia*. I have been unable to procure any of his works or see their titles. Hence I merely insert his name here, hoping to be able to give further details in the second part of the *Bibliographia*. It is said that he took the Hon. Mr. Cameron in hand when a boy, and educated him. Allibone has not the name.]

DAVID, J. B.

[See the interesting life of this great missionary of the West in Dr. Spalding's *Sketches of Kentucky*. Suffice here to remark that he was born near Nantes, France, A.D. 1761. He came to this country in 1792, was consecrated Bishop Coadjutor to Dr. Flaget, of Bardstown, Ky., Aug. 15, 1819, and d. July 12, 1841, æt. 81. See *Life of Bishop Flaget*, by Abp. Spalding, and Baltimore *Catholic Almanac*, 1842, p. 167, and 1846, p. 50. His very likeness betrays the soul of a saint. In 1809 he published a prayer-book, the *True Piety*. It is a reprint of the Cork edition of 1797. I have before me the copy used by Bishop David, with the alterations in his handwriting. It only forms the groundwork of the much enlarged American edition. Here I give the title, with the portion omitted or altered *in italics*:

True Piety; | or, the | Day Well Spent. | *A Manual* | of |

Chosen Prayers, Devout Practices, and | Solid Instructions. | Adapted to every State of Life. | — | *By the Right Rev. Dr. C.....* | Taken partly from the French. | — | *The eighth edition, with additions.* | — | Ask and you shall receive, that your Joy may be | full. St. John, xvi. 24. | — | *Cork:* | *Printed for the Proprietors.* | — | 1797. pp. ix–286.]

True Piety; or, The Day Well Spent. Being a Catholic Manual of Chosen Prayers, Devout Practices, and Solid Instructions. Adapted to every State of Life. Taken partly from the French. "Ask and you shall receive, that your joy be full." —St. John, xvi. 24. First American Edition. With considerable Additions. By a Catholic Clergyman of Baltimore, and with the Authority of the Right Rev. Bishop Carroll. Baltimore: Printed and sold by Warner & Hanna, at the Bible and Heart Printing-Office. 1809. pp. iv. and 528. 18mo. F.

[Against the title-page, a horrid representation of the Crucifixion.]

A Second Edition, same plates, same paging, on inferior paper. In my copy, first and last pages torn off. F.

—— —— Same title to St. John xvi. 24. From the Second American Edition. By the authority of the Rt. Rev. Bishop David. Lexington: Printed at *Kentucky Gazette* Office. 1824. pp. 327. 18mo. F.

Contemporaneous to the Lexington edition appeared,

True Piety. . . . Adapted to all Ranks and Conditions. Ask . . . Copyright Secured, According to Law. Stereotype Edition. Philadelphia: Published by Eugene Cummiskey. 1824. pp. 213. 18mo. F.

and

True Piety . . . John xvi. 24. Approved by Bishop Kenrick. Philadelphia: Eugene Cummiskey, 130 S. Sixth Street. 1832. pp. 424. 18mo. F.

[These two editions differ from the Cork and the David editions, and from each other. In Bishop Spalding's *Sketches*, at page 256, we read that "Fr. David's *Prayer-Book*, like many other works, has since been improved for the worst; and Fr. David was wont to call the new editions, with a smile, the *false True Pieties*."]

—— —— *Catholic Hymn-Book.* Bardstown. 1815.

[I have been unable to find a copy of it. But Archbishop Spalding has favored me with a copy of the edition, published in Louisville by Webb & Levering, 18—. "Compiled chiefly from Bishop David's original volume," write the publishers. If I well remember, I think I saw at St. Sulpice, in Baltimore, a catechism in the handwriting of Bishop David, and composed by himself.]

DEPONS, F.—*Voyage to the Eastern Part of Terra Firma, or the Spanish Main, in South America, during the Years* 1801, 2, 3, 4. Containing a Description of the Territory under the Jurisdiction of the Captain-General of Caraccas, composed of the Provinces of Venezuela, Maracaibo, Varinas, Spanish Guiana, Cumana, and the Islands of Margaretta; and embracing everything Relative to the Discovery, Conquest, Topography, Legislation, Commerce, Finances, Inhabitants, and Productions of the Provinces, together with a View of the Manners and Customs of the Spaniards, and the Savage as well as the Civilized Indians. By F. D., late Agent of the French Government at Caraccas. Translated by an American Gentleman. New York: Printed by and for I. Riley & Co., No. 1 City Hotel, Broadway. 1806. 3 vols. 8vo. F.

I. Map; pp. xxxii. and 348. II. 256. III. 293.

[It is evidently the work of a Catholic writer, although he may at times write with inaccuracy. Nor can any one find fault with his touching upon what he honestly considers an abuse. Chapter VII. will give the keytone of the work, which is introduced by a letter to the publisher (was I. Riley a Catholic in profession, as he was in name ?), by the celebrated sceptic, Dr. Sam. L. Mitchill, who gives it as a source of recommendation to many that the author writes more like a man of business than a man of science. The introductory remarks are a hasty translation by the doctor. The text does not seem to bear evidence of perfect English style, and much less of one well acquainted with Catholic terms. Of the author I have been unable to find any information. My copy bears the autograph of W. Irving. The original edition is entitled "*Voyage à la partie Orientale de la Terre-ferme, dans l'Amérique Meridionale, fait pendant les années* 1801, 1802, 1803, *et* 1804: Contenant la Description de la Capitainerie générale de Caracas, composée des Provinces de Venezuela, Maracaibo, Varinas, la Guiane Espagnole, Cumana, et de l'Ile de la Margarite; et renfermant . . . par F. Depons, ex-Agent du Gouvernement Français à Caracas. Avec une Carte géographique, et les Plans de la ville Capitale et des ports principaux. *Bonus historicus est qui de iis scribit rebus, quibus ipse interfuit.* Polib. Hist. lib. 12. A Paris, Colnet, etc., etc., etc., etc. 1806. 3 vols. 12mo. F.

An English edition appeared in 1807. London: Longman, Hurst, Rees & Orme. 2 vols. 8vo. F.

The title differs from the American. It does not avow it to be "A translation by an American gentleman," although the text is the same, with the exception of the preface, which is given at full length, whilst Dr. Mitchill's, in the American edition, is not only hasty, but cramped and curtailed.]

DIAZ DEL CASTILLO, CAPT. BERNAL—*The True History of the Conquest of Mexico.* By ——, one of the Conquerors. Written in the year 1568.

"Labore, et Expensis, et damno, Tempore, veritatis cognitio adquiritur." Translated from the Original Spanish, by Maurice Keatinge, Esq. Printed in London. Reprinted at Salem, by Joshua Cushing for Cushing & Appleton. 1803. 2 vols. 8vo. F.

Vol. I. pp. viii. and 333; facing title-page, "Ancient Plan of the City of Mexico." II. iv. and 440.

[Original title, *Historia Verdadera de la Conquesta de Nueva Espagna.* Madrid. 1632. Folio. It was edited by a friar of the Order of Mercy, who disentombed the MSS. from an old library.]

DOCTRINE, *An Abridgment of the Christian*—By Bishop Hay. Philadelphia: Printed for Mathew Carey, No. 118 Market Street. 1803. pp. 143. 18mo. S. S. B.

——— ——— ——— With some Alterations in the Language. Published with the approbation of the Rt. Rev. Bp. Carroll. Printed for Bernard Dornin, and sold by him at his Roman Catholic Library, No. 30 Baltimore Street, Baltimore. Geo. Dobbin & Murphy, Printers. 1809. pp. 108. 24mo. S. S. B.

DOCTRINE, *Summary Proofs of the Catholic—from Scripture.* Price 12½ cents. Dornin's advertisement. 1810.

DOCTRINE, CATHOLIC — *and Catholic Principles Explained.* To which is added *The Conversion of the Duchess of York,* written by herself; of *A. M. de Ramsay,* by Abp. Fénelon (1709), as given by Ramsay himself. New York: Higgins, 16 Barclay Street. 1817. A. Spooney, Printer. pp. 92. 24mo. G. T. C.

DRYDEN, J.—*Prose Works.* Philadelphia: Sanford. 1819.

[Dryden became a Catholic under James II., and d. May 1, 1707, æt. 70. His translation of the *Life of St. Francis Xavier,* from the French of Père D. Bouhours—a penance imposed on him, it is said, on his conversion, to atone for reproachable compositions—appeared in London, 1683, with the title, "*Life of S. Francis Xavier, of the Society of Jesus;* translated from the French of Dominick Bouhours into English. London, 1683. 8vo." Did Mr. Sanford republish it? Allibone, in a fair notice of Dryden, does not mention this item of his life.]

DUBOIS, Abbe J. A.—*Description of the Characters, Manners, and Customs of the People of India,* and of their Institutions, Religious and Civil. By the A. J. A. D., Missionary in the Mysore. Translated from the French Manuscript. Philadelphia: Published by M. Carey & Son, No. 126, Chesnut Street. 1818. 2 vols. 8vo. F.

I. pp. iii.–x., Advertisement, dated London, Dec. 2, 1816; pp. xi.–xxiv., Preface and Contents; Text, 25–390.

II. pp. ii.–viii., Contents; Text, 9–368.

[Rev. Mr. Dubois "escaped from one of the fusillades of the French Revolution, and then lived among the Hindoos as one of themselves." He was highly esteemed by both the officers of the East India Company and those of the British army and Government. The work was written before 1807, and remained in the East India Company Library until it was translated. This edition is a reprint of the English of 1816, which was made on a translation of the French MS. entrusted by the author to the hands of Major Wilks, Acting President at Mysore, in 1806. In December, 1867, I bought, at the sale of Dr. Jenk's library, the following work, on the fly-page whereof we read, "From the author to his respected and venerated brother, the Rev. Dr. Baldwin, Boston"; and then, in Dr. Jenk's handwriting, "Bo't at sale of late Rev. Dr. B.'s books." Here is the title: *Reply to the Abbé J. A. Dubois's Letters on the State of Christianity in India, originally published in the "Friend of India."* Serampore: Printed at the Mission Press. 1824. pp. 208. 8vo. Was it printed at the expense of the A. B. F. M.? Then, surely, money never was more wantonly thrown away.—The Hon. and Rev. Ignatius Spencer, a Passionist, made the following entry in his diary:

"*Thursday, Oct.* 3, 1844, PARIS.

"Took the omnibus to Rue de Bac. Had an interesting conversation with the Abbé Dubois, now 80 years old. . . He receives a pension of £100 from England."]

DUBOURG, MOST REV. W. LOUIS VALENTINE.

[Born February 14, 1766, at Cape Français, San Domingo; entered St. Sulpice Seminary, in Paris; arrived in Baltimore,

December, 1794; entered St. Sulpice, 1795. Whilst superintendent of St. Mary's Seminary, if any attack was made on the Catholic Church by the papers, and if refused insertion to a reply, by a courteous note that the reply would be sent to another paper, with notes of explanation for such a course, his rejoinders were always inserted, and it was a case often repeated. Was he the author of *St. Mary's Seminary and the Catholics at large Vindicated;* also of *The Sons of St. Dominic?* (*v.* Brute and titles *infra.*) Dr. Dubourg was consecrated Bishop of New Orleans, in Rome, September 24, 1815; November 19, 1826, he took possession of the Diocese of Montauban, in France, formerly occupied by Dr. Cheverus; February, 1833, transferred to the Archdiocese of Besançon; he there died the 12th of the following December, æt. 65. (*Cfr. Catholic Almanac,* Baltimore, 1839, page 50; *Catholic Telegraph,* Cincinnati, 1834. In a pamphlet, *Battle of New Orleans: A Poem,* Dr. Dubourg's address to General Jackson is reported at page 33; *Annales de la Propagation de la Foi,* ii., 405, and his letter to the Council, *ib.* i. and ii., page 394. *v.* Clarke's *Deceased Bishops.*]

DUPONCEAU, P. S.

["As far as our literature is concerned, we owe much to Duponceau, who first drew the attention of the learned to the philosophical and ethnological labors of early Catholic missions in America, China, and the East at large."—*Prize Essay on American Catholic Literature, Baltimore Metropolitan Magazine, March,* 1854. "Du Ponceau, claimed as a Catholic author, was a very bad Catholic, to say the least, having neither lived (at least for forty years) nor died in the communion of the Church."—*Ed. Metropolitan Magazine.* Be this as it may, he has contributed to the knowledge and value of Catholic literature, never joined any particular sect, never professed anti-Catholic sentiments (unless for the limited part he took in the Hogan schism), and for what regards his last hour, what do we know? Peter Stephen Duponceau, b. in France, June 3, 1760, d. in Philadelphia, April 1, 1844; made studies preparatory for the priesthood; landed at Portsmouth, N. H., December 1, 1777; was attached to Baron Steuben's staff. In July, 1781, he became a citizen, and since 1785 was one of the most successful members of the American bar. In the Hogan imbroglio he sided with the schismatics, until he became disgusted with the whole affair, and, with M. Carey, and others, withdrew his name and influence. M. Duponceau, whilst practising law, translated several valuable books on law, and published original essays on the same subject. In connection with the American Philosophical Society, of which he had been a member since 1791, he published, in 1819, a report on *The Structure of the Indian Language.* On the occasion of Citizen Genet's reception at Philadelphia, Duponceau wrote an ode, which was translated by Philip Freneau. For more details about Mr. Duponceau's literary labors, *v.* second part of this *Bibliographia.* I am informed, from a creditable source, that the late Right Rev. Dr. Bruté, of Vincennes, took great interest in the spiritual welfare of Peter S. Duponceau, with what result we may yet find out.]

ELEVATION *of the Soul.* *v.* Baudran.

ENGLAND'S *Conversion and Reformation Compared;* or, The Young Gentleman Directed in the Choice of his Religion. To which is premised, *A Brief Inquiry into the General Grounds of the Catholic Faith,* in a Conversation between a Young Gentleman and his Preceptor. Divided into Four

Dialogues. The First American Edition. Revised and Corrected from the Fifth Dublin Edition. "Examine yourselves whether you be in the Faith."—2 Cor. xiii. 5. "Prove all things: hold fast that which is good."—Thess. v. 21. Lancaster: Printed for George Daly, by Jesse Kendall. 1813. F.

Pp. 318; 12mo; eight pp. unnumbered; Subscribers' names.

[Sixteen pages are taken up with subscribers' names. A seventh edition was published, revised and corrected, in Belfast, by Joseph Smith, 34 High Street, 1817. Is not this work by Thomas Ward, author of the *Bible Errata* and *England's Reformation: A Poem.* 2 vols. 12mo. London: Printed in the year MDCCXV. ?]

EXERCISE — *Short Daily.* Advertised by Dornin, 1808.

ESSAI *du Michigan.* *v.* Richard.

ESPRIELLA, DON MAN. ALO.—*Letters from England.* Translated from the Spanish. First American Edition. Boston: Printed by Munroe & Francis, No. 10 Court Street. 1807. pp. 384. 12mo. F.

EUSTACE, REV. JOHN CHETWODE.—*A Classical Tour in Italy.* An. MDCCCII. "Haec est

Italia diis sacra, hae gentes ejus, haec oppida populorum."—Plin. Nat. Hist. iii. 20. First American from the Third London Edition, Revised and Enlarged. Illustrated with ten Engravings, an Index, etc. Philadelphia: Published by M. Carey, No. 121 Chestnut Street. For sale by him and Wells & Lilly, Boston. J. Robinson, printer, Baltimore. 1816. 2–8vo. pp. ix.–538 and 584. F.

[Rev. J. C. Eustace, a Catholic priest, b. in Lancaster, had charge of several young English noblemen, and with them visited the Continent. An edition of Eustace, 2 vols. 12mo, was published in Leghorn, by Glaucus Mosi, 1817. H. ✠ C.]

ETRENNES *Spirituelles, Petites*—Contenant les Prières et Offices, et la Messe, Latin-François. A l'usage Universel. 32mo. Price 44 cts. Carey's advertisement, 1816.

EXERCICIO *Quotidiano.* Oraciones y Devotiones para Antes y Despues de la Confesion y Sagrada Comunion. 24mo. Price 63 cts. Carey's advertisement, 1816.

FENELON. 1736 (?).

[At a sale by Bangs, Merwin & Co., March 7, 1870, *The Tales and Fables of Fénelon, in English and French.* Illustrated with Copper-plates. 8vo. 1736. (American?) My order miscarried.

The work was bought by a Worcester firm; wrote to them; the book could not be found.]

1750. —— *Dissertation on Pure Love.* With an Account of the Life and Writings of a Lady for whose sake the Archbishop was banished from Court, and the Grievous Persecutions she Suffered in France for her Religion. Also, Two Letters written by one of the Lady's Maids during her Confinement in the Castle of Vincennes, where she was a prisoner for eight years; one of the Letters was written with a Bit of Stick instead of a Pen, and Soot instead of Ink, to her brother; the other to a Clergyman. Together with an Apologetic Preface, containing divers Letters of the Archbishop of Cambray to the Duke of Burgundy, the present French King's Father and other persons of distinction. Also, divers Letters of the Lady to Persons of Quality, relating to her Religious Principles. Germantown, Pa. 1750. pp. 217. 12mo.

Gowan's Catalogue, No. 19. 1860.

1796–7. —— *Telemachus, The Adventures of*— From the French of F., by the celebrated J. Hawkesworth, LL.D. Corrected and Revised by G. Gregory. With a Life of the author, and a complete Index, historical and geographical. Embellished with engravings. In two vols. Printed by T. & J. Swords for David Longworth, No. 66 Nassau Street, New York. 8vo. F.

Vol. I. n. d. Milus, sculptor; Roberts, sculptor; Telemachus's Portrait from vision, and eight Engravings, seventh marked "D. Longworth, 66 Nassau Street, 1796." pp. 357.

Vol. II. Facing title-page, two basso-rilievos of Ulysses and Telemachus, from the antique; beneath, "Engraved by Thos. Clarke, N. Y. New York: Published by David Longworth, No. 66 Nassau Street. 1797;" in title-page, "Printed and Published by D. Longworth, No. 11 Park. Roberts, sculptor;" four Engravings, besides the title Medallion. pp. 318.

[It will prove difficult to find in America a work more elegantly printed than this up to twenty years ago. It is a gem of typography.]

1797. —— *Les Aventures de Telemaque. . . .* Nouvelle Edition. . . . Revue et Corrigée par Joseph Nancrede, Maître de Langue François, en l'Université de Cambridge. A Boston: Chez Joseph Nancrede, Libraire, No. 49 Marlborough Street. 1797. pp. 375. 12mo. F.

[*v.* Nancrede, *infra*, and Charles Butler, *supra.*]

1804. —— *Extracts from the Writings of Francis Fénelon, Archbishop of Cambray.* With some Memoirs of his Life. To which are added:

Letters Expressive of Love and Friendship. The writer not known. Recommended to the perusal and notice of the religiously disposed. By John Kendall. Philadelphia: Printed and sold by Kimber, Conrad & Co., No. 170 South Second Street. 1804. pp. xiii.–223. 12mo. F.

[Mme. de la Mothe Guyon's *Poems*, by W. Cooper, advertised in said book.]

1806. —— *The Adventures of Telemachus, Son of Ulysses.* By the Abp. of Cambray. Second American Edition [after Longworth's?]. Philadelphia: Printed for Mathew Carey, No. 122 Market Street. Wm. F. McLaughlin, printer. 1806.

[Advertised by M. Carey, 1816. Hawkesworth's translation, 2 vols. 18mo., also advertised by M. Carey; also, *Les Aventures de Telemaque;* par Fénelon; nouvelle edition revue et corrigée par Charles Le Brun. 12mo. 138 cts. And *Les Aventures,* etc., *en François et en Anglois.* Seconde edition Amer. soigneusement comparée avec les meilleures eds. Françoises . . . par L. C. Wallon, prof. en l'Univ'é de Pennie. 2 vols. 12mo. 225 cts.]

1806. —— *Treatise on the Education of Daughters.* Translated from the French, and adapted to English Readers. With an original Chapter, *On Religious Studies.* By the Rev. T. F. Dibbin. . . .

Albany: Printed and published by Backus & Whiting. 1806. pp. xi. and 250. 12mo. F.

[It was lately sold for $12. I think there is another copy in G. T. C.]

1810. —— *Dialogues Concerning Eloquence in General, and Particularly that kind which is Proper for the Pulpit.* By M. de Fénelon, Abp. of Cambray. Translated from the French, and illustrated with Notes and Quotations. By W. Stevenson, M.A., Rector of Morningthorp, in Norfolk. First American Edition. Published by Farrand, Mallory & Co., Boston; Lyman, Mallory & Co., Portland; B. B. Hopkins & Co., Philadelphia; P. H. Nicklin & Co., Baltimore; D. Farrand & Green, Albany; and Williams & Whiting, New York. 1810. pp. v. 174. 12mo. S. J. Armstrong, printer. F.

1811. —— *Conversation with Ramsay.* *v. supra Catechism of Foundation, etc.*

J. G. S., B. M.

1814. —— *Pious Reflections.* Newburg. *v. Doctrine, Catholic* —.

FENWICK, Rev. B. J.—*A Sermon* delivered in the Roman Catholic Church, New York, on

Sunday evening, February 25, 1810, for the benefit of the City Dispensary. New York: Published by Williams & Whiting, at their Theological and Classical Book-store, No. 118 Pearl Street. J. Seymour, printer. 1810. pp. 22. 8vo.

B. P. L.

[Rev. Benedict Joseph Fenwick succeeded Bishop Cheverus in the Episcopal See of Boston in 1825. For a notice of this eminent prelate see R. H. Clarke's *Lives of Deceased Bishops*, and the truly eloquent tribute paid to his memory by Dr. O. A. Brownson (*Brownson's Quarterly Review*, October, 1846). The following Latin eulogy, written by a young Italian on the occasion of his death, and privately circulated, was never published. It was intended for a scroll to be placed in the coffin at the Bishop's burial in the grave-yard attached to the Jesuit College of Holy Cross, near Worcester, Mass. The Bishop's grave, although not neglected, was for many years left unadorned by any monument. The lamented Rev. Mr. Boyce alludes to this neglect in his *Mary Lee* (p. 319, Balt. ed., 1868) in words of much feeling, indeed, but, perhaps, in not very good taste. However, a reparation has been made by the Rev. John Brady, in 1867, under the superintendence of Rev. John Powers, of Worcester. An elegant and costly monument of white marble adorns the grave of one of the very best of men.

D. M.
heic
Benedictus J. Fenwick
In . S . Mariæ . Com . Oræ . Maryl . Ortus . Modestam . Sed . Dudum . Amatam . Corpori . Requietem . Voluit.

Religione . Auctoritate . Sapientia . Summis . Viris . Æquatus . Vixit . A . p . m . LXIIII.

Soc . JESU . In . Ipso . Ætatis . Flore . Nomine . Dato . Post . Neoborac . Et . Georgiop . Lyceorum . Præfecturas . In . Karopol . Expeditone . Animis . Pacatis . Religione . Constabilita . Multis . Ad . Religionem . Virtutem . Que . Excitatis . Et . Institutis.

Eum . Doli . Nescium . Prudentia . Incomparabilem . Mitissimum . Ingenio . Propositi . Tenacem . Pontificem . Bostoniensem . A . LEONE . XII . P . M . Renunciatum . Patrem . Alti . Pauperes . Et . Sanctissimum . Omnes . Prædicaverunt.

Pontificatu . XXI . An . In . Exemplum . Perfunctus . De . Plebe . Klero . Et . Ecclesiis . Arduis . Exantlatis . Laboribus . Vitiis . Plurimis . Profligatis . Sontibus . Debellatis . Patrimonio . Que . Omni . Profuso . Optime . Meritus . Dec . III . Non . Aug . A . R . S . M.DCCC.XXXXVI.

In . Funere . Publico . Vel . Acatholicorum . Lacrimis . Honestatus.

S . T . ✠ . I . P .

Sodales . Veteres . Seniori . Pientissimo.

Alumni . In . Vigorn . Ephebeo . Per . Eum . Inchoato . Et . Omni . Cultu . Exornato . Parenti . Suæ Salutis.

Have . Et . Vale . Anima . Suavissima.

FIELD, M.—See *Almanac.*

FLEMING, REV. FRANCIS A.—*The Calumnies of Verus;* or, Catholics vindicated from certain old Slanders revived; in a Series of Letters published in different Gazettes at Philadelphia. Collected and revised by "Verax," with the addition of a Preface and a few Notes. Philadelphia: Johnson & Justice. 1792.

[J. G. Shea, Esq., is the fortunate possessor of this extremely rare work; he writes: "The Rev. Fr. F. was, it seems, a Father of the Company of Jesus, but his name does not appear in Oliver's Collection," nor in the more recent work of Carayon, *Bibliographie Historique de la C. de J.*, Paris, 1864. For a history of Fr. Fleming's work, see *The Catholic Church in the U. S.*, by De Courcy, and J. G. S., pp. 220, 221. The following will prove interesting:

"LOYOLA COLLEGE, BALTIMORE, MD., July 29, '71.

"*Rev. Dear Father, P. C.:* All I can find in relation to Rev. F. A. Fleming is his name in the list of clergymen, Anno 1791, and in 1793 there is the entry of his death. No place of residence, etc. He seems to have been a secular priest.

"I am sorry that this information is so meagre, and that I have no idea where you might find more. The good old missionaries seem to have cared little about records of their acts in this world—their labors are recorded in heaven.

"Yours in Dno.,

"JOS. E. KELLER, S.J."

FLETCHER, REV. J.—*Works of the Rev. John Fletcher.* The First American Edition. Philadelphia: Printed by Joseph Cruksank. Sold by John Dickins, No. 182 in Race Street, near Sixth Street. 3 vols. 12mo. n. d. Abp. B.?

—— *Reflections on the Spirit, etc., etc.* [sic] *of Religious Controversy.* With Observations on the

Discourses of Doctor Proteus, Bishop of London; Doctor Watson, Bishop of Landaff; Doctor Shute Barrington, Bishop of Durham; and Doctor Rennell, of London. By the Rev. Dr. Fletcher, of Hexham, England. New York: Printed and published for Bernard Dornin, Bookseller, 136 Pearl Street. 1808. pp. xvi.–252. 12mo. F.

—— *A Comparative View of the Grounds of the Catholic and Protestant Churches.* "Look at the Rock, from which you have been separated." —Is. Baltimore: Published by F. Lucas, Jr. J. Robinson, printer. 1820. pp. xii.–366. 12mo. F.

[For a very scanty notice of F., see Allibone, ad n.]

FLEURY. — *Catechismus Historicus Minor.* Auctore Abate Fleury. Philadelphia: Impensis Joannes Conrad et Soc.; M. et J. Conrad et Soc., Baltimore; Rapin, Conrad et Soc., Washington; Somerwell & Conrad, Petersburg; et Bousal, Conrad et Soc., Norfolk. Excudebat J. et G. Palmer, 116 Vico Alto [High Street?]. 1805. pp. 73. 18mo. F.

[It is a spurious work. See *St. Mary's Seminary and Catholics at Large*, Baltimore, Dornin, 1811, pp. 5, 6.]

—— *Catechisme Historique.—Historical Catechism.*

Verso of this simple title-page: *Petit Catechisme Historique, contenant en abrégé l'Histoire Sainte, et la Doctrine Chrétienne.* Par M. Fleury, Prêtre, Prieur d'Argenteuil. Nouvelle edition. Detroit: Imprimé par Theophile Mettez. 1812. pp. 201. 12mo; 4 pp. unnumb. Index.

The work is both in French and English. Evidently opposite to the above title was another in English; but the copy kindly lent me by Father Hecker (this rare book belongs to the Library of the Congregation of St. Paul, N. Y.) is torn from p. 3 to 10 inclusive.—*v. infra*, Richard. Bound with the *Catechism* we find *Les Ornemens de la Mémoire; ou, Les Traits Brillans des Poetes François le plus Célèbres.* Avec des Dissertations sur chaque Genre de Style. Pour Perfectionner l'Education de la Jeunesse. Au Detroit. Imprimé par A. Coxshaw. 1811. pp. i. ii., Introduction; 3–132. 12mo. Wretched paper and ink; types seem worn. The two last pages, unnumbered, contain, in French and English, "Proposals for printing, in French and English, *The Epistles and Gospels*, for all Sundays and holydays throughout the year." See Appendix for collation of this from a copy in the possession of Mr. Shea.

—— *Short Historical Catechism:* Containing a summary of the sacred history and Christian Doctrine. Translated from the French. Revised by the Right Rev. Bishop Cheverus. Baltimore: Published by F. Lucas, Jr., 138 Market Street. n. d. 12mo. B. P. L.

[E. Cummiskey, 130 South 6th Street, Philadelphia, republished it.]

—— —— Containing a Summary of the Sacred History and Christian Doctrine. Translated from the French, and revised. Published with the approbation of the Right Reverend Bishop. Boston: Printed by J. Belcher. 1813. pp. 120. 32mo. Abp. B.

[Since 1820, P. Cunningham published it, pp. 71, 18mo, as translated from the French, and revised by the Rt. Rev. Bishop Cheverus.—F.]

—— —— Another edition. N. Y.: W. H. Creagh. 24mo. [Date?] G. T. C.

[In 1828, Ezra Lincoln, of Boston, published "*A Brief Summary of the Sacred History, And Christian Doctrine.* Published for the use of the Catholic Sunday School, with the approbation of the Right Reverend Bishop. pp. 32. 16mo." I am told that it is a new edition of one formerly published by Bp. Cheverus. *v. supra* the title of Detroit ed.]

FRANCIS DE SALES, St.—*An Introduction to a Devout Life.* From the French of St. Fr. de S., Bishop and Prince of Geneva. To which is prefixed an Abstract of his Life. First American

from the sixth London edition, revised and corrected. Baltimore: Published by Bernard Dornin, and for sale at his Catholic bookstore, No. 5, Saratoga Street, within a few yards of the Arch-Bishop's. J. Robinson, printer. 1806. 1–18mo. pp. xv.–393.
F.

[Was not this the last work published by Dornin in Baltimore? *v. supra,* Elevation, etc. John Yates, S.J., is thought to be "The translator of the *Introduction* in 1613, 12mo, pp. 695. It is dedicated to Miss Ann Roper, great-grand-daughter of Sir Thomas Moore." *v.* Dr. Oliver, ad n.]

GAHAN, Rev. W., O.S.A.—*A Compendious Abstract of the History of the Church of Christ, from its First Foundation to the Eighteenth Century.* With a faithful and circumstantial account of the Acts of the Apostles; of the Lives of the Primitive Christians; of the General Persecutions raised against them by the Pagan Emperors; of the Œcumenical Councils; of the Chief Pastors; of the Condemnation of the Ancient Heresies; of the Defective Systems of Pagan Philosophy; of the Dispersion of the Jews, the Destruction of the Temple of Jerusalem, and the vain attempt of the Emperor Julian to rebuild it; of the Downfall of Idolatry; of the Suppression of Schisms; of the Conversion of Nations; of the Rise of Mahometanism; of the Crusades; with several other remarkable events and occurrences, illustrated with a brief detail of the eminent virtues and apostolic labors of the Holy Fathers, learned Doctors, ecclesiastical Rulers, renowned Martyrs, and other great Saints, who have flourished in every age down to the present, etc. "Upon this Rock I will build my Church, and the gates of Hell shall not prevail against her."—St. Matt. c. 16 v. 18. From the last Dublin ed., with very considerable additions. New York: Printed by T. Seymour, No. 49 John Street. 1814. pp. xii.–408. 12mo. F.

v. Baker, *supra.*

GALLITZIN, REV. DEMETRIUS ALEXANDER.—*A Defence of Catholic Principles in a Letter to a Protestant Minister.* Pittsburgh: Printed by S. Engles. 1816. pp. iv.–5–144. 18mo. F.

—— —— Winchester: Heiskell. 1818. 12mo. G. T. C.

—— *A Letter to a Protestant Friend on the Holy Scriptures:* Being a continuation of the *Defence of Catholic Principles,* in opposition to the *Vindication of the Doctrines of the Reformation.*

"The foolishness of God is wiser than men: and the weakness of God is stronger than men."—1 Cor. i. 25. Ebensburg: Printed by Thomas Foley. 1820. pp. xxiv. and 150. 12mo. F.

[It is dated March 29, 1819.]

[*v. supra*, Brosius. *Catholic World*, Nov., 1865 (translated from the *Revue Contemporaine*, Bruxelles), Very Rev. Thomas Hayden's Discourse, 1848. In February, 1866, Dr. Hayden delivered a Lecture on the Life of D. Gallitzin, at Birmingham, Penn.; but we think, to our great disappointment, it was not published. An interesting memoir of "The Pastor of the Alleghanies" will be found in the *Biographical Annual*, 1841, by the eloquent and classical pen of the late Charles Constantine Pise, D.D. The fourth volume of the *Metropolitan*, anno 1856, p. 201, May, contains a notice of that saintly missionary by my excellent friend and college-mate Richard H. Clarke, Esq., of the New York bar. The *Cornhill Magazine* contains an interesting memoir of Rev. D. Gallitzin's mother, copied into *Littell's Living Age*, Boston, December, 1871. At p. 44 of *The Catholic Family Almanac*, for 1872, New York, Cath. Pub. Society, we have a striking engraving representing the meeting of Rev. Fr. Lemcke, O.S.B., now of Elizabeth, N. J., with the Missionary Prince. The anxiety which is felt for the preservation of all that refers to American Catholic history will warrant the insertion here of the following words copied from the New York *Freeman's Journal:*

"Fr. Lemcke gathered all he could get hold of here of Prince Gallitzin's missionary life in America, and was perfectly posted on the *early* history of Prince D. Gallitzin in Europe. He published in Munster, if we recollect aright what was told us, a most interesting and connected history of this hero of the Cross."

Notice of "*A Memoir on the Life and Character of the Rev. Prince Demetrius A. de Gallitzin,* Founder of Loretto and Catholicity in Cambria Co., Pa., Apostle of the Alleghanies. By V. R. Thomas Heyden, of Bedford, Pa. Baltimore: J. Murphy & Co. 1869."

Rev. Mr. Gallitzin's name will recur in the second part of the *Bibliographia.*]

GANDOLPHY, P.—*Sermons on the Ancient Faith.* Advertised by Dornin, 1815, for imminent publication, in last page of *Poor Man's Catechism.* I doubt whether they were published.

[Peter Gandolphy, an English priest, was educated at Stonyhurst, and died at Eastsheen, England, July 9, 1821, aged 41. He wrote polemics on the limits of temporal authority in matters concerning church discipline. The V. A. of London put a censure on his work, but G. appealed to Rome, where he personally defended his position. In the library of the Archbishop of Baltimore I found "*A Series of Letters addressed to the Protestant Community on the Secret Causes of the Increase of Catholics;* Intended to Counteract and Expose the Gross and Calumnious Misrepresentations of Catholics and their Doctrine. By a Catholic Priest. 'Redimentes opportunitatem quoniam dies mali sunt.'—Eph. 5th chap. 18th ver. New York: Reprinted from the London copy. James Bloomfield, printer, 1826, pp. 108, 12mo." Page 2 states that "The following pages are offered to the American public as the production of *one of the most eminent and valuable of men.* . . . New York, Sept. 16, 1826." The italics are underlined by Abp. A. Marechal, who adds: "This Rev. Gandolphy was condemned by the See; they say he died penitent." Allibone gives a list of his works; so does De Feller; but two of his works were put on the *Index,* July 27, 1828—1st, that advertised by Dornin ; 2d, *An Exposition of Liturgy. . . . Una cum testificatione seu Epistola quadam alterius auctoris (qui tamen eandem epistolam laudabiliter retractavit) sive conjunctim sive seorsim impressa, quæ incipit Omnibus et Singulis Anglice et Latine scripta, et Romæ data* 13 *Nov.*, 1816, *in qua temere et falso asseritur dicta opera amplam approbationem a Sede Apostolica obtinuisse.* Since writing the above, I have met with the work announced by Dornin: *A Defence of the Ancient Faith; or, A Full Exposition of the Christian Religion, in a Series of Controversial Sermons.* 4 vols., 8vo. London. 1813.]

GARDEN *of the Soul.* *v.* Challoner.

["Coyne, on his way to London, paid Dr. Milner a visit at Wolverhampton, and in the morning the Bishop said: 'Now, Mr. Coyne, I am going to say Mass; you need not come down to the chapel.' And, opening a door in the wall, he said: 'Here is a little tribune opening on the chapel where I say my prayers.' Coyne found on the Bishop's kneeling-place a *Following of Christ*, a *Think Well On't*, and a *Garden of the Soul*, all worn and blackened with the Bishop's thumbs. When Dr. Doyle heard this, a tear burst into his eyes, and he exclaimed, 'That gives me a greater idea of Dr. Milner than his *End of Controversy* and all he has written—that he should constantly nourish his soul with those simple, but solid manuals of the people."—From a letter of Dr. Ullathorne to Mr. Fitzpatrick, reported in his *Life of Bishop Doyle*, vol. ii. p. 14, Boston, P. Donahoe, 1864.]

GASS, PATRICK.—*A Journal of the Voyages and Travels of a Corps of Discovery*, under the Command of Capt. Lewis and Capt. Clarke, of the

Army of the United States, from the mouth of the river Missouri through the interior parts of North America to the Pacific Ocean, during the years 1804, 1805, and 1806. Containing an authentic relation of the most interesting transactions during the expedition, a description of the country, and an account of its inhabitants, soil, climate, curiosities, and vegetable and animal productions. By Patrick Gass, one of the persons employed in the expedition. With Geographical and Explanatory Notes by the publisher. (Copy-right secured according to Law.) Pittsburgh: Printed by Zadoc Cramer, for David McKeehan, Publisher and Proprietor. . . . 1807. F.

Pp. viii. 262. *v.* Allibone, ad n.

—— 1810. Title as above. Words *by the publisher* omitted; added, *Second Edition. With six Engravings.* Philadelphia: Printed for Mathew Carey, No. 122, Market Street. 1810. F.

Same types and paging as above. At p. iii., "Preface by the publisher of the First Edition." Although the publisher is David McKeehan, who also entered the title in the Clerk's Office (District of Pennsylvania), April 11, 1807, yet the preface reads like the style of M. Carey. It contains two engravings, curiosities of the art.

[The larger work by Lewis & Clarke has gone through many editions, both in England and America. I have more than a dozen titles in my list. Gass was the first narrator. It seems he put his *crude and uncouth MS.* in Mr. Carey's hands, who *licked* it into some shape. However, Gass had the honor of a French translation :

" *Voyage des Capitaines Lewis et Clarke* . . . fait dans les années 1804, 1805, et 1806 . . . Redigé en Anglais par Patrice Gass, employé dans l'Expedition . . . traduit en français par A. J. N. Lallemant, l'un de Secrétaires de la Marine. Avec des Notes . . . et une Carte gravée par J. B. Jardien. A Paris : Arthus-Bertrand. 1810." 12mo, pp. 443. F. I think I have seen a Dutch translation of it. Mathew Carey published a fourth edition, Philadelphia, 1812.]

GASTON, William.—*Speech of the Hon. W. G., of North Carolina,* on the Bill to authorize a Loan of $25,000,000, delivered in the House of Representatives of the U. S., February, 1814. Washington City: Printed at the office of the *Senator.* pp. 53. 12mo. F.

[He opposed the bill intended to place that sum in the hands of the President for the purchase of Canada.—W. G. b. in Newbern, N. C., September 19, 1778, died in Raleigh, January 23, 1844. He was "the first student who entered his name in the rolls of Georgetown College" (corresp. *Baltimore Mirror,* Jan. 11, '68); graduated in Princeton, N. J., in 1796; U. S. Senator in 1813. Although laboring under Catholic disabilities, he became Judge of the Supreme Court, and with him the clause in the Constitution of N. C. against Catholics became a dead-letter.

Allibone does not mention him, as, in fact, Catholic names are slightly considered by that compiler. Mr. Gaston was baptized in his infancy in the Catholic Church, his mother being a Catholic, educated by the Dominican Nuns in France. His father was an Irish Presbyterian, and formerly a Surgeon in the British Navy. Judge Gaston's accomplished daughter, Mrs. E. G. Graham, lives in Upper Marlborough, Md.

In O'Conor's *War of* 1812, p. 179, 4th ed., we read the following: "Mrs. Gaston, of Newburn, wife of the Member of Congress, being told that the British had landed and would shortly be in possession of Newburn, fell into convulsive fits, and expired in a few hours."

"HON. WILLIAM GASTON, N. C.—The Washington correspondent of the *Baltimore Catholic Mirror* made an excellent suggestion when he wrote that some memorial of William Gaston should be erected in Georgetown College—he having been the first student who entered his name on the roll of that time-honored Alma Mater. Judge Gaston was one of the greatest men of his time: Representative in the councils of his own State, United States Senator, Judge of the Supreme Court, and a lawyer inferior to none, and—the best of all—an excellent Catholic. We suggest that the next anniversary of his birth (Sept. 19, 1878) should be *kept;* or that of his opening the list of so many brave young men who have honored Georgetown College. Invite some distinguished man who will do honor to the name by skilful arrangement of diligent researches made of the particulars of his life, to deliver a *biographical* oration on that day. It should be some old student, and, if possible, a member of the Philodemic Society from the same State. We Catholics (and our Catholic institutions are to be blamed for it) neglect too much those memories of great and good men whose deeds should be treasured in the hearts of posterity. William Gaston has been lying in his grave four-and-twenty years. Should not Georgetown College show her appreciation for the honor of having been the Alma Mater of such a distinguished son? We remember the reverence with which the lamented Dr. Ryder always mentioned the name of Judge Gaston. It was a household name with him. Let the members of the Philodemic Society take the matter in hand at once. We feel confident that none will refuse to contribute his quota to defray necessary expenses, nay, it will be a source of pleasure with them as it will be with

"HON. MEMBER PHILOD. SOCIETY.

"MASS., Jan. 12, 1868."—*Boston Pilot.*

For a more extended and very interesting notice of Judge Gaston, *v. The Metropolitan*, Baltimore, 1856, vol. iv. pp. 585 *seqq.*, 681 *seqq.* It is from the pen of R. H. Clarke, of the New York bar.]

—— *Speech of the Hon. Judge Gaston*, delivered in the recent State Convention [1835] of North Carolina, assembled for the purpose of revising the constitution. Baltimore: Fielding Lucas, Jr. pp. 50. 8vo. F.

[n. d. of course, à la Lucas. The amendment substituted the word "Christian" for "Protestant," 74 against 51.]

—— *An Address* delivered before the American Whig and Cliosophic Societies of the College of New Jersey, September 29, 1835. By William Gaston, LL.D. Second edition. Princeton, N. J.: R. E. Hornor. 1835. pp. 32. 8vo. F.

GAUDENTIO DI LUCCA.—*The Life and Adventures of Sig.* ——. Written by Himself. Giving an Account of a Country in the midst of the vast Desarts of Africa, being unknown to any persons except Sig. Gaudentio, and its inhabitants, altho' as Ancient, Populous, and Civilized, as the Chinese. With a particular Account of their Antiquity, Origin, Religion, Customs, Policy, etc.; the manner how they got first over those vast Desarts, and their method of travelling. Interspersed with several most surprizing and curious Incidents. Copied from the Original Manuscript kept in St. Mark's Library at Venice. First American Edition. Norwich: Printed and sold by John Trumbull, at his Printing-office, few rods west from the Court House. M,DCC,XCVI. pp. 130. 16mo.

F.

[At p. 3, "*Life and Adventures of Sign. Gaudentio di Lucca.* Wrote at Bologna, in Italy."]

—— —— *The Adventures of Sig.* ——. Being the Substance of his Examination before the Fathers of the Inquisition at Bologna, in Italy: Giving an Account of an Unknown Country, in the midst of the Deserts of Africa, the Origin and Antiquity of the People, their Religion, Customs, and Laws. Copied from the Original Manuscript in St. Mark's Library at Venice. With critical notes of the learned Signor Rhedi. To which is prefixed: *A Letter of the Secretary of the Inquisition*, shewing the reasons of Signor Gaudentio's being apprehended, and the manner of it. Translated from the Italian. Philadelphia: Reprinted by William Conover, No. 71 Walnut Street. 1799. pp. 320. 12mo. F.

[The work is very interesting, seemingly written at the Inquisition in Bologna, and giving details of the economy of that tribunal as it existed in the Roman States. The Preface is written by an Englishman.]

—— —— The same as above, with the words "A Letter . . . the manner of it," omitted. Wilmington: Printed and sold by Bonsal & Niles. 1800. pp. xxii and 234. 12mo. F.

[An English edition in my possession bears this title: *The Adventures of Signor Gaudentio Di Lucca ;* being the Substance of his Examination before the Fathers of the Inquisition, at Bologna, in Italy. By Bishop Berkeley, author of *The Minute Philosopher*, etc. Dublin: for John Cumming, 16, Lower Ormond Quay, 1821, pp. xxiv and 215. 12mo.

It is divided into unnumbered chapters, each chapter having at its end "Remarks of Signor Rhedi." The various editions differ in many things as to the matter. Bp. Berkeley, in 1713, accompanied the Earl of Peterborough to Italy as Chaplain and Secretary of Legation (to Sicily. Allibone); but remained scarcely a year. Was he the author of *Gaudentio?* All the sources of information at my disposal have failed me. The work evidently belongs to the category of the works contained in this *Bibliographia;* Catholic matters are mixed up in it; it is "A Curiosity of Literature."]

GAVIN.—*The Master-Key of Popery;* Giving a full Account of all the Customs of the Priests and Friars, and the Rites and Ceremonies of the Popish Religion. In four parts. By Anthony Gavin, one of the Roman Catholic Priests of Saragossa. To which is added an account of the Inquisition of Goa, extracted from a recent work entitled *Christian Researches in Asia.* Printed for the publisher. 1812. pp. x and 300. 12mo. F.

[By an affidavit embodied in the Preface, and signed "John London" (Bp. ?), it appears A. G. was reconciled (!) to the Church of England on the 3d day of January, 1715–16.]

—— —— Another edition. Phila.: Printed for the booksellers. 1816. F.

—— —— Another edition. Hagerstown, Md. 1828. And another, with an additional preface and plates, and large additions. Boston: Samuel Jones, 86 Washington Street. 1854.

[A Protestant lady found the work so infamous that she

burned it.—I have some indistinct recollection that the poor wretch died reconciled with Mother Church.

Since the above was in print, I have obtained the following edition: "*A Master-Key to Popery:* in five Parts. . . . By D. Antonio Gavin, Born and Educated in Spain, some years Secular Priest in the Church of Rome, and since 1715, Minister of the Church of England. The Third Edition, carefully corrected. London, Printed: Newport, Rhode-Island: Reprinted and Sold by Solomon Southwick, in Queen-Street, 1773." Allibone quotes, "Lond., 1725–26. 3 vls. 8vo."]

GOBINET'S *Instructions for Youth* are advertised by Dornin to be published with all rapidity. 1815.

[I never saw a copy of it. The book was afterwards republished in Philadelphia and Boston.]

GOETZ, John Nepomucen.—*Sermon* [German] *on the Sanctity of Christian Churches.* On the anniversary of the solemn opening of the German Catholic Church of the Holy Trinity, Philadelphia. Preached Nov. 20, 1796, by J. N. Goetz, Secular Priest, and formerly Professor and Preacher at the Royal Academy of Wienerisch, Neustadt. Phila.: H. Schweitzer. 1796. pp. 20. 8vo. R.

[Was not Goetz implicated in the Trinity Church schism?]

GOTHER, Rev. John.—*A Papist Misrepresented and Re-Presented;* or, A Two-fold Character of Popery—the first containing a Sum of the Superstitions, Idolatries, Cruelties, Treacheries, and wicked Principles laid to their charge; the other laying open that Religion which those termed Papists own and profess, the chief articles of their faith, and the principal Grounds and Reasons which attach them to it. By the Rev. J. Gother. First American edition from the nineteenth London edition. Revised and published by a Catholic clergyman of Baltimore. Baltimore: Printed for the publisher by J. W. Butler. 1808. F.

Pp. ii–iv, Amer. Pref.; v–xi, Introduction; blank and 13–95.

[Gother had been brought up at Douay, and was instrumental in receiving Challoner into the Church. Dryden, no ordinary judge, is said to have been an admirer of Gother's style.]

GRAMMAR—*Portuguese and English*—compiled . . . by a Professor of the Spanish and Portuguese Languages, in St. Mary's College. Baltimore: published for the author, by Fielding Lucas, Jun'r, No. 138, Market Str. 1820. John D. Joy, printer. pp. viii–229. Abp. B.

GUIDE, *The Pious—to Prayer and Devotion.* Containing various Practices of Piety and Devotion calculated to answer the various Demands of the different devout Members of the Roman Catholic

Church. *Permissu Superiorum.* Georgetown, [Potowmack]: Printed by James Doyle. MDCCXCI. pp. 281. G. T. C.

[This work is said to have been prepared by the Jesuit Fathers of Georgetown College, who had shortly before opened the institution. After the tenth page, it opens with *Devotions to the Sacred Heart of Jesus*, extending over fifty pages. The Doyles sold to the Fathers the land on which Trinity Church now stands. Alexander Doyle was a Georgetown printer of same year; *v. infra* J. Thayer. Were they any kin to the famous John Doyle of N. Y.?]

[Rev. F. J. Sumner, S.J., Librarian of Georgetown College, D. C., has kindly furnished me with the following title: *Pious Guide.* Georgetown: "(Potowmack,)" printed by Jas. Doyle. 1792.]

GUIDE, *The Pious*—to prayer and devotion, a Roman Catholic Prayer-Book, containing various practices of piety, calculated to answer the demands of the devout members of the Catholic Church; with a compleat collection of Hymns sung in the Roman Catholic Churches. 2d ed. New York: Dornin. 1808. G. T. C.?

[Dornin has advertised it in 1809 and 1814. Price 87½ cts.]

—— 1813. J. G. S.–B.M.

—— 1815. G. T. C.?

GUION.—*Poems.* Translated from the French of Madame de la Mothe Guion, by the late William

Cowper, Esq., author of the *Task.* Philadelphia: Kimber, Conrad, & Co., No. 170, South Second Street. (Price 40 cents.)

Advertised in *Fenelon's Extracts*, 1804, as "already published."

HAROLD, Rev. W. V.—*Sermon* preached in the Catholic Church of St. Peter, Baltimore, Nov. 1st, 1810; on Occasion of the Consecration of the Rt. Rev. Dr. John Cheverus, Bishop of Boston. By the Rev. W. V. Harold, one of the Pastors of St. Mary's Church, Philadelphia, and Printed at the Request of the Rt. Rev. Bishops Attending on this Solemn Occasion. Baltimore: Printed for Bernard Dornin, and Sold at his Roman Catholic Library, 30, Baltimore Street. G. Dobbin and Murphy . . . Print. . . . 1810. pp. 20. 8vo. (Copyrighted.)

Abp. Balt.

[William Vincent Harold, O.S.D., a very eloquent man. "Dr. Archibald Alexander (of Princeton College, N. J.) told John Nagle he never knew what true pulpit oratory was until he had heard Harold; he said his logic, rhetoric, diction, grace, were all superlative."—*Lippincott's Magazine*, May, 1868. The University of Pennsylvania conferred upon him the degree of D.D. He rather committed himself previous, and during the famous Hogan-St.-Mary's affair, by an imprudent zeal. Left America, and died superior of a convent in Denmark Street, Dublin. *v.* De Courcey & Shea, p. 229. Allusion is made to him in *Dr. Doyle's Life*, by Fitzpatrick, pp. 154, 183, 241, vol. ii., Boston, P. Donahoe, 1865. *v. infra* Hoganiana.]

HAY, Rt. Rev. George.—*v. Doctrine, An Abridgment of Christian* —.

—— *An Abridgment of Christian Doctrine.* By Bishop Hay. Philadelphia: Printed for Mathew Carey, No. 118, Market Street. 1800. pp. 152. 18mo. F.

—— *Pious Christian, The*—instructed in the Nature and Practice of the Principal Exercises of Piety Used in the Catholic Church. By Bishop Hay. Philadelphia: Printed for Mathew Carey, No. 118 Market Street. By James Carey, Nov. 10, 1800. pp. xii and 298 (?). F.

[James was a brother to Mathew Carey. *v. infra* App.]

HOGANIANA.

[William Hogan has gained too great a notoriety in one of the severest trials of the Catholic Church in this country, and his rebellious attempts at subverting the fundamental laws of Church discipline have such bearings on the history of the Catholic Church in the U. S. that I have deemed it *operæ pretium* to give the titles of such pamphlets issued in connection with Hoganism as may prove good reference to the future historian. My information is drawn from my own collection, from that of the late G. W. Richards, Esq., of Philadelphia, who courteously supplied me with some titles, and, above all, from *five* thick octavo volumes of documents preserved in the library of the Bishop of Boston. See a detailed history of the schism in the *History of the Catholic Church in the U. S.*, by H. de Courcey & J. G. Shea; New York, Dunigan & Bro., 1856, pp. 217 *et seqq.; Rt. Rev. Dr. England's Works;* Baltimore, J. Murphy & Co., 1849, vol. v., pp. 108 *et seqq.* Poor Hogan ended his play by the usual farce, as Erasmus would say, became a Protestant, and *married.* His life was not the most moral: he escaped from Bridewell in New York; held an office in the customhouse in Boston; died in a public-house in Nashua or Peterboro, N. H., about the close of 1847 or the beginning of 1848. He was the author of *High and Low Mass in the Roman Catholic Church;* with Comments [F.]; Concord, N. H.; Ch. J. Sill, 1846. *Synopsis of Popery as it Was and as it Is;* 12mo pamphlet; Boston, 1845 [F.] *Auricular Confession and Popish Nunneries;* London, 1846, 12mo [F.]; 5th ed., 1851; *Allibone's Catalogue.* Works republished in Hartford, by Silas Andrus & Son, n. d., but during the Know-Nothing excitement, I believe.]

1812. *Sundry Documents,* submitted to the Consideration of the Pewholders of St. Mary's Church, By the Trustees of that Church. Phila.: Print. by Lydia R. Bailey, No. 10, North Alley. 1812. pp. 26. 8vo. F.

[This pamphlet fixes the start of the schism, on Sept. 15, 1812. Rev. Wm. Harold, uncle to Rev. Wm. Vincent Harold, both O.S.D., was, in all probability, the principal mover in the matter.]

1820. HOGAN, Rev. William.—*A Sermon on the Intercession of Saints.* Delivered in the Roman Catholic Church, Albany. Lansinburgh: Print. by Tracy & Bliss. 1820. pp. 16. 8vo. F.

[On the testimony of Rev. G. D. Hogan, W. Hogan's cousin, "This sermon, which he (W. H.) gave as his own production, was given by the Rev. Justin McNamara, of Cork, with many other sermons." It ends by exhorting his hearers "to adhere to the religion of their forefathers. Be not the dupes of any enthusiast who calls himself a minister of the Gospel." Rev. W. H., on his arrival from Limerick to New York, was employed for some time in Albany, which place he left towards the close of 1819 (?) against the Bishop's wish, and received temporary jurisdiction by the Vicar Administrator of Philadelphia to minister in St. Mary's Church. Bishop Conwell arrived in the latter part of 1820, and in December 14th he withdrew Mr. Hogan's faculties, on account of dubious morality (suspicions fully justified by subsequent disclosures). Mr. H. continued to officiate . . . and on the 11th of February, 1821, he was excommunicated. These few hints will give the key to the history of the pamphlets, a list whereof I have endeavored to put together in chronological order.]

—— Aug. 8. An autograph letter calling Rev. Mr. Roloff to account for having spoken "in an ungentlemanlike and unchristian manner" of the writer, Wm. Hogan. To it is annexed an autograph copy of Mr. R.'s reply (Aug. 8, 1820) endorsed: This note was received by him who subjoins his answer thereunto a considerable time before Rev. Mr. Hogan's suspension.

—— An Address to the Congregation of St. Mary's Church, Philadelphia. pp. 35. 12mo.

At p. 35 signed "William Hogan. (To be continued.)"

—— Dec. 21. *Address to the Rt. Rev. the Bishop of Penna., and the Members of St. Mary's Congregation.* [Mathew Carey.]

Abp. N. Y., R. H. C.

—— Another edition. *Ib.*

[M. C. afterwards withdrew his opposition.]

1821. Continuation of an Address to the Congregation of St. Mary's Church, Philadelphia. pp. 36. 12mo. Headed "Continuation"; signed "Wm. Hogan. Philadelphia, Feb. 2, 1821. A P.S. (To be continued.)"

—— Continuation of an address to the Congregation of St. Mary's Church, Philadelphia. pp. 31. 8vo. Headed "Continuation," signed "Wm. Hogan," and a postcript.

—— Feb. 11. *Sundry Documents* addressed to St. Mary's Congregation. Philadelphia: published by B. Dornin. pp. 30. 8vo.

[The most damaging evidence against poor Hogan. P. 30,

note: "The correspondence between Rev. W. Hogan and Keating Rawson, Esq., will shortly be published." To the *Sundry Documents* Mr. H. announced, in a brief newspaper notice, *To the Public*, that he will reply in a few days, March 12, it. Hence—]

—— *A Brief Reply* to a Ludicrous Pamphlet compiled from the Affidavits, Letters, and Assertions of a Number of Theologians, with the Signature of Henry, Bishop, and entitled "Sundry Documents, addressed to St. Mary's Congregation." pp. 48. 8vo.

[In the Appendix, p. 48, it draws a parallel in favor of Mr. W. H. from the case of a church, Charleston, S. C. *v.* Bp. England's *Works.*]

—— Feb. 11. Pastoral Charges Delivered by the Rt. Rev. Henry, in St. Mary's Church, Nov. 2, 1820, and Feb. 11, 1821.

Pp. 8. 8vo. No title. At the end, "Phila.: Pub. by Rob. Desilver, No. 110, Walnut St."

[It is a forgery, to cast ridicule on the Bishop. The true charges were afterwards published in Philadelphia papers, and are to be seen in Dr. England's *Works.*]

—— An Inquiry into the Causes which led to the Dissensions actually existing in the Congregation of St. Mary's, and Observations on the Mode best calculated to prevent its Increase. *Fiat Justitia.* By a Layman of the Congregation. pp. 12. 12mo.

[*Pro* Hogan; signed "A Layman." Written immediately after the 11th of Feb. Carey's?]

—— March 10. *A Reply to the Accusations of John T. Sullivan, Esq.*

Pp. 4. 8vo. Signed "The Teacher of the Free School. (To be Continued if Necessary.)" *Anti* Hogan.

—— April. *Proceedings of a Meeting of the Congregation of St. Mary's Church,* Favorable to the Restoration of the Rev. W. Hogan. Held at Washington Hall, Wedn. ev'g, Feb. 14, 1821. And at an Adjourned Meeting. Held as above, on Wed. ev'g, Feb. 28, 1821.

Pp. 12. 12mo. Signed "C. W. Bazeley, Chairman; Archibald Randall, Secretary." It contains also an address to the Rt. Rev. Dr. England, signed "W. Hogan, Ap. 27, 1821." Also, "The Opinions [not judicial] of W. Tighman, J. B. Gibson, and Th. Duncan, Esqrs., Judges of the Supreme Court of Pa., on the Charter of St. Mary's Church." *v. ante*, p. 29.

[These opinions were given in full in a pamphlet containing "The Memorial of the Members of the Roman Catholic Society worshipping at the Church of St. Mary's, in the City of Philadelphia." pp. 46. 8vo.]

—— April 9. *To John Leamy, Esq.*

Pp. 3. 8vo. Signed "A Pew Holder." It is a dignified protest against a *pro* Hogan meeting, held April 7th at Washington Hall.

—— April 12. *An Explanation of some Canon Laws concerning Excommunication and Suspension.* Respectfully Dedicated to the Congregation of St. Mary's Church, Phila. By M. F.

Pp. 25. 8vo. Signed "Your Devoted Servant, M. F." It is a temperate exposition of facts. *Anti* Hogan.

—— April 13. *To the Members of St. Mary's Congregation.*

A *caveat* by William Hogan against crediting a letter purported as written by Bp. Cheverus. The *caveat* appeared in a newspaper; appended to it we find: *To the Members of St. Mary's Church,* . . . in which, after a short preamble, the genuine Letter of Condemnation is given, signed, "✠ John, Bishop of Boston"; directed "To the Rt. Rev. Dr. Conwell, Bishop of Phila."; dated "Boston, April 6, 1821."

—— April 14. *Letter to Henry, Bishop of Phila.* By a Lady. "Let none of you imagine evil in your hearts against his neighbour, and love no false oath: for all these are things that I hate, saith the Lord."—Zechariah, c. viii, v. 17. Phila.: Printed for the Author.

Pp. 10. 12mo. Signed "Mary, Phila., April 14, 1821."

—— May 2–7. *The Opinion of the Rt. Rev. Dr. John Rico*, of the Order of St. Francis, D.D., and Vicar-General of the Armies of Spain, on the Differences existing between the Rt. Rev. Dr. Conwell and Rev. Wm. Hogan, Relative to the Canons quoted by him, and their application in support of his Claims to St. Mary's Church, with other Documents. pp. 11. 8vo.

[Rico's name not signed ; but Jos. Leamy testifies to having taken down the deposition at the above date, and R. W. Meade (*v. infra*) certifies, May 7, to the exalted character and high position of the friar. *Pro* Hogan.]

—— May 7. *To the Editor of the Aurora.*

A letter signed "John, Bishop of Charleston, S. C.," and written by him in reply to an *Address* by W. H. to himself, pub. in the *Aurora*, Ap. 28 (*v. supra*). It is directed "To Mr. Duane, Phila."

[W. Duane, born of Catholic parents, near Lake Champlain, N. Y.; married a Presbyterian; discarded by his mother; editor of the *Aurora;* died 1835, in Philadelphia.]

—— May 10. *To the Congregation of St. Mary's*, "On the Banks of the Rubicon." [M. Carey.] Abp. N. Y., R. H. C.

—— July 11. *The Opinion of the Rt. Rev. Servandus A. Mier, D. S. T.*, in the Royal and

Pontif. Univ'y of Mexico, and Chap. of the Army of the Right, 1st Army of the Peninsula, On certain Queries proposed to him by the Rev. W. Hogan, Pastor St. Mary's Ch. Phila.: July 11, 1821.

Pp. 12. 8vo. p. 3, Letter of W. H. to Dr. M.; pp. 4–12, Reply, signed "Servandus A. Mier." [*Pro* Hogan.]

—— *Remarks on the Opinion of the Rt. Rev. Servandus A. Mier, Dr. of S.J., etc.*, On certain Queries, proposed to him by the Rev. W. Hogan. Phila.: pub. by B. Dornin. 1821. pp. 8. 8vo.

[*Anti* Hogan. The Dr. appears to have been a *mauvais sujet.*]

—— Aug. 17. *A Word Relative to an Anonymous Pamphlet printed in Phila.*, entitled *Remarks, etc.* [as above]. "Super omnia charitatem habete." —St. Paul. Phila.: Aug. 17, 1821. pp. 11. 8vo.

[The Doctor himself speaketh, but signeth not his name. *Pro* Hogan.]

—— *Address of the Communicants of St. Mary's Ch., Phila.*, to their Brethren of the Rom. Cath. Faith throughout the U. S. of America, on the Subject of Reform of Sundry Abuses in the Administration of Church Discipline.

10

—— *Address to the Rom. Catholics of the U. S.* By a Layman of St. Mary's Congregation, Phila. pp. 18. 8vo. G. W. R.

[A noble reply to the above.]

—— *A Republication of Two Addresses* lately published in Phila.; the 1st, by a Committee of St. Mary's Ch., on "Reform of Church Discipline"; the 2d, by a Layman of St. Mary's Congregation, in Reply to the same, with Introductory Remarks by a Layman of New York. New York: Printed by Wm. Grattan, No. 8, Thames Str. 1821. pp. 18. 8vo. F.

[The "Layman of New York" prefaces some well-seasoned remarks—*anti* Hogan—and then gives the two above pamphlets, which he "had both printed and stitched together."]

—— July 27. *An Address to "An Address by a Catholic Layman to the Rom. Catholics of the U. S."* By a Member of St. Mary's Church, Phila.

Pp. 22, 8vo. *Pro* Hogan. "To be continued."

[I have not seen the continuation.]

—— *Hoganism Examined according to the Canons of Criticism, Sacred and Profane;* or, A Short Letter to a Late Reverend Pamphleteer on the Republication of his famous Pamphlet. "The creature is at his dirty work again."—Pope. Phila.: Published by Bernard Dornin. pp. 12. 8vo.

[*Anti* Hogan—probably Mr. Harold's—headed "Ostendam gentibus nuditatem tuam.—Nahum, c. iii, v. 5"; signed "The Detector," and "(To be continued, if the illustrious writer continues to republish)."]

—— *Hoganism Defended;* or, The Detector Detected. *Medice Cura Teipsum.*—Turn, coward, turn; nor from a woman fly. Philadelphia: Printed for the author. 1821.

Pp. 8. 12mo. Headed: Teque conjectis in Te sordibus ita ignominiose tractabo ac ostentui exponam. Nahum c. iii. v. 6—signed "Mary," and "To be continued, if the illustrious writer continues to publish." *Pro* Hogan.

—— *Last Appeal to the Members of St. Mary's Church.*

Pp. 12. 8vo. No t. p.; addressed to "Gentlemen and Ladies"; signed "An Independent Catholic." The writer insists upon having an "Independent Catholic Church"!

—— *The True Sentiments of the Writer of the "Last Appeal to the Catholic Congregation of St. Mary's Church."* Phila.: Published by Bernard Dornin. 1821.

Pp. 8. 8vo. Signed "A Sincere Catholic and no Traitor."

——? *The Hoganite Star.*

1 f. 8vo..

[A poem of four stanzas, *pro* Hogan, and side by side with it another four stanzas, *anti* Hogan.]

——? *To the Members of St. Mary's Congregation.*

1 f. 4to. *Pro* Hogan.

1822. January 1. *Decision of the Supreme Court of Pennsylvania* in the Case of the Corporation of St. Mary's Church (Roman Catholic) in the City of Philadelphia, on a proposed Alteration of its Charter.

TILGHMAN, Chief-Justice (adverse). From *The National Gazette and Literary Register.* Phila.: Tuesday afternoon, Jan. 1, 1822.

GIBSON, Justice (favorable). *Ib.* Jan. 2. (Opinion.)

DUNCAN, Justice (refers to the Legislature). *Ib.* Jan. 5. (Opinion.)

[The following quotations are inserted to give an idea of how far things were carried when, on the part of Hogan, every restraint seemed to have been thrown away, and his party resorted to the most scurrilous squibs and innuendoes. At the same time, scribblers indulged in sarcasm against both parties.

From the *Balance,* Jan. 2, 1822, "Churches Militant," "The Dutch," "The Bishopites and Hoganites." Jan. 9, *The Lay Preacher* began a serious of six sermons of low and weak witticism. Feb. 6, "The Bishop *versus* I. T. S. Damages for the Plaintiff, $10,000. Counseller Botherim's Speech." Feb. 13, a forged and ridiculous form of excommunication, partly from Sterne. "Cheap Clerical Shoes: Rev. Dr. Crispin returns to his Trade." Feb. 20, "An Anecdote of the Rev. Rebel Harrow. Defence for publishing the forged Excommunication." March, "A Letter to Rev. Dr. Cabbage Stalk." "A Hole in the Wall; or, The Cabbage Stock in Council," poetry. *Montes parturent* [sic], *et nascitur mus.* "Victor Harold was three weeks in labor, and at last brought forth a scandalous pamphlet." It is a communication, and it "regrets that he (V. H.) has abused Mr. Mathew Carey," signed "A Friend." "A Medley of Characters well known to the Public." Old Harry, Bishop of Phila."; signed "Dryden."—"Friar Tuck."—A *pro* Hogan "Catholic" protests against the filth of "Lay Preacher." Communication against "Dominic" (Rev. W. V. H.); ditto to "Dear Friend Dominic." "The Priest," signed "Buffon's Natural History." "*Mene, mene, Teckel Upharsin!*—Prior Dominic, thou hast been weighed in the *Balance*, and wast found wanting!" April 8, "Letter from Prior Dominic." "A letter from Ptk. McIlheny on the riots of April 9." (Dr. Cabbage is meant for Dr. Conwell), etc., etc., etc., etc.]

—— Feb. 4. No. 1. *A Letter to the Roman Catholics of Philadelphia and the U. S. of America.* By a Friend to the Civil and Religious Liberties of Man. "For modes of faith let furious bigots fight, Their's can't be wrong whose life is in the right."—*Pope.* Philadelphia: Published by Robert Desilver, No. 110, Walnut Street. 1822. T. Town, printer. F.

Pp. 60. 8vo. *Pro* Hogan, contains *Letter I.*, giving Rich. H.

Bayard's opinion on the amendment of the Charter; *Letter II.*, dated Phila., Feb. 5, 1822, rambles through the history of the churches in Phila., signed "Pacificus"; *Letter III.*, Washington Feb. 8, 1822, signed "M. F." (a curiosity).]

—— No. 2. *Letters to the Roman Catholics of Philadelphia, etc.* Same title as precedent. F.

Pp. 61–82. 8vo. *Pro* Hogan. *Letter IV.*, Wash., Feb. 20, 1822 [another curiosity], signed "Z. A."

—— No. 3. March 20. *Strictures on a Pamphlet written by W. V. Harold,* entitled "*A Reply to A Catholic Layman.*" [Seven long quotations.] By W. Hogan, Pastor of St. Mary's Church. Philadelphia: Published by Rob't Desilver, No. 110, Walnut Street. March 20, 1822. T. Town, printer. F.

Pp. 28. 8vo. Ends "(To be Continued)."

—— No. 4. March 25. *Address of the Lay Trustees to the Congregation of St. Mary's Church,* On the subject of the approaching Election. Philadelphia: Published by Robert Desilver, No. 110, Walnut Street. 1822. pp. 25. 8vo. F.

[Signers: Jno. Doyle, Jno. Dempsey, Augustine Fagan, Jno. Ashley, Ptk. Connell, Jno. Leamy, Joseph Dugan, Jos. Strahan.]

—— Feb. 13. *Reverendissimo Domino Archipresuli;* admodum Reverendis episcopis suffraganiis, Diocesum, ac Reverendis dominis parochiarum administratoribus, Catholicis Romanæ ecclesiæ, in Federata Respublica Americana. Salutem in Christo Jesu, et apostolicam benedictionem [sic].

Pp. 2, 4to. Signed, "Quibus sum divinctissimus in Christo Jesu, filius Ecclesiæ. GULIELMUS HOGAN, Pastor Ecclesiæ Sanctæ Mariæ, Philadelphia, 13th Februarii, A.D. 1822." It is a request, in shockingly bad Latin, for a National Synod to depose Dr. Conwell, otherwise Mr. H. will provide the Diocese of Philadelphia with priests.

—— Feb. 23. *Address to the Rt. Rev. the Bishop of Pennsylvania,* the Catholic Clergy of Philadelphia, and the Congregation of St. Mary's in this City. By a Catholic Layman. "Iliacos intra muros peccatur et extra." "That mercy I to others show, that mercy show to me." "If ye forgive not men their trespasses, neither will your Father forgive you your trespasses."—Matt. xi. 25. Philadelphia: Printed by H. C. Carey & I. Lea. 1822.

Pp. iii, iv, v, Pref.; Text, pp. 7–31.

[Neither *pro* nor *con*—a "sutor ne ultra crepidas" production. M. Carey's ?]

First reply:

—— *Brief Remarks addressed to a Catholic Layman*, on his late *Address to the Rt. Rev.*, etc. (title *ut supra*). By a Protestant Episcopalian. "Fortuna nimium quem fovet, stultum facit." "Repent ye therefore, and be converted, that your sins may be blotted out."—Acts iii. 19. Philadelphia: Published by B. Dornin. 1822. pp. 48. 8vo.

[A dignified and effective paper. Who is the author? R. Mead?]

Second reply:

A Reply to A Catholic Layman, on his late Address to the Rt. Rev., etc. (title *ut supra*). By William Vincent Harold, Pastor in St. Mary's. "Atqui vultus erat multa ac præclara minantis."—*Q. Horat. Sat.* lib. 2. "Chi ha le pupille viziate trova la caligine tra'l meriggio."—*Pallavicino.* "Nothing extenuate, nor set down aught in malice." —*Shakespeare.* Philadelphia: Published by B. Dornin.

Pp. 64. 8vo. An Appendix contains correspondence between the Bishop and Trustees.

—— March 28. *Rejoinder* to the *Reply* of the Rev. Mr. Harold to the *Address to the Rt. Rev.*

the Cath. Bp. of Pa., the Cath. Clergy of Phila., and the Congreg. of St. Mary's. In which are detailed the inflammatory and violent proceedings of the Rev. Mr. H. in the year 1812, whereby discord and disunion were introduced into the Congregation of St. Mary's. By a Catholic Layman. Phila.: H. C. Carey & I. Lea, Chesnut Street. 1822.

Pp. iii–viii, Pref.; 9–44 Text and Appendices. 8vo.

[In G. W. Richard's collection it is styled "2d ed. corrected."]

Appendix E. No. I. Address to the Rt. Rev. Bishop of Pa., and the members of St. Mary's Congregation. "Hear me for my cause." "My peace I leave with you, my peace I give you." "Follow peace with all men." "Every kingdom divided against itself is brought to desolation; and every city or house divided against itself shall not stand."

No. II. "Have peace with one another."—Mark ix, 30, etc., etc. 3 pp. Dated "Phila. 14, 1821." A Catholic Layman.

No. III. To the Congregation of St. Mary's, "On the Banks of the Rubicon." 2 pp. Dated "May 10, 1821." A Catholic Layman.

[All Carey's Work.]

—— March 30. *A Letter* to the Rev. W. V. Harold, of the Order of Dominican Friars, on reading his late *Reply to A Catholic Layman.* By an admirer of Fenelon. . . . "Come on, Macduff, And damned be he who first cries hold—

enough." Phila. : Pub. by Rob't Desilver, No. 110, Walnut Str. March 30, '22. T. Town, printer. F.

Pp. 32. 8vo. *Pro* Hogan.

—— *A Reply to the "Cath. Layman's Rejoinder."* By W. V. Harold, Pastor in St. Mary's. ——; Primi clypeos mentitaque tela Agnoscunt, atque ora sono discordia signant.—*Æneidos,* lib. ii. Ma; pero'ch' egli disarmata vede La man nemica, si riman sospeso; Chè stima ignobil palma, e vili spoglie Quelle ch' altrui, con tal vantaggio, uom toglie.—*Gerusalemme liberata,* Canto 7. Philadelphia: Printed by B. Dornin. 1822. pp. 28. 8vo. F.

—— May 10. *A Desultory Examination of the Reply of the Rev. W. V. Harold to A Catholic Layman's Rejoinder.* By a Catholic Layman. To which is annexed an Appendix, containing the above *Reply* verbatim. "You skulk into a corner to play the assassin."—*Harold.* "A vulgar mind finds it easy to utter foul aspersions—for in doing so, it follows its natural bent."—*Idem.* "Eh! quoi! grand Dieu! d'un prêtre est cela le langage?—*Racine.* "Fortiter calumniare, aliquid remanebit." "Curst be the lines, how smooth so'ever they flow, That tend to make one honest man foe, Give virtue scandal—innocent a fear, Or from the soft-ey'd virgin steal a tear."—*Pope.* Phila.: H. C. Carey & I. Lea, Chestnut Street. 1822.

P. ii advises the reader to read first Mr. Harold's reply. pp. iii–viii, Pref.; Text, pp. 9–53, 8vo, ends with; *Graviora manent.* pp. 55–72, Mr. Harold's Reply.

May 15, "A Catholic Layman" published another pamphlet, pp. 8, 8vo, containing "Extracts from the Desultory Examination of the Rev. W. V. Harold's Reply to the Rejoinder of the Catholic Layman," preceded by an Advertisement.

[Mr. C. goes too far, and allows the heat of controversy to get the better of himself; he makes charges which cannot be substantiated, and rambles a good deal.]

—— *Remarks on the "Catholic Layman's Desultory Examination."* By W. V. Harold, Pastor in St. Mary's. "Ira furor brevis est; animum rege: qui, nisi paret, Imperat, hunc frænis, hunc tu compesce catenæ."—*Hor.* Epp. l. i. ep. 2. "He's in a fit now, and does not talk after the wisest."—*Shakspeare—Tempest.* Phila.: Pub. by B. Dornin. 1822. pp. 33. 8vo.

—— *Review of Three Pamphlets* Lately pub'd by the Rev. W. V. Harold. 1. *Reply to a Catholic Layman's Address.* 2. *Reply to the Cath. Layman's*

Rejoinder. 3. *Remarks on the Cath. Layman's Desultory Examination.* Embracing a view of the canon law on the subject of suspensions, and the requisites for clerical sentences of condemnation. By a Catholic Layman. "Though I speak with the tongues of men and angels, and have no charity, I become as sounding brass or a tinkling cymbal."—1 Cor. xiii. 1. "Mark them which cause divisions, . . . and avoid them."—Rom. xvi. 17. "Thou which teachest others, teachest thou not thyself?"—Rom. ii. 21. "The servant of the Lord must not strive, but be gentle, apt to teach, patient."—2 Tim. ii. 24. "Another would have whipped you with scorpions, but I merely put a little wire in the lash."—W. V. Harold. Phila.: H. C. Carey & I. Lea, Chestnut Street. 1822.

Pp. ii–viii, Pref.; Text, pp. 9–40. 8vo. *Graviora manent,* at the end.

—— *Strictures on "Strictures of William Hogan upon the Rev. Wm. Harold's Pamphlet."* By A Catholic "of the Olden Time." Phila.: Pub. by B. Dornin. 1822.

Pp. 16. 8vo. (To be continued if necessary.)

1822. March 16. [Advertisement in the *Balance* (?).]

This Day is Published, and for Sale by Robert Desilver, No.

110 Walnut Street, price 12½ cents, Letters to the Trustees and Electors of St. Mary's Church, and Friends to Religious Liberty. By the Author of A Friend to the Civil and Religious Rights of Man. . . .

An Answer to the Pastor of St. Mary's Church will appear next week. Quis risum teneatis ?

—— April. *The Trial of the Rev. W. Hogan,* Pastor of St. Mary's Ch., for an Assault and Battery on Mary Connell. Tried before the Mayor's Ct. in and for the City of Phila., on Monday, 1st of Ap'l, 1822, and succeeding days. Including the Speeches of Counsel on both sides at length; the Examination, Cross-examination, and Re-examination of the witnesses, verbatim; together with the Anonymous Correspondence, etc. To which is added a Digested Index. The whole taken in Short Hand, by Jos. A. Dowling, Stenographer, 44 So. Sixth Str., Phila. Philadelphia: Pub. by R. Desilver, 110 Walnut Street. 1822. F.

Pp. 271, 8vo, and pp. 1–8 containing "The Charge."

[David Paul Brown told Mr. G. W. R. that during the trial Mr. Hogan showed an astonishing imperturbability.]

—— *An Answer to a Paragraph Contained in the "U. S. Catholic Miscellany,"* edited by the Bishop of Charleston. By the Rev. W. Hogan,

Pastor of St. Mary's Church, Phila. "Thou shalt not be false witness against thy neighbour."—Exodus. Phila. 1822. pp. 39. 8vo.

[I doubt the correctness of this title, as it is torn off the copy in the collection before me. It was given by G. W. R.]

—— *A Reply to Sundry Letters of the Rt. Rev. Dr. England to the Bishop of Phila;* in which he assigns his Reasons for having Detracted him and several other Clergymen. By the Rev. Wm. Hogan, Past. of St. Mary's Ch., Phila. Phila.: Pub. by E. F. Crozet, No. 4 North Sixth Str. 1822. pp. 56. 8vo.

[It is a sequel to the precedent pamphlet. At the end he gives the two *pretended* charges, of a most ridiculous style, (*never*) delivered by Dr. Conwell in St. Mary's Church, Nov. 2, 1820, and Feb. 11, 1821.]

—— *Brief Address to the Rom. Cath. Congregation worshipping at St. Mary's,* on the Approaching Election for a Board of Trustees. "Justum et tenacem propositi virum Non vultus instantis tyranni Mente quatit solida."—*Hor.* Phila.: 1822.

Pp. 10. 12mo. *Pro* Hogan. Signed "A Catholic Layman."

—— *A Short Address to the Rom. Cath. Congregation of St. Mary's Church,* on the Approaching Election for Trustees, written in consequence of two late Addresses from the Pastor and Lay Trustees of the said church. By an Irish Catholic,

Who is proud of having been a Soldier in the Revolution,
Who is proud of being a Citizen of the United States,—
Who is proud of, and zealous for, the Religion of his Fathers.

"And ye shall take to you all who observe the law, and redress the wrongs of your people; And the Lord himself will overthrow them before our face; but as for you, fear them not."—1 Machabees. "I, and my Sons, and my Brethren, will obey the law of our Fathers."—2 Machabees. Phila.: Printed by B. Dornin. 1822. pp. 8. 8vo.

—— March 25. *Address of the Lay Trustees to the Congregation of St. Mary's Church*, on the Subject of the Approaching Election. Phila.: Pub. by Rob't Desilver, No. 110 Walnut Str. 1822.

Pp. 25. 8vo. *Pro* Hogan.

—— Ap. 9. Election of Trustees. *v.* Acc't of the two bloody scenes, in the Church Yard, and Fifth Street, in the *American Sentinel and Mercantile Advertiser*, and in *The Democratic Press*, both under date of April 10.

—— *Meeting of Catholics.* pp. 22. 8vo.

G. W. R.

1822. Aug. 9. The Regular Trustees, lawfully elected, on the Bishop's part, give a public statement of the affair of April 9.

1822. Nov. 30. The *Catholic Herald and Weekly Register* was started by E. F. Crozet; it seems to advocate Hogan and St. Mary's schism. The three first numbers, and the only ones I have seen, not only continue upholding the schism, but are of a blasphemous tone in Catholic matters generally.

[The true *Catholic Herald* was started about ten years afterwards, and flourished for many years as a sterling Catholic paper. Mr. Spellissy, I believe, was the last editor, and buried it.]

—— Dec. 17. The Brief of His Holiness, Pope Pius the Seventh, addressed to Ambrose, Abp. of Baltimore, to his Suffragan Bishops, to the Administrators of the Temporalities of the Churches, and to all the Faithful in the United States of America.

The Brief is given in both Latin and English, pp. 3–14. Then, in the copy before me, follow two pages numbered 9 and 10, stating the decision of the Pope, against W. H., to be final, and given after a careful perusal of documents on both sides, all endorsed by a Letter from Mgr. Pedicini, Secretary of Propaganda. Mr. Hogan then gives a Correspondence, pp. 11 ?–34, endeavoring to prove that he had *submitted*, but that the absence of authenticity in the Brief, and other causes, induced him to adopt another course!

—— In *Poulson's American Daily Advertiser* and the *Franklin Gazette* are given summary reports of the proceedings in Court against W. H. for his continuing to celebrate in St. Mary's after having been excommunicated, May 27, 1822. When the decision of the Supreme Court was given against him, he persisted in being in the Sanctuary with the Bp. and the Clergy—6th, 13th, and 20th, 1823—Mass could not be said. The people grew tumultuous. Hence the charges against H., who employed in his behalf Messrs. Du Ponceau, C. J., and J. R. Ingersoll, whilst the Bp. was supported by Messrs. Hopkinson, Chauncey, Kittern, and Keating. The Court bound W. H. to appear before the Mayor, and advised the friends of Bp. Conwell not to worship in St. Mary's until the trial before the Mayor's Court, in March, shall be determined. The opinion of the Court, in courteous style, is given in full in the *Democratic Press.*

—— The *Democratic Free Press* published, with sober remarks by B. A. M., what purports to be the genuine copy of the Excommunication pronounced against W. H., May 27, 1821. If it is genuine, Dr. Conwell did not follow the formula given in the Rom. Pontifical. In a subsequent number of the *D. F. Press*, B. A. M. confirms the genuineness of the copy aforesaid, on the testimony of the Bishop and the Clergy, and adds: "This form is *not* to be found in the Pontif. Rom. . . . It was prepared in this city, and adapted not only to the case of the Individual, but to the age and the country in which it was read." *v.* Dr. England, who shows the orthodoxy of the Formula.

Battle, The—of St. Mary's. A Serio-Comic Ballad, with Desultory Remarks on the Dissensions in the Church. By an Observer wholly unconnected with the Parties, but wishing well to Liberty and Peace. Pub. at 11 South Sixth Street. pp. 8. 8vo. G. W. R.

1822–23. At the latter part of '22 and during '23 the battle waxed very hot, and it received new impulse from the publication of the Pope's Rescript. The following papers were engaged: *The Democratic Press*, *The Aurora*, *The National Gazette*, *The Gazette and Daily Advertiser*, *The Franklin Gazette*, *The Erin* (with an angel's name and a devil's tongue), *The American Sentinel and Mercantile Advertiser* (in which "Catholicus" wrote *six* letters in behalf of the schism—M. Carey's ?), *The American Daily Advertiser*, all of Philadelphia; *The Shamrock*, of New York, against the Hoganites and with telling force (Th. O'Conor's); *The Columbian Observer*, Phila.; *The Advocate and Irishman's Journal; The Baltimore Federal Gazette*—reporting a meeting of the Catholics at the Cathedral in Balt. condemning the schism, and conveying their resolutions through Charles Carroll of Carrollton, which resolutions were replied to with insult by the Hoganites. *The Columbian Observer* gives Peter S. Duponceau's opinion, based on a wrong interpretation of the *jus patronatus.* At this time the case was laid before the Grand Jury of Philadelphia, and from thence was carried to the Senate, where an amendment was passed in opposition to the laws of the Catholic Church, vetoed by Gov. Hiester (Mch. 27, 1823), reconsidered in the Senate, and *lost.*

1823. July and Aug. *Letters, etc.*—viz.: from Bishop England, on Captain Rock's Proclamation; from the Rev. W. Hogan, In Reply to the Rev. Bishop; from an Irishman to the Rev. W. Hogan; and from An Irish Catholic to an Irishman: copied from the *Charleston Mercury*, the *Columbian Observer*, and the *Democratic Press.* Print. and pub.

at No. 11, S. Sixth Street, Phila. 1823. pp. 28. 8vo.

—— Aug. 30. The following appeared in the Philadelphia *Democratic Press:* "In consequence of a communication which appeared in the *Democratic Press*, the Congregation of St. Mary's Church are hereby duly notified that the Rev. Wm. Hogan continues as sole Pastor of said Church. The correspondence upon the subject of a conditional resignation tendered by the Rev. Mr. Hogan will be laid before the public in a few days. By order of the board of Trustees. (Signed) Archibald Randall, Sec'y."

The subject alluded to is explained by a note of the Chairman of the Trustees, Aug. 28, in which it is stated Rev. Mr. Hogan's "*resignation has been admitted* BY US [*sic*], and we have this day nominated the Rev. A. Inglesi, and requested him to officiate at said Church"!!! But then Mr. Inglesi declined, and Mr. Hogan reinstated BY US, Aug. 29.

—— September. *Address of the Trustees of St. Mary's Church, to their Fellow-Citizens.* Containing a Correspondence between them and the Right Reverend Bishop Conwell, on a Late Attempt at a Reconciliation between the Contending Parties of the Congregation of said Church. Phila.: Print. by Lydia R. Bailey, No. 10, North Alley. September, 1823. pp. 25. 8vo.

—— *Appendix to an Address of the Lay Trustees of St. Mary's Church to their Fellow-Citizens.* n. d. pp. 15. 8vo. F.

[Contains particulars about Rev. Mr. Inglesi, a *mauvais sujet.*]

—— Oct. 3. *An Address to the Roman Catholics of Philadelphia.* By the Rev. W. V. Harold, Pastor of St. Mary's and Vicar-General. Phila.: Printed for the Trustee of Harriet and Jane Dornin. Bernard Dornin, Agent. 1823. F.

Pp. 56. 8vo. An Appendix (pp. 43–56) gives a correspondence in reference to Rev. Mr. Inglesi, and contains information about De Abbate, Rico, and R. W. Meade.

—— Oct. 22. *An Address to the Roman Catholics of the City of Philadelphia,* in Reply to Mr. Harold's Address. By Richard W. Meade. Philadelphia, October 22, 1823. pp. 33. 8vo.

[R. W. Meade was a wealthy merchant, and father to the present Major-General Meade, U. S. A. He was also Consul to Cadiz for several years.]

—— Nov. 4. *A Postscript to the Rev. Mr. Harold's Address to the Roman Catholics of Philadelphia.* pp. 32. 8vo. F.

[It is in reply to the above: demolishes Mr. Meade.]

—— Nov. 15. *Continuation of an Address to the Roman Catholics of the City of Philadelphia,* in Reply to Mr. Harold's Address. Containing the Documents of the Reverend A. Inglesi. By Richard W. Meade. pp. 40. 8vo.

[Mr. M. is inferior to none in *abusive* language.]

—— Oct. "One of the principal leaders of this party, Mr. Augustine Fagan, was found dead at the place of his residence in Phila., on the morning of Sunday, the 11th inst. . . . Mr. Fagan had, we understand, just finished a *Pamphlet, addressed to Governor Schultze,* of Pennsylvania, who exerted himself lately in the Legislature of that State against the rights of his Roman Catholic fellow-citizens. This pamphlet is, we understand, now in progress towards publication." Dr. England Section xix., p. 187, *ut supra.* *v.* 1824, January, *Reflections, etc.*

—— Nov. Rev. W. Hogan resigns, departs for Europe, thence goes to Charleston, S. C. *v.* Ap. 6, 1824.

—— *A Fair and Full View of the Votes of John Andrew Schultze,* in the Senate of Pa., Respecting the Charter of the Rom. Cath. Congregation Worshipping at St. Mary's Church, in the City of Phila. 1823. pp. 26. 8vo.

A View of the Application for an Amendment of the Charter of Incorporation of St. Mary's Cath. Congregation. pp. 15. 8vo. G. W. R.

An Act to Incorporate the Members of the Religious Society of Roman Catholics, belonging to the Congregation of St. Mary's Church, in the City of Philadelphia.

Pp. 7. 8vo. A copy of the "Act enacted into a law, at Philadelphia, on Saturday, the thirteenth day of September, in the year of our Lord one thousand seven hundred and eighty-eight."

—— *The Rights of the States to Alter and Annul Charters Considered*—And the Decisions of the Supreme Court of the U. S. therein examined by the Principles of the Am. Constit., Common Law, Common Sense, with some Observations on the Dispute Concerning the Alteration of the Charter of St. Mary's Church, Phila. By Thomas Earle. Phila.: Pub. by Carey & Lea; Ed. Parker & Hogan; and J. Potter & Co.; G. Little & Abraham Small. J. Hardin, Printer, 1823. pp. 31. 8vo.
G. W. R.

[Earle was a Quaker, a man of note; he first originated the amendment of the Constitution of the State, of the Assembly whereof he was a member.]

1824. *A Concatenation of Speeches, Memoirs, Deeds, and Memorable References, Relative to St. Mary's Church in Phila.* Submitted to Consideration. Philadelphia: 1824. pp. 109. 8vo.

—— January. *Reflections on the Dissension actually existing in St. Mary's Congregation:* respectfully addressed to H. E. the Gov'r of the State of Penn. To which are added Notes on the Right of Patronage and Presentation, as established in the Rom. Cath. Ch. By a Roman Catholic. Phila.: Printed by Lydia R. Bailey, No. 10, North Alley. pp. 28. 8vo.

—— March 22. *An Address to the Public of Phila.:* containing a Vindication of the Character and Conduct of the Rev. Mr. Inglesi, from Charges and Strictures lately reported and pub'd against him by the Rev. Mr. Harold. Transl'd from the French. Hic respondere voluit, non lacessere. Benedictis si certâsset, audîsset bene. He has wished to defend himself, not to attack; if his adversary had begun the combat with civility, it would have redounded to his praise. Phila.: Printed for the Author. 1824.

Pp. 36. 8vo. Signed "A. Inglesi."

—— Ap. 6. At a meeting of the Trustees a communication (d. Charleston, S. C., Mch. 28) was received from Rev. W. H. tendering his resignation . . . *Resolved*, The Sec'y will inform Mr. H. that his resignation is *formally* accepted, but was considered unnecessary by the Trustees, who conceived his abandonment of the Church in Nov'r last as a virtual resignation, etc.

Several communications, dated from Charleston, S. C., during this year, and published in the Phila. *U. S. Gazette*, openly aim at planting an American Cath. Church, independent of Rome, Episcopal authority, law of celibacy, etc., written by W. Hogan.

—— June 26. The Trustees of St. Mary's Church publish a card protesting against Rev. W. Hogan's purpose of preaching to that congregation; to which W. H. replies with a letter, June 28, and concludes: "I value your menaces as little as I do your opinions on polemical subjects," etc. Which protest is followed by letters in the public papers, replete with criminations and recriminations between W. H. and the Trustees.

—— July. Rev. W. Hogan was one of the Judges (!) in the public Dispute between Rev. Messrs. W. L. McCalla and Abner Kneeland, Prot. Ministers, on the Following Question: *Is the punishment of the Wicked absolutely Eternal? or is it only a Temporal Punishment in this World for their Good, and to be succeeded by Eternal Happiness after Death?* A substance of this *Discussion* was Printed and Published for the Author, by T. S. Manning, 11 South Sixth Street, Philadelphia. 1824. pp. 40. 8vo. [In the B. B. collection.]

—— July 22. William Hogan publishes an address to the Congregation of St. Mary's Church on the subject of a new-fangled *The American Catholic Church*, which called forth severe and sarcastic rebuffs from even the Hoganites, who twit Hogan even on the stability of his *amours*. Yet he met with some encouragement, although only *on paper*.

—— Dec. *An Address, Explanatory and Vindicatory, to Both Parties of the Congregation of St. Mary's.* By the Rev. Thadeus J. O Meally, Officiating Pastor. "With those who hated peace, was I peaceful" . . .—Psalm 119. Phila.: Printed for the Author, by Wm. Brown. 1824. pp. 85. 8vo.

1825. January 27. *A Series of Letters Relating to the Late Attempt at a Reconciliation between the Members of the Congregation of St. Mary's and St. Joseph's;* with a Brief Notice of the Present State of the Controversy between them: Being an Abstract of an Address delivered by the Rev. J. J. O'Meally, at the Meeting held in St. Mary's, on Thursday ev'g, the 23d ult. Phila.: Printed by W. Brown. January, 1825. pp. 42. 8vo. F.

—— July 25. *Declaration of Priest O'Meally,* making in Rome ample amends for his past conduct in America; endorsed by the Cardinal Prefect of Propaganda. pp. 2. 8vo.

A Clear View of the State of the Rom. Cath. Succursal Church styled St. Mary's, in Phila.:

deduced from facts, connected with the Schism in that Church. pp. 15. 8vo. G. W. R.

[Dr. England's ?]

1828. July 15. "The Rt. Rev. Dr. Conwell, Bishop of Phila., sailed from New York in the packet ship *France*, Capt. Funck, for Havre, being invited to Rome by the Pope, and having appointed *Elder Pastor* of St. Mary's Very Rev. W. Matthews, of Washington, who had been chosen Administrator of the Diocese by the Holy See." All the letters concerning thereto were previously published by Dr. Conwell. Hence dates the funny episode of the Dominican Fathers Harold and Ryan, which may be read in Dr. England's *Works*, "The Harold Correspondence," Vol. V.

1827. November. *A Continuation of References relative to St. Mary's Church.* F.

Pp. 13. 8vo. No title-page. It contains five Doc's: No. I., dated 1804; No. V., giving Bp. Conwell's summons to Rome, Mch. 8, 1828. This pamphlet supposes another, which I have not seen.

1829. "The Correspondence between the late Archbishop [A. Marechal] of Baltimore and Rev. W. V. Harold was printed in pamphlet form, and widely circulated though not formally published." Dr. England: *note* to Letter to Rev. Mr. Harold,

Sept. 17, 1829. *Works*, t. v. p. 227. "Harold Correspondence."

1829 or 1830. *Address of Rt. Rev. F. P. Kenrick, Bishop of Arath.* pp. 12. 8vo.

G. W. R.

1831. April 16. *Address of the Trustees of St. Mary's Church, to the Congregation.* pp. 22. 8vo.

F.

[It is a protest against Bp. Kenrick's authority. All the old names disappear, a new set subscribe themselves.]

1831. April 31. *Pastoral Address of Rt. Rev. F. P. Kenrick interdicting the Church of St. Mary's.* *v.* Dr. England. *Ib.*

—— May 28. *Charge of Rt. Rev. F. P. Kenrick, on the re-opening of St. Mary's Church.* 3 pp. 8vo. G. W. R.

[From hints read here and there through this irksome investigation of Hoganian documents, I come to the conclusion that scarcely one-half of the titles of writings on the subject have I been able to collect. A rich source of information will be drawn from the columns of the Philadelphia, New York, and Baltimore papers of the times from 1821 to 1832.]

1834. November 9. The substance of *The Farewell Sermon,* delivered at St. Mary's Church, Philadelphia, on Sunday, Nov. 9, 1834. By the Pastor, the Rev. Mr. [Jeremiah] Keily. To which is prefixed the Correspondence between the Board of Trustees and the Rev. Gentleman, on his Resignation of the Pastorship of the Church. Philadelphia : Printed by L. [Lydia] R. Bailey, 26 North Fifth Street. 1835. Pp. 17, 12mo. F.

Historical Note.—NORAH.—"Crazy Norah" died in Phila. Feb'y, 1865. "She sported either an immense *stove-pipe* [the same week died Geo. Munday, who never wore a hat], or, in summer, a broad-rimmed straw hat, which, together with a long woollen cloak, and the inevitable accompaniment of a couple of huge carpet-bags stowed full of novels and bills for collection, set off her gaunt, raw-boned figure rather conspicuously. . . . She was the daughter of Mr. Gower, a respectable farmer, Co. Limerick, Ireland. After his death she came to this country. . . . She espoused Mr. Hogan's cause, but when she saw the officers of the law, who had been called upon to quell the riot, trampling on the sanctuary, her reason gave way, and from that time she wandered in the streets . . . an especial favorite with children. . . . Her ostensible business was that of collector. . . . She would present her bill, and, on payment being refused, would take up her station, opposite the debtor's house, surrounded by a crowd of children. . . . Shame would soon bring the debtor to terms, and Norah would hand over to the principal the amount, *minus her commission.* . . .

The Litany of the Saints was her favorite prayer. She frequently repeated it over insolvent debtors . . . enumerated among the celestial inhabitants her *grandmother.* Up to a few days of her death, . . . a regular attendant at St. John's . . . She was buried from her sister's house: a hearse and a solitary carriage composing the funeral cortege." Phila. Corr. Cinc. *Cath. Tel.*, Mch. 8, 1865.

HORNYHOLD, RT. REV. JOHN.—*Real Principles of Catholics;* or, A Catechism of General Instructions for grown persons: Explaining the principal points of the Doctrine and Ceremonies of the Catholic Church. "I will teach the unjust thy ways, and the wicked shall be converted to thee."—Psalm i. 15. By the Rt. Rev. J. H., Author of the *Decalogue and Sacraments Explained.* "Haec est via, ambulate in ea."—Isa. xxx. 21. Philadelphia: Published by Bernard Dornin, North-East Corner of Fourth and Walnut Streets. 1819. F.

Pp. x.–326. 12mo. 3 pp. A General Index; 1 blank; 5 unnumbered, Subscribers.

[*v. Life of Bp. Hornyhold,* by Dr. Milner; also, Canon Flanagan's *History of the Church in England,* vol. ii. Dr. H. is also the author of the *Commandments* and *Sacraments.* It is related of him that the pursuivants having come to arrest him, as a priest, at the conclusion of Mass, he saved himself by throwing a portentous woman's cap over his flowing wig and a woman's cloak over his vestments, and throwing himself in a corner in attitude of prayer. He died a holy death, Dec., 1778.]

HOUDET. *A Treatise on Morality:* chiefly designed for the Instruction of Youth.

"To blend improving Morals with Delight,
And with kind Precept set the Heart aright."

By the Reverend René Houdet. Philadelphia: Printed for the author by T. Dobson, No. 41, S. Second-street. 1796. pp. vi. and 120. 12mo.
H. ✠ C.

[Copyright secured according to law.

Pp. iii.-vi., Preface. Signed "R. Houdet, Philadelphia, November 21st, 1796; last page "Translated by Michael Fortune." M. F.'s name appears among the subscribers to *The Grounds of the Old Religion*, by Fagan, in 1814. Rt. Rev. Bp. Woods, of Philadelphia, kindly transcribed for me the following: "Rev. R. Houdet apud S. Josephum a 15a Octobris, 1795.]

HOWARD, Col. Jno. Eager—*An Oration.* Delivered before the Washington Society of Alexandria, Febr'y 22d, 1815. Printed by Allen & Hill, *Telegraph* office. pp. 16. 8vo. F.

[Object not to my reckoning Col. H. among Catholics, for I know not the precise circumstances of his death, and because his wife and son, Major E. Howard, were Catholics. I have performed the sad office of closing the eyes of the former and consigned the remains of both to rest, in Holyhood Cemetery, Brookline, Mass. Col. H. was the oldest son of Col. J. E. Howard, one of the heroes of the Revolution; two medals were decreed to him by the U. S. Senate. They descended from the Catholic family of the Earls of Arundel. Mrs. Col. H., Jr., became a convert with her brother, W. G. Read, under the guidance of Dr. England, S.C. For these items I am indebted to the courtesy of W. G. Read, Esq., of Baltimore, Md.]

HUBY.—*The Spiritual Retreat of the Reverend Father Vincent Huby, of the Society of Jesus.* Translated from the French. Philadelphia: Printed for Mathew Carey, No. 118, Market Street. 1795. F.

Pp. v. and 222. 18mo. Last page "Printed by R. Folwell, No. 33, Mulberry Street."

HYMNS, *for the Use of the Catholic Church in the United States of America.* A New Edition, with Additions and Improvements. Baltimore: Printed by John West Butler. 1807. pp. 112. 12mo. F.

—— A neat pocket edition of the —— adv'd by Dornin, 1815, "to be shortly published."

—— *v. David.*

IMITATION, *The—of the Blessed Virgin:* composed on the Plan of *The Imitation of Christ.* "Unius vita, omnium disciplina."—*St. Ambr. de Virg.*, L. II. From the French. Philadelphia: Published by Bernard Dornin, Corner of Fourth and Walnut Street. 1819. pp. ii.–v.–387. 18mo. F.

[Preface contains also the approbation of the *Sorbonne*, 1772, by Dr. Jean Réné Asseline, afterwards Bp. of Boulogne, who died April, 1813, in Aylesbury, where he had accompanied, as his confessor, Louis XVIII. But who is the author ?]

[C. P. Soc. now publish this work from Lucas's Plates.]

INSTRUCTIONS *on the Erection of Four New Catholic Episcopal Sees* in the U. S., and the Consecration of their First Bishops, Celebrated in Baltimore on the 23d Oct., 1st and 4th November. In which the signification of the various ceremonies used in that Sacred Rite is fully explained and developed, and the principal Formulæ and Prayers transcribed in English for the convenience of the Laity. Baltimore: Printed for Bernard Dornin, and sold at his Roman Catholic Library, 30, Baltimore Street. . . . C. Dobbin & Murphy, Print. . . . 1810. pp. 23. Small 12mo. F.

[This little work, even to the title, is printed both in French and English. The four bishops were—Dr. Concanen, for New York, who died in Naples on the eve of his sailing for America, not without suspicion of poison; Dr. Egan, for Philadelphia, consecrated October 28; Dr. Cheverus, consecrated November 1st; Dr. Flaget, consecrated November 4th. See *Cath. Church in the U. S.*, by DeCourcy & Shea.]

INSTRUCTIONS *upon the Sacrament of Confirmation.* "By the imposition of the hands of the Apostles, the Holy Ghost was given."—Acts viii. 18. Authorised by Superiors. Washington, District of Columbia: Printed by Way & Groff, North E Street. . . . 1802. pp. 42. sm. 12mo. F.

JOURNEE, *La—du Chrétien, sanctifiée par la Prière et la Meditation.* Nouv. ed. Baltimore: W. Pechin. MDCCXCVI. J. G. S.

24mo, 311 pp., last folio erroneously given as 284. Followed by Catechism (ante p. 81). The Catechism is followed by *Cantique sur la Passion de N. S. J. C.*, pour être chantée le Vendredi Saint. 12 pp. J. G. S.

JOURNEE *du Chrétien, Sanctifiée par la Prière et la Meditation.* Nouvelle edition en Latin et François, augmentée de plusieurs prières. 18mo. 75 cts. Carey's adv't. 1816.

IRONSIDE, GEO. E., A.M.—*Observations on*

Bishop Hobart's Charge entitled, Corruptions of the Church of Rome, Contrasted with certain Protestant Errors, in a Letter to that Prelate. "The Spirit of Truth shall guide you into all Truth."—St. John 16, v. 18. Washington: Printed for David & Force, Pennsylvania Avenue. . . . . 1820. pp. 43. 8vo. F.

—— —— *Epitome Historiæ Sacræ*, Auctore L'Homond. Editio nova, quam Prosodiæ signis, novaque vocum omnium interpretatione, adornavit Georgius Ironside, A.M. Novi Eboraci: Impensis Eastburn, Kirk & Co. Typis N. Van Riper. 1814. F.

Pp. iv.–249. 18mo. Last page "Van Riper, Print., Greenwich cor. Vesey."

[The text is from the Vulgate. Here is a Bible adopted as a text-book in our schools in the U. S. in 1814. Oh! how the Papists are opposed to the Bible! Rev. James Ward, S.J., of Frederick, Md., has (March 1, 1871) kindly placed at my disposal the following items: "There ought to be an obituary in the papers between '26 and '29, for I remember I was sent by my uncle (?) to G. T. C. somewhere about that time to give, in his name, to the Rev. F. Smith the Book of Common Prayer that had belonged to Mr. Ironside. All I know of him is that he was a Protestant minister in New York, and when he was converted that he came to Washington City, where my uncle's family visited him, and that he died in Washington. . . . We G. T. C. boys knew him as the editor of the *Gloucester Greek Grammar*, called by us 'Ironsides.'" Sister M. de Chantal, of the V. B. M. (sister to the ever lamented J. Cummings, D.D.), informs me that Mr. Ironside was born in Aberdeenshire, Scotland, and served as a chaplain in the British Navy. He was a distinguished Episcopal minister, and officiated in St. George's Church, New York, in 1815; became a Catholic in 1817, and was forsaken by all his former admirers. He removed with his family to Washington, where he was much esteemed, and President Adams appointed him to the office of translator in the State Department, an important office which he occupied for many years." Among the remains lately transferred from St. Patrick's old burying-ground to a new Catholic cemetery in Washington those of Mr. Ironside are mentioned. *v. Balt. Cath. Mirror,* November, 1871, "Washington Correspondence."

ISLA, REV. JOHN FRANCIS, S.J. *The Adventures of Gil Blas of Santillane.* A new Translation, by the author of *Roderick Random* [T. G. Smollett]. Baltimore: Published by Fielding Lucas, Jr., J. Cushing, and J. & T. Vance. R. W. Pomeroy, printer. 1814. F.

4 vols. 18mo. I.—pp. 275; II.—229; III.—269; IV.—246.

[Fr. I. born April 11, 1714, in Segovia, Spain; died Dec. 20, 1783, in Bologna, Italy. He was a hard student, finished scholar, and great preacher. He was author of *Fray Gerundio,* a satire on the foolish way of preaching then in vogue, translated into English by Barrett (and I think there is an American edition previous to 1820), and into other European tongues. *Gil Blas de Saltillana buelto a su patria,* finished in Bologna, 1781, appeared at Madrid only in 1805. In consequence of the writer's assumptions in his Preface, *Gil Blas* was ascribed to Le Sage. P. François de Neufchateau has demolished this opinion, 1820; but W. Scott attributes the work to Le Sage. *v. Précis de la querelle*

Literaire sur la propriété nationale de Gil Blas, by Pichot, in his translation of W. Scott's *Notice* of Le Sage: also Llorente *Observations Critiques sur le Roman de Gil Blas de Santillane*, Paris, 1822, where he attributes it to Le Sage. Here is a title copied from Sabin's *American Bibliopolist*, Dec., 1871: "*The Adventures of Gil Blas of Santillane.* Translated from the French of Le Sage, by B. Malkin. With Smirke's illustrations. Fine steel plates. 4 vols. 4to. Lond. 1809. $55.00." Le Sage (Alarin Réné de) born May 8, 1668, near Vannes, died at Boulogne-sur-Mer, Nov. 17, 1747, æt. 79. His *Gil Blas* bears the date of 1715, 1724, and 1735, 4 vols. 12mo. It is said that this work was based on "*History of the Squire Marcos de Obregon*, by Vincent Espinal," a Spanish work. In 1803 appeared "*Compendio Historico de la vida, caracter moral y literario del celebre P. Josef Francisco de Isla:* con la noticia analitica de todos sus escritos compilado par D. Joseph Ignacio de Sales, Presbitero. Dalo a luz D[a] Maria Francisca de Isla y Losada hermana del mismo P. Isla. Y lo dedica al publico. Madrid: Ibarra, 1803. 18mo." And Venezia, 1803. But the real author was Fr. Tolra: *cf.* also Christoph Gottlieb von Murr, *Journal zur Kunstgeschichte und zur Allgemeinen Litteratur*. Eilfter Theil. Nürnberg, 1783, pp. 231–289.]

KEATING, Rev. Thomas.—*Extract from a Sermon* preached in St. Mary's Church, Philadelphia, Sunday, August 20, 1790. Carey's Am. Museum, v. viii, p. 112. Sept. '90. F.

["I find the name of Rev. *Christ. V. Keating* among the priests for the year 1791. He was not a Jesuit apparently, nor is his name found as a Jesuit in any of the books of our archives. His name appears only once. R. F. Keller, S.J."]

KEMPIS, THOMAS A.—1749. *The Imitation of Jesus Christ,* being an Abridgement of the *Works of Thomas à Kempis.* By a Female Hand. London: Printed M.DCC.XLIV. Germantown: Re-Printed by Christophor Sowr. 1749. pp. (2), 278. 8vo. J. G. S.

[Only three books, fourth omitted. The whole adapted to the use of Protestants. J. G. S.]

1802. *The Imitation of Christ.* In three Books. Translated from the Latin of Thomas à Kempis. By John Payne. New Bedford: Printed by Abraham Shearman, Jun. 1802. F.

Pp. iii.–ix., Contents; 1–28, Preface; 29, 30, extract from the *Amaranth;* 31–287, text. 12mo.

Another edition, in 1805. 12mo, viii, pp. 256.

1803. —— —— Stanford (Dutches County, N. Y.): Printed by Daniel Lawrence, for Henry & John F. Hull. M.DCCC.III. F.

Pp. xxxi., Preface; 33–40, Contents; xli., xlii., extract from the *Amaranth;* 1–210, text. 12mo.

1805. —— Challoner's Translation. 1st Am. ed. Phila.: Carey. Hist. Mag. ix, pp. 279.

1808. —— *The Following of Christ*, in four books. Written in Latin by Thomas à Kempis. Translated into English, by the Right Rev. Father in God, Richard Challoner, D.D., Bishop of Debra and V. A. The Thirteenth edition. Published by and with the authority of the Right Rev. Bishop Carrol. New York: Printed for Hopkins and Seymour, for B. Dornin, Bookseller, 136, Pearl-street. 1808. F.

Pp. ii.–v., Life; 1–271, text; 273–81, Contents; i.–vi., subscribers. 18mo.

—— Another ed. adv'd by Dornin, 30 Baltimore Str. Baltimore: 1809.

1810. —— *The Following of Christ*, in Four Books. Written in Latin by Th. à K. Transl. into English by the Rt. Rev. Father in God, Richard Challoner, D.D., Bp. of Debra and V.A. The second [!] American edition. Published with the approbation of Rt. Rev. Archbishop Carroll. Baltimore: Printed for Bernard Dornin, and sold at his Roman Catholic Library, 30, Baltimore Street. G. Dobbin & Murphy, Print. 1810. Pp. 246. 24mo. F.

[Are not the types those used by Carey, who is said to have

been the first printer in the U. S. who preserved plates? A description of Carey's edition would explain all.]

—— This same edition advertised by Longworth, of New York, 1816, in a Catalogue of all kinds of books; evidently he had a supply from Dornin.

1812. —— *The Christian Pattern;* or, A Treatise of the Imitation of Jesus Christ; with Meditations and Prayers for Sick Persons. By George Stanhope, D.D., Charlestown. 8vo.

1813. —— *L'Imitation de Jesus-Christ.* Traduction avec une Pratique et une Priere à la fin de chaque Chapitre. Par le R. P. De Gonnelieu, de la Compagnie de Jesus. Baltimore: Imprimé par A. Miltenberger. 18mo. F.

12 pp. Table; pp. 1–539 text.

1816. —— —— in three books. Transl. from the Latin of Th. à K. by John Payne. New York: Manlius. Print. by Leonard Kellogg. 1816. Pp. 231. 12mo. [Prot.]

[K. b. A.D. 1380, d. A. 1471, æt. 91. A Canon Regular of St. Augustin. His authorship of this excellent work (read as universally as the Scriptures) has been controverted. But it seems at last generally agreed that he wrote it. The first printed edition is fixed at the year 1471, fol. in Gothic characters. An old French transl. seems to have existed, contemporaneously with the author's life, under the title of *Interior Consolation.*]

KEY TO PARADISE. Philadelphia: 1812.
J.G.S.—B.M.

[A London ed., printed in the year M.DCC.LXXII. Permissu superiorum (no printer), bears the following title-page: "The Key of Paradise opening the Gate to Eternal Salvation. Carefully corrected." At the beginning of the *second part,* a "*Preface to the Reader*" ends with a "N.B. This Preface is above 100 Years old." But this preface was supplanted by another in a later Belfast edition. Ed. 1840, printed by Simms & McIntire, has the same title, is stereotyped, and carefully revised and corrected [and so it appears by the text]. Both eds. are in two parts, which division appears only in the title-page and in the index.

Longworth of New York advertises in 1816, thus: "The Key of Paradise, opening the Gate to Eternal Salvation. 1 dollar. This edition is carefully corrected and considerably improved."]

KOHLMAN, REV. ANTHONY, S.J.—*Centurial Jubilee,* to be celebrated by all the Reformed Churches, throughout the United States, on the Thirty-first of October next, in commemoration of the Reformation—which was so happily commenced by Dr. Martin Luther on the Thirty-first of October, Anno 1517. Respectfully dedicated to the Lutheran Synods of New York, Pennsylvania, and the adjoining States, which have passed resolves at their late sessions, recommending the observance of the ever-memorable *Thirty-first* of August ensuing to the members of their respective congregations; of all which, notice is given in the Federal Gazette of Baltimore, on the *Sixteenth* of July. By a countryman of Martin Luther. *Quot.* from Horace. Printed for the author. 1817. G. T. C.

—— *The Blessed Reformation.* Martin Luther portrayed by himself. By the Rev. John Beschter [*nom de plume*]. Philadelphia: B. Dornin. 1818. G. T. C.

[*v.* Sampson, *infra.*—A. K. b. July 13, 1771, at Kayersberg, near Colmar, Departm't Haut-Rhin.: ordained in Fribourg April, 1796: joined FF. of the Sacred Heart, under Fr. Tournely: joined in their fusion with the FF. of *The Faith:* worked in the military hospitals of Italy, exposed to every kind of insults, privations, and incredible sufferings; reconciled hundreds of Protestants with the Church; worked in the ministry, and teaching, at the order of his superior, in Dillingen, Berlin, England, and Amsterdam; in 1805 joins the Novitiate S. J. in Dunébourg, the Company having been acknowledged in Russia by Pius VII. (1801); in 1807 sent to the U. S., where he remained until 1825, when he was called to occupy the chair of Mor. Theol. in the Rom. College, restored to the Jesuits by Leo XII., who had placed his private library at the disposal of Fr. K.; in Rome he filled posts of importance. He was truly a holy man, an excellent confessor, and "it did people good only to look at him." He was instrumental in the conversion of the famous A. Theiner, P. O. (*v.* his Notice of Ecclesiastic Seminaries). Attacked by a severe cold in April, 1836, he yet went out on the 8th to hear confessions in the cold church of Del Gesù;

on the 10th he died, æt. 65.—The famous Mattingly miracle of 1824 took place when K. was Sup. of the Semin'y in Washington—*v.* Ann. de la Religion, T. xli., p. 8, and *Affidavits,* etc. *The Catholic Almanac* (Cath. Pub. Soc., N. Y.) for 1872 gives a succinct but accurate biographical notice of good and dear Father Kohlman.]

LAROCHEJAQUELEIN, *Memoirs of the Marchioness de.*—With a map of the Theatre of War in La Vendée. Translated from the French. Philadelphia: Published by M. Carey, and for sale by Wells & Lilly, Boston. 1816. F.

8vo, v, vi, *Preface of the Transl'r.* . . . *Edinburgh, April* 1816; vii, viii, *To my Children.* . . . Donnissan de Larochejaquelein, August 1, 1811; Text 406, at p. 375, she adds a Supplement, bringing the Memoirs to June, 1815.

[This work is styled *admirable* by Dr. Bayley, in his "Life of Bishop Bruté," p. 12, *ad calcem.*]

? LATOUR (MAJOR A. LACARRIERE).—*Historical Memoirs of the War in West Florida and Louisiana in* 1814–'15. With an Atlas, written originally in French, and translated for the author by H. P. Nugent, Esq. Philadelphia: Conrad. 1816.

2 vls. in 1 (from J. A. Rice's Catalogue).

LETTER *addressed to the Most Rev. Leonard*

Neale by a Member of the Roman Catholic Congregation of Norfolk, in Virginia. G. T. C.

[n. d. but headed *Norfolk*, 1816. It belongs to that schism. It is endorsed *Defence of Jasper Moran.*—Fr. Sumner.]

L'HOMOND.

v. supra, *Epitome*, *Bibles*, 1814, and *Appleton.*

M. Carey, in 1816, advertised as *printed for M. C.: Elemens de la Grammaire Française.* Par M. L'Homond, Prof. émérite en la ci-devant Univ'é de Paris. Dixième édition, 12mo, 50 cts.

?LIANCOURT, F. A. FRED.—*Duc de la Rochefoucauld.* A comparative view of the Mild and Sanguinary; and the good effects of the former exhibited in the present Economy of the Prisons of Philadelphia. London: Darton & Harvey. 1796.

First printed in Philadelphia: O. Rich, " Biblioth. Amer. Nova." pp. 48. 12mo.

? McCULLOCH'S *Pocket Almanac*, for the year 1794, etc.

*
* *
* * *
* * * *
* * * * *

While kindred stars in heav'n shall glow,
This Pyramid will shine below.

Philadelphia: Printed and sold by John McCulloch, No. 1 North Third-Street. Pp. 32. 64mo. Abp. B.

McNEVEN, Wm. James, M.D.—*Chemical Examination of the Mineral Water of Schooley's Mountain.* New York: 1815. 8vo. B. P. L.

—— *Exposition of the Atomic Theory of Chemistry.* New York: 1819. 8vo. *Ib.*

—— *Pieces of Irish History.* New York: Dornin. 1807. 8vo. G. T. C.

[A copy was sold in Boston, at the auction of Giles' Library, at a high rate.]

He had published in Dublin in 1803, *Rambles through Swisserland in the Summer and Autumn of* 1802. 8vo.

[McN., b. at Ballynahowne, Co. Galway, March 21, 1763, was educated in Germany, arrived in N. York July 4th, 1805; d. at the house of his son-in-law, Thos. Emmet, N. York, July 12, 1849, æt. 79.—Besides the above works, he pub'd an ed. of Brande's "Chemistry," and was co-editor for three years with Dr. De Witt, of N. Y., of the *Medical and Philosophical Journal* [previous to 1819], *v. New Am. Cycl.* and Allibone.]

MANNOCK, John, O.S.B.—*The Poor Man's Catechism;* or, The Christian Doctrine Explained. With short admonitions. *First American from the Fifth London Edition.* "Blessed are the poor in spirit, for theirs is the Kingdom of Heaven."—St. Matthew, v. 3. "Hath not God chosen the poor of this world, rich in faith, and heirs of the kingdom, which he hath promised to those that love him?"—St. James ii. 5. Baltimore: Published by Bernard Dornin. J. Robinson, printer. 1815. pp. 342. 12mo. F.

[Allibone mentions his name. My copy has the following autograph of Dr. Matignon: "Mary Ann Farmer has received this book as a reward of her good behaviour, and a memorial of her first communion, June the 16th, 1816.

"FRANCIS A. MATIGNON.

"I have attended Mrs. Farmer on her death-bed, Nov. 25, 1869."]

—— —— *Poor Man's Controversy;* or, Religious and Moral Instructions and Exhortations. By J. Mannock, O.S.B., author of the Poor Man's Catechism. A posthumous work, published by his friends. *Be always ready to give an account of your faith.* George-Town, D. C.: Printed by Wm. Duffy, Book-seller and Stationer. 1817. pp. 106. 12mo. F.

[At p. 107, "Catalogue of Roman Catholic Books, for sale by William Duffy, *Printer, Book-binder, and Stationer,* High Street, Georgetown. (List follows)—at the bottom:

"W. Duffy has now in Press a splendid Edition of the Douay Bible, in Quarto, illustrated with Plates by the first artists in America, which will be delivered to subscribers at $10, elegantly bound." Was it ever published? There is no vestige of it in the oldest Catholic libraries, nor have the "oldest inhabitants," like the venerable Fathers A. Elder and J. McElroy, any remembrance of its publication. Perhaps some of the beginning sheets have been, long ago, used to wrap up red herrings.]

MAN'S *Only Affair;* or, Reflections on the Four Last Things to be Remembered. *Translated from the latest French edition,* and enlarged with a chapter on the Devotion to the Blessed Virgin; several edifying Histories; Morning and Evening Prayers; Prayers of Mass, accompanied with a short explanation of its ceremonies; and Vespers. *Tolle, et lege—Take and Read.* First American edition. New York: Printed by J. Seymour, No. 49, John-Street. 1813. pp. v.–288. 24mo. F.

[The "Preface to the New Edition," p. ii., remarks: "As it was originally published at a time when several authors were rather too free in their citations, many doubtful facts have been expunged and others substituted, drawn from the most authentic documents. . . . Heaven grant that the present ENGLISH publication, . . . etc." At p. 169, where the work proper ends, is given the Approbation, signed LEONARD (NEALE, Coadj. Bp. of Baltimore), *Bishop of Gortyna.* May 14, 1807.]

MANUAL *of Catholic Prayers.* Philadelphia: Printed by A. Bell. 1774. 12mo. G. T. C.

—— *Roman Catholic*—or, Collection of Prayers, Anthems, Hymns, etc. Boston: Printed by Manning & Loring, No. 2 Cornhill. Dec. 1803. pp. 287. 24mo. J. G. S.

—— *Rom. Cath.*—or, Collection of Prayers, Anthems, Hymns, et. With the approbation of the Rt. Rev. Bishop [Dr. Cheverus]. Boston: Printed by J. T. Buckingham, Winter-Street. . . . 1811. pp. 184. 18mo. F.

[Dr. Cheverus wrote to Eliz. Seton, under date of June 1, 1806, that he desired Mr. Tisserant to give her "one of the prayer-books, printed here for the use of our church." My edition begins the Table of Movable Feasts with 1812. Ezra Lincoln: Boston, 1823, republished this manual from the same plates, adding, however, 213 pp. (18mo—F.); another edition, same number of pages, and to pp. 221 (pp. 395. 12mo. F.), same plates, was published in Boston: Devereux & Donahoe, 1836.]

"*Dornin* is now *printing* the *Catholic Christian's Pocket Manual*, being a Collection of Devout Prayers, for Mass, Confession, and Communion. With the Litanies, Vespers, and Hymns, revised and corrected by a Catholic Clergyman of Baltimore, and will be found in every respect an epitome of real Catholic Piety. Price 37½ *cents*."—*Dornin's Adv.* 1810.

[I never saw the printed copy, nor did D. advertise it in subsequent notices as published, at least in such editions of his works as I have seen.]

—— —— *Christian's—of Faith and Devotion.* New York. 1814. 18mo. J.G.S.—B.M.

Manuale Clericorum Seminarii S. Sulpitii Baltimorensis. Continens: 1. Varias preces, quæ in illo Seminario recitari solent. 2. Officium parvum

B. Mariæ Virginis. 3. Ordinem devotionis Viæ Crucis, seu Calvarii, quæ ex Indulto Pii VII. in prædicto Seminario instituta est. 4. Brevem expositionem Indulgentiarum quas singuli Fideles lucrari possunt; speciatim vero earum, quæ Seminario S. Sulpitii a Pio VI. concessæ fuerunt. Baltimori: Typis Johannis W. Butler. 1808. pp. 217. 24mo. F.

MARECHAL.—*Pastoral Letter of the Abp. of Baltimore* [Dr. Ambrose Marechal] *to the Rom. Catholics of Norfolk, Sept.* 28, 1819. Baltimore: Printed by J. Robinson, Circulating Library, 94 Market Street, corner of Belvidere-Street. 1819. pp. 62. 8vo. Abp. B.

[An important document bearing on the plan of *schismatizing* the church in the U. S. by bringing over a bishop consecrated at Utrecht. The Pastoral gives a history of the transaction: The Abp.'s copy has additional notes in the hand of Dr. Marechal.]

—— —— 2d ed., by Robinson. *Ib. it.* 1820. Republication of Abp. Carroll's Letter to Trinity Church, Phila., and Marechal's to Norfolk. pp. 88. 8vo. F.

v. supra, Carroll and Marechal.

[For a succinct biographical sketch of Abp. Marechal, see *Catholic Almanac.* Baltimore: 1836, p. 49., and R. H. Clarke's Memoirs, etc.

MARTIN, François-Xavier—*The History of Louisiana, from the earliest Period.* By F. X. Martin. *Hæc igitur formam crescendo mutat, et olim Immensi caput orbis erit. Sic dicere vates.* Ovid. Metam. xv. 434 and 435. New Orleans: Printed by Lyman & Beardslee. 1827. F.

I. Preface, to p. viii, *dated* Gentilly, near New Orleans, June 20, 1827. *Contents:* pp. ix–xxiii. *Preliminary Chapter*, xxv–lxxxiii. *Text:* 364 to A.D. 1769.

II. Printed by A. T. Penniman & Co. 1829. *Contents:* xv. *Text*, 429 to A.D. 1815.

[Whether by an *auctioneering* legerdemain, or really through an honest competitor against an *unlimited* bid, I know not; but this copy was bought in New York, April, 1872, for the trifling sum of $222! O ye bibliomaniacs!]

—— *The History of North Carolina, from the earliest Period.* New Orleans: Printed by A. T. Pennyman & Co., corner of Chartres and Bienville Streets. 1829. F.

2 vols. 8vo. I. pp. xii and 325; app. civ. II. pp. 411.

[Mr. Martin's attention was engaged in this work as early as 1791, as he says in his *preface*, dated Gentilly, near N. O., July 20, 1829. Mr. Martin was born in Marseilles, France, March 17, 1762, died in N. O., La., Dec. 11, 1846. Previous to 1820 he published Reports of the Superior Court of New Orleans, from 1809 to 1813 (2 vls.) As to his Catholicity, so far all my enquiries in N. O. have proved unsuccessful. But the author of *Catholic Literature* (*supra*) says that "Martin, a Catholic, was the first historian of North Carolina and then of Louisiana, whilst *as a jurist* he was without a rival."—p. 133.

MASSILLON.—*Sermons* by Jean-Baptiste Massillon, Bishop of Clermont. To which is prefixed The Life of the Author, selected and translated by William Dickson, and dedicated, by permission, to her Grace the Dutchess of Buccleugh. Complete in two volumes. Brooklyn: Printed by T. Kirk for John Conrad & Co., Booksellers, Chesnut-street, Philadelphia. 1803.

1st vol., pp. 487. 12mo. 2d vol., pp. 546. 12mo. Printed for Thomas S. Arden, No. 186 Pearl-Street, New York. T. Kirk, Printer. 1803. (2 copies.) H. ✠ C.

MASSILLON.—*Sermons by J. B. Massillon*, Bishop of Clermont. To which is prefixed the Life of the Author. Selected and Translated by William Dickson. Second American Edition. Revised and Materially corrected. In Two Volumes. Philadelphia: Published by M. Carey & Son, Corner of Fourth and Chestnut Streets. D. Allison, Printer. 1818. F.

8vo. I. pp. xxi.–2. Contents, unnumb. Text, 17–303. II. Same title, but *J. Bakestraw, Printer.* Text, 1–544.

—— *The Charges* of J. B. M., Bishop of Clermont. Addressed to his clergy. Also two Essays—the one on the Art of Preaching, from the French of M. Reybaz, and the other on the Composition of a Sermon, as adapted to the Church of England, etc., etc. . . . By the Rev. Teops. St. John, LL.B., etc. New York: Printed by D. & G. Bruce, for Brisban and Brannan, 186 Pearl-street. 1806. pp. xix.–330. 8vo. F.

[Not having this part of Massillon's works at hand, I cannot institute a comparison as to the fidelity of the translation. The editor and translator, it must be borne in mind, was no Catholic.]

—— *Sermons* of J. B. Massillon and Lewis Bourdaloue, two celebrated Preachers. Also a Spiritual Paraphrase of some of the Psalms, in the form of Devout Meditations and Prayers. By J. B. Massillon. Transl. by Rev. Abel Flint, Pastor of a church in Hartford. Hartford: Printed by Lincoln & Gleason. 1805. pp. xi.–310. 12mo. F.

[Prot. transl.]

MATIGNON—*Rules of the Confraternity;* or, Association of the Holy Cross. Established in Boston, with the approbation of the Rt. Rev. Bishop (Cheverus). [Printed by Buckingham? A.D. 1817.] pp. 8. 18mo. F.

[For notices of Dr. Matignon see Creagh's *Laity's Directory* for 1822, p. 133; also, Lives of Card. Abp. Cheverus—*Catholic Observer*, Boston, 1847; contemporary secular papers of Boston (Sept., 1818); and the "History of the Catholic Church in New England," by Rev. James Fitton, East Boston, Mass., published by Mr. Donahoe, which is a very valuable addition to the monuments of Catholic History in this country.]

MILNER, Rt. Rev. John—D.D., Bp. of Castabala, V.A., F.S.A., Lond. and Cath. Acad. Rome. *Letters to a Prebendary;* being an answer to Reflections on Popery by the Rev. J. Sturgess, LL.D., Prebendary and Chancellor of Winchester, and Chaplain to His Majesty. With Remarks on the Opposition of *Hoadlyism* to the Doctrines of the Church of England. First American edition. Baltimore: Published by Bernard Dornin, and sold at his Roman Catholic Library, 30, Baltimore-street. G. Dobbin & Murphy, Print. 1810. F.

Pp. xvi. and 384. 12mo. Pp. 385–'94, Subscribers' Names; '95–400, Adv'ts.

—— *The End of Religious Controversy,* in a Friendly Correspondence, between A Religious Society of Protestants, and A Roman Catholic Divine. In Three Parts. Part I. On the Rule of Faith; or, The Method of Finding Out the True Religion.

Part II. On the Characteristics of the True Church. Part III. On Rectifying Mistakes concerning the Catholic Church: Addressed to the Rt. Rev. *Dr. Burgess, Lord Bishop of St. David's*, in answer to His Lordship's *Protestant Catechism.* Accompanied by an elegant Engraving of the Apostolical Tree [not in my copy]. Philadelphia: Pub'd by Bernard Dornin, No. 58, South Fourth Street. 1820. Pp. xxxiv, 35–419. 12mo. F.

[It was published by subscription.]

—— *A Brief Summary* of the History and Doctrine of the Holy Scripture. In two parts. New York: Printed for William H. Creagh. [C. N. Baldwin, Printer.] 1820. Pp. viii.–230. 12mo. F.

[M. b. in Lond., 1752; studied at Douay; ord. priest 1777; consecrated Bishop of Castabala *in part.* and Vicar Ap. of the Middle District; died Ap. 19, 1826, æt. 74, at Wolverhampton. For accurate notices of this wonderful man, *cfr. Ami de la Religion*, vl. 53, and Can. Flanagan's *History of the Church in England*, vl. ii. and his recent Life by Dr. Husenbeth.]

1. MIRANDA'S EXPEDITION, *a General Account of*—including the Trial and Execution of Ten of his Officers. And an Account of the Imprisonment and Sufferings of the Remainder of his Officers and Men who were taken Prisoners. *Upon the autho-*

rity of a person who was an officer under Miranda, who was taken and condemned to ten years' imprisonment, and who, after suffering nearly two years, effected his return home. New York: Printed by McFarland & Long, No. 308 Broadway. 1808. Pp. 120. 8vo. F.

[Miranda was a Catholic, and died as such. Many of his followers were Catholics, including several Irish. Those who were executed were attended by three Catholic clergymen.]

2. *The History* of Don Francisco de Miranda's Attempt to Effect a Revolution in South America. In a series of Letters. By a gentleman who was an officer under that General, to his friend in the United States. To which are annexed Sketches of the Life of Miranda, and Geographical Notices of Caraccas. Boston: Published by Oliver & Munroe, No. 70, State Street, 1808. pp. xi, and 300. F.

3. *The History* of Don Francisco de Miranda's Attempt to Effect a Revolution in South America. In a series of Letters. By a gentleman who was an officer under the General, to his friend in the United States. To which are annexed Sketches of the Life of Miranda, and Geographical Notices of Caraccas. Second edition. "Thoughts tending to ambition, they do plot unlikely wonders."—Shak.

Boston: Published by Oliver & Munroe, No. 70, State Street. 1809. 12mo. F.

Verso of t. p., *license* given to Oliver & Munroe; iii–xi, contents and preface; p. 300 *text*.

4. —— Same title as above, but differs in type and arrangement. The *second edition*. Boston: Edward Oliver, No. 70, State Street. 1810. F.

[This ed. of equal format with the above, changes at p. 285, and adds 12 pages to the text, and shows a change in the printing firm. In fact, a *third* ed.]

5. —— Same title, different type, but Third edition. Boston: Edward Oliver. 1811. F.

Same as above, only different type in the last 12 pp.

MIRROR, *The Spiritual*—of the Confraternity of St. Augustine and St. Monica, under the Invocation and Patronage of the Blessed Virgin, Mother of Consolation. *Let every one of you please your neighbor, for his good, unto edification.*—Rom. xv. 2. Philadelphia: Printed for the Confraternity by A. Fagan, 133 South Front Street. 1812. Pp. 108. 18mo. F.

[It is evidently connected with the early history of St. Augustine's Church, Philadelphia. About A. Fagan, *v.* App.]

MOLINA, Don J. Ignatius.—*The Geographical, Natural, and Civil History of Chili.* Illustrated by a half-sheet Map of the Country. With notes from the Spanish and French versions, and an Appendix containing copious extracts from the Araucana of Don Alonzo de Ercilla. Translated from the original Italian by an American gentleman. Middletown (Conn.): Printed for S. Riley. 1808.

F.

2 vols. 8vo. I., xii. and 271; II., viii. and 306. (2d vol. contains "An Appendix to the Civil and Political History of Chili, consisting of a Sketch of the Araucana of Don Alonzo de Ercilla, with copious Translations from that Poem, by William Hayley, Esq., and the Rev. H. Boyd. New York: Published by Alsop, Brannan & Alsop, City Hotel, Broadway. 1808. *Verso:* Printed by Richard Alsop, Middletown, Connecticut." Pp. iv–69.)

[Padre Molina was a very learned Jesuit of the Province of Chili, South America, whence he was ostracised with all his brethren, in 1765, by the Bourbon Charles III. After much suffering and many trials, he at last found rest in Bologna, Italy, where with several other members of the Company he devoted himself to study and scientific pursuits. He died very poor, Sept. 13, 1829, and was buried in a pauper's grave, at the Certosa. Some years after the Municipality of Bologna caused his bust to be placed in the Pantheon, among the illustrious men of Bologna. But no inscription records his merits. The book whereof the title is given above seems to be a translation of an original work published in 1782, a second edition of the first part of which Molina printed in large quarto, Bologna: Masi e comp. 1810 (F.) pp. v. and 307, with a new map, and dedicated to "Eugenio Napoleone figlio di Napoleone Augusto."

It has also a beautiful portrait of the author by the celebrated engraver J. Rosaspina, taken in 1805. In 1776 Molina had already published a *Compendio della Storia Geografica Naturale e Civile del Regno del Chile. Bologna:* MDCCLXXVI. *Stamperia di S. Tommaso d'Aquino.* Pp. viii. and 246, with a map and ten illustrations (F.) A 2d ed. of this work, pub. in 1787, is mentioned at p. 272 of the 4to map ed. Molina's history was translated into French by Gravel, in 1792, also into German and Spanish. It is quoted by Gmelin in his enlarged ed. of *Systema Naturæ.*]

MONITOR, *The Christian's*—*v.* Taylor.

MOREAU, DE SAINT-MERY, *Mederic Louis Elie* ——.

—— *Description de la Partie Française de Saint-Domingue.* Philadelphie. 1798–99. 2-4to. pp. 788–756.

—— *Description de la Partie Espagnole de Saint-Domingue.* Philadelphia. 1796. 2-8vo.

A Topographical and Political Description of the Spanish Part of St. Domingo. Translated from the French by William Cobbett. Vol. I. 8vo. Phila. 1798.

—— *Idée generale,* ou Abrégé des Sciences et des Arts à l'usage de la Jeunesse. Philadelphie. 1795. 1-12mo.

—— *Relation de l'Ambassade de la Compagnie des Indes Orientales Hollandaises à la Chine.* Redigée par Van-Braam. Trad. en Français. Philadelphie. 1796–97. 2-4to.

—— *De la Danse.* Philadelphie. 1797. 2-12mo.

This work aims at proving a similarity between the colonial dances and those of the Moors, Africans, and Greeks.—*v. Encyclopédie Catholique.*

[M. L. E. Moreau, b. Jan. 15, 1750, in Martinique ; d. in Paris (?), Jan. 28, 1819. An extraordinary man ; *v.* Feller. He discovered Colombo's grave, in San Domingo. In 1789 he had Lafayette appointed commander-in-chief of the National Guard. Arrested, in those troublous days, and afforded the opportunity of escape by a guard who was under obligation to him, he sailed the same day for the U. S.—1793. He suffered a great deal in New York, and went to Philadelphia, where he became bookseller and printer. As some calm appeared on the French horizon, he returned, and, being related to Josephine, Napoleon I. appointed him, in 1800, to the Council of State, and sent him to Parma. There he was beloved by the people ; but, opposed to Junot's tyranny, he was recalled, and fell into great poverty, from which he was relieved by Louis XVIII. sending him 15,000 francs. He was the author of many works published in France and Italy.]

MOREAU, J. V.—*Comparison of Moreau and Bonaparte* [Napol. I.], of their political and military lives. To which is added " Moreau's Speech on his Trial at Paris." Albany. 1806. 1-12mo. B.P.L.

[The greatest blame attached to Moreau is that he might have crushed Bonaparte on his outset, and did not do it. M. b. at Morlaix, France; d. at Laun in Bohemia, Sept. 2, 1813. In 1804 he travelled in the U. S., and lost a son, who is buried beside St. Patrick's Cathedral, New York. He is buried in the Cath. Church of St. Petersburg.]

MOORE, TH.—*Odes of Anacreon.* Translated into English Verse, with Notes, by Th. M., Esq., of the Middle Temple. Philadelphia: Printed and published by Hugh Maxwell, opposite Christ Church. 1804. Pp. xvi.–301. 12mo. F.

[A splendid edition. Odes arranged in the order of the Vatican MS. Surely not a Catholic work, yet translated by a Catholic, *the* Poet of Erin. We believe poor Tom has repeatedly, and in writing also, expressed regret for this translation of Anacreon.]

MUMFORD, J., P.S.J.—*The Catholic Scripturist;* or, The plea of the Roman Catholics: shewing the Scriptures to hold the Roman Faith in above Forty of the chief Controversies now under Debate. "*Now I beseech you, brethren, mark them which cause divisions and offences, contrary to the doctrine which ye have learned, and avoid them.*" Rom. xvi. 17. By J. M., P.S.J. Revised by a Catholic Clergyman of Baltimore. Baltimore: Printed for Bernard Dornin, and sold by him at his Catholic

Library, No. 30, Baltimore Street. . . . Geo. Dobbin & Murphy, Printers. 1809. 12mo. F.

P. vii., containing Title and Author's Preface; p. viii. *A* Note to *the Catholic Reader*, by the Am. Edr.; Text, pp. 9 to 291; pp. ccxciii. to ccxcvii., *Table of Points;* p. ccxcviii., *To the Protestant Reader.*

[James Mumford, b. in Norfolk, England, 1606; joined the Co. of Jesus 1626; prof. Sept. 29, 1641; d. March 9, 1666, in Engl. He was once apprehended in his sacerdotal vestments, and, amid a shouting rabble, cast into prison; afterwards released on bail. He was the author of several works. The *Scripturist* was first pub. Ghent, 1662, and passed through several editions.]

MURPHY, A. — Translation of *Vaniere's Georgics.* Published by J. Riley, of New York, in Middletown, Conn., quoted in Simpson's work [*v. infra*]. pp. cxxi.

NAGOT, REV. FRANCIS—Founder and Superior of the Catholic Seminary (of St. Sulpice) of Baltimore, b. at Tours, Ap. 1734, arrived in Baltimore, in 1791, and d. Ap'l 9, 1816—He was the author of the *Narratives of Remarkable Conversions* and of a *Life of Rev. Mr. Olier,* he translated the *Catholic Christian,* some of Bp. Hay's Works, and Alban Butler's *Moveable Feasts* into French, etc. *v.* Creagh's Laity's Directory. New York. 1822. pp. 129.

NANCREDE.—

Joseph Nancrede, bookseller of Boston. In 1797, his place of business was at 49 Marlborough Street. The same year he published an edition of Telemaque, "revue et corrigée" by himself. He was also "Maître de la Langue Françoise, en l'Université de Cambridge." In 1799, he published Anderson's *Essay on Quick Time*, 12mo.

"MR. FINOTTI:

"MY DEAR SIR: I don't know as the above will be of any service to you. I made it the next day after you were here, in expectation that you would call in a day or two.

"Respectfully and truly,

"SAM. G. DRAKE.

"17 Bromfield St., 3 July, 1871."

Allibone adds: "J. N. d. in Paris, 1841, æt. 81, came to Am'ca in the army of Rochambeau, and was wounded at Yorktown. About 1800 [*a*] he was Prof. of French at Harvard; and he also resided for some time in Philadelphia [*b*]. He edited a French Reader—*L'Abeille Française*, 1792—and some other books."

[*a*] Not in 1800, but in 1792: "L'Abeille Française, ou Nouveau Recueil, De Morceaux Brillans des auteurs Français le plus celebres . . . à l'usage de l'Université de Cambridge. Par P. J. G. de Nancrede, Maître de Langue Française en cette Université. . . . A Boston: De l'imprimerie de Belknap et Young, rue de l'Etat [State Str.], vis-à-vis de la Banque Nationale. MDCCXCII. F.

Pp. 352. 12mo. i.–v., Table des Matières, 1–3, Subscripteurs. [At p. 10, we read: "The late M. *de la Luzerne*, Minister Plenipotentiary from the Court of France, did, by M. Silas Deane, make an offer to found a professorship at New Haven College, the object of which was to be to teach the French language and the history of France. The trustees of this college refused the generous offer, alleging that such an establishment would tend to introduce *Popery* into the State." *Per contra*, in the *Courier de Boston* . . . . No. I. Jeudi, 23 Avril, 1789, p. 2, in a *note*, we read : "*plusieurs imprimeurs de l'Amerique qui ont réimprimé differens ouvrages tres-considerable ; entr' autres M. Thomas* [Isaias ?] . . . *vient de réimprimer l'histoire Romaine, par l'Abbe Millot.* Cet auteur a été introduit à l'Université de Cambridge." However, it should be borne in mind that the ex-Jesuit Claude François X. Millot wrote in a strain that caused him great uneasiness at the point of death.—Who was the editor of the *Courier de Boston*, publ. by Sam. Hall, 53 Cornhill ? M. Carey was its agent in Phila. On the 15th Oct., 1789, the 26th number was pub., completing six months (4to, double col. pp. 8 each No. F.) A new Prospectus is issued, the edr. appealing to Bostonians to give him the means of living, he being a citizen of Boston, also. I am inclined to think the *C.* was discontinued, not being able to secure 400 subscribers.]

[*b*] In the Life of Abp. Hughes (by Hassard. N. Y. 1866) we read (p. 394) : " My dear Mr. Frenaye : Feb. 13, '57. I received your letter of the 2d inst., announcing the death of my old and honored friend, Dr. Nancrede . . . . Had I known of his illness, I certainly should have had the melancholy satisfaction of seeing him once again before his death. . . . . With all his peculiarities, *he clung nobly to the faith of his fathers from childhood* to old age, and this amidst many temptations to abandon it. During the period of our difficulties in the erection of St. John's Church, the doctor stood by us with great constancy and great fidelity.—✠John, Abp. N. Y." Was the Dr. any relation to the J. Nancrede of Harvard ? In reply to an enquiry of mine, Dr. Bayley, Bp. of Newark, writes : " Dr. Nancrede,

alluded to in the Life of Abp. Hughes, was quite a distinguished physician in Phila., and was received into the Church [? *v. supra*], I believe, by the Abp. himself, when P. P. of St. John's Church, Phila. Dr. Nancrede used to visit Bp. Hughes, when I was his Sec'y in New York, and I remember him very well. He was a fervent Catholic. . . . I know nothing of Dr. Nancrede's family, or of the connection between him and the Prof. of French at Harvard."—Is he the author of "An Address delivered before the N. E. Soc'y of Phila, at their semi-annual meeting, May 1, 1820. By Jos. G. Nancrede, M.D. . . Phila. W. Fry. 1820." pp. 35. 8vo ? F.

At p. 4, the Dr. clearly alludes to his N. E. origin.

v. Fénelon, ante.]

NERINCX, Rev. J.

NEERINCKX, C.—*De Zegepraal van het Catholijk Geloof, ter Beschaming van Ongeloof en Dwaling, ter Bevestiging van Godvruchtige, en ter Opwekking van trage Christenen;* of Verhaal van de uitbreiding der H. Kerk in Kentucky. Uit eenen eigenhandigen Brief van den eerw. Heer Neerinckx, R. C. Priester en Zendeling. Met eene voorrede van J. G. Lesage ten Broek, Notaris te Naaldwijk. Te Amsterdam, Bij A Schievenbus. 1819. Ten voordeele der Amerikaansche Missie.

J. G. S.

[The Triumph of the Catholic Faith to the confounding of Infidelity and Error ; to the Strengthening of the Pious, and to the waking up of Slothful Christianity ; or, Sketch of the Extension of the Holy Church in Kentucky, with a Letter of Rev.

Mr. Neerinckx, R. C. Priest, etc. With a Preface by J. G. Lesage ten Broek, Notary. 8vo. vi. 48 pp.]

NERINCKX, CHARLES.—*Nagelaten Brief van den weleerw. Heer Carolus Nerinckx, in Leven Missionaris in Kentucky ;* aan zijne Bloedverwanten en Vrienden in Nederland. Te's Gravenhage, ter Drukkerij van de Gebs. Langenhuysen, Achter de Groote Kerk, No. 23. MDCCCXXV. J. G. S.

[Letter of the late Ch. Nerinckx, Missionary in Kentucky, to his friends in Netherland.

This letter is written in 1820, and treats of the state of the Catholic Faith in Kentucky, the Order of the Nuns of Loretto founded by Nerinckx, etc.

Vide Sketches of Kentucky and *Life of Bishop Flaget.* By Archbishop Spalding.]

O'BRIEN, M.—*Oration on the Death of General George Washington,* addressed to the Catholic Congregation of St. Mary's Church, of Albany, by the Rev. Matthew O'Brien, D.D., Pastor of the same, for February 22, 1800, the day appointed by Congress. *N. York State Library.*

Albany *Gazette*, February 27, 1800.

[A MS. copy of it has been furnished me by my reverend friend, Dr. E. B. O'Callaghan. As relates to Rev. M. O'Brien, cfr. *The Cath. Church in the U. S.*, by De Courcy & Shea, p. 359. Rev. M. O'Brien died in Baltimore, Oct, 20, 1815. *v.* Creagh's Directory, New York: 1822. p. 135. He had published in Ireland "Sermons on some of the most Important Subjects of Morality and Religion. Cork: James Haly. 1798. 8vo–viii. 229 pp.

O'CONOR, Thomas.

I hope I shall not be charged with impropriety because I transcribe in full the following:

"New York, Feb. 25th, 1867.

"Dear Sir:

"My father emigrated in 1801, and died in this city in 1855, at the age of 85. I think he never aspired to the character of an author. He first resorted to his pen as a means of earning a scanty subsistence for his family. This must have been about the year 1811. He was connected with the press at intervals thenceforward until he had reached a very advanced age.

"War was declared against Great Britain June 18th, 1812. Samuel Woodworth, a printer, but subsequently well known as a poet, novelist, and Swedenborgian preacher, at once commenced a [quarto] weekly newspaper called *The War.* My father was its editor for two or three months. His connection with that paper then ceased; and, in conjunction with Stephen Wall, a countryman of his, he edited for a couple of years, beginning about Sept., 1812, a weekly paper called *The Military Monitor.* Subsequently he edited for two or three years, commencing in 1815, a weekly called *The Shamrock.* In January, 1819, he commenced the publication of a monthly magazine called *The Globe.* Its proprietors avowed no particular views; but its contents indicate that it was *The Shamrock* in a new form. Ireland and Catholicity were its leading topics. It lasted about a year. In 1815 he wrote for one John Low, a publisher, a single volume entitled a 'History of the War.' It had a good circulation. . . .

14

"The book of which you particularly enquire must have been issued in numbers to subscribers. Its title page is 'The Inquisition Examined by an Impartial Reviewer. *Religionis non est Religionem cogere.* New York: Printed by J. Desnoues, 23 Provost-Street. 1825.' I have a single bound copy. In May, 1824, I was admitted to the bar; and from that time my father had no business connection with the press, nor any resort to literature except to gratify some emotion of his heart. I presume he wrote the 'Inquisition Examined' gratuitously, at the request of Mr. Desnoues, who was an old friend.

"He was brought up by his grandfather, 'the Irish antiquarian. . . . He was a devoted Catholic, an enthusiastically patriotic Irishman, and, as a necessary consequence, was averse to the government of Britain, and deeply attached to the republican institutions of his adopted country. These characteristics exhibit themselves in all his literary efforts. Whether employed in procuring bread for his family or in the freely chosen pursuits of easy leisure, his pen was always under the influence of these sentiments. It was ever directed in vindicating the fame of Ireland, the honor of our United American States, or the truth and purity of his cherished Mother the Apostolic Church. . . .

"I am, dear sir, yours truly,

"CH. O'CONOR."

To my esteemed friend, Michael Hennessy, Esq., of New York, I am indebted for the following additional items: "I had, at one time, in my possession, copies of both *The War* and *The Military Monitor*. *The War* was established at the sole suggestion of O'Conor, who edited it up to the 10th number. With a Mr. Wall, who 'had been induced by him . . . to associate his talents and military knowledge with him,' *The Military Monitor* was started by him. The new paper had a sub-title more like a table of contents than anything else. It was first printed and published for the proprietor by Joseph Desnoues, No. 6, Church

St., rear of St. Paul's church-yard, commencing with Monday, Aug. 17, 1812, and weekly thereafter. It was in small 4to form, 3 cols. to a page. For a few Nos. of the 1st vol. Hardcastle & Van Pelt, No. 63, Pine-Street, printed the paper, but by No. 9, it was back again in the hands of Joseph Desnoues, as printer, then temporarily at No. 61 Church-Street, near Murray. By Febr'y 8, 1813, Desnoues returned permanently to No. 6 Church St., where he had bought a printing office. By No. 33, April 12, 1813, O'Conor's name disappeared from its columns. Wall had retired soon after the paper was started or before the date of 1812.

"O'Conor published in the *Monitor*, under date of May, 1813, a prospectus of a 'History of the Revolutionary War in America,' which he contemplated relating in a 12mo of some 300 pp., to be sold at a dollar a copy. I know not whether it was ever given to the public. Relative to O'Conor's 'History of the War' of 1812–15, . . . within the last ten years I have seen at least four copies of it. One of them is in my own collection. It is a 12mo, of some 336 pp., '*fourth* edition, revised and improved.' It is introduced by a wretched copper-plate 'likeness' of Maj.-Gen. Andrew Jackson, and an unusually elaborate title, beginning with 'An Impartial and Correct History of the War between the United States and Great Britain.' My copy has this imprint: 'New York: Printed and Published by John Low, No. 62 Vesey-Str. 1817.' [*Infra.*] The narrative affords a very satisfactory outline sketch of the history of the war, and it is authentic.¶ The Irish-American element is not treated with indifference. Many interesting documents are supplied. . . . A fair portrait of Decatur faces p. 63, and 'middling' of Perry p. 117. An index is also supplied."

—— I. *An Impartial and Correct History of the War between the United States of America, and*

Great Britain; declared by a Law of Congress, June 18, 1812, and concluded by a ratification and exchange of a Treaty of Peace, at the City of Washington, Feb. 17, 1815. Comprising A Particular Detail of the Naval and Military Operations, and A Faithful Record of the Events Pro | duced During the contest. And including the following important doc's: 1. The President's Message to Cong. of 1st June, 1812. 2. The Report of the Comm'ee of Foreign Relations of 3d June, 1812. 3. The Act declaring War, between the U. S. and Gt. B. 4. The Treaty of Peace. 5. Niles's List of Prizes, captured during the War. 6. The Treaty of Peace of 1783. Caref'y compiled from official doc's. New York: Printed and pub'd by John Low, at Shakespear's Head, No. 17 Chatham-Street. 1815. pp. 304. 12mo. F.

T. p. copper-plate engagement of Jackson at N. O.

II. —— —— *Second edition, revised and corrected.* 1815. pp. 312. 12mo. F.

Title same as above, with omission of *And including* to *Peace of* 1783. Same engraving facing t.-p.

[At a N. Y. sale Oct. 15, 1869, an ed. of 1816 sold for more than $5.—Was not an 8vo ed. pub'd in Hartford, 1865?—A work seems to have been written in opposition to O'Conor's:

"History of the Am'an War of 1812, from the commencement, until the final termination thereof, on the memorable Eighth of Jan'y, 1815, at N. O. Embell'd with a strik'g likeness of Gen. Pike, and six other engrav'gs. *Third ed.* Phila.: pub. by Wm. McCarty. Printed by McCarty & Davis, S.W. corn. of 5th and Cherry Strs. 1817. pp. ix—252, 12mo." F.]

IV. —— —— *Fourth edition.* Same title as 2d ed. as far as the words *during the Contest,* then "By T. O'Conor. *Fourth edition, revised and corrected.* . . N. York : Printed and published by John Low, No. 62, Vesey-Street. 1817. pp. 336. 12mo. F.

[I am indebted to Jeremiah Colburn, Esq., Pres't of the Boston Numismatic Society, and member of the N. E. Historical and Genealogical Society, for the following very interesting notice of

THE O'CONOR FAMILY.

Memoir of Gabriel Beranger and his Labours in the cause of Irish Art, Literature, and Antiquities, from 1760 *to* 1780. By Sir W. R. Wilde, M.D., *Vice-President of the Royal Irish Academy.*

In the *Journal of the Royal Historical and Archæological Association of Ireland*—(Vol. I., Part I., 4th Series. 1870)—I find the following notice of the ancestors of one of New York's distinguished citizens, which I have never seen in print before. It is from a series of articles, under the title quoted, of much interest, communicated to the Association by the above-named gentleman. J. C.

18 *Somerset Street.*

"Went on, and arrived at Belinagar, the residence of Charles O'Conor, Esq. (descendant of the ancient Kings of Connaught, and well known in the literary world by his publications concerning Ireland)."—*Beranger.*

Next day, August 3, having first worked at their Sketches, they set out on horseback with Mr. O'Conor and his son Denis.

At the time of Beranger's visit, the Belinagar family had not adopted the title of Don, which was then used by the Clonalis branch at the male head of the line.

Owen O'Conor, the eldest grandson of Charles, was the first of the Belinagar branch who assumed the title of Don, or *Dun*, on the death without issue of Alexander O'Conor, the last male of the Castlerea branch. Owen was a most courteous, refined gentleman, and immediately after the passing of the Relief Bill was elected M. P. for Roscommon—an honor which has since descended to his son Denis J. O'Conor Don, and is now worn by Charles, his grandson, the present esteemed O'Conor Don, of Clonalis. The first named, Denis, had two other sons. Matthew, the second son, with whom I had the honor of an intimate acquaintance, and who resided at Mont-Druid, was a distinguished lawyer, a man of great erudition, of refined tastes, and an accomplished writer. The third son, Charles, was the well-known author of the *Rerum Hibernicarum Scriptores.*

Having been born in the locality, I am perhaps the last writer who retains a personal recollection of three of the following lineal descendants of Cathal Crove-Dearig, one of the last Kings of Connaught.

Daniel, one of the direct descendants of Sir Hugh of Ballintubber, was The O'Conor Dun. . . . He lived in great state at Clonalis, near Castlerea, and died in 1769. He had three sons, Dominick, Alexander, and Thomas, and two daughters, Jane and Elizabeth. The former married Mr. William Eccles, a solicitor and a Protestant, and was never afterwards seen by her father; my aunt, who died several years ago at a very advanced age, remembered having seen her coming in to "cry" her brother Dominick, when he was "laid out" in the barn at Clonalis. . . . In the old house I remember seeing a beautiful Spanish picture of the Madonna; a large gold snuff-box, representing on the lid *the landing of Columbus in America*, said to have been given by the King of Spain to one of the O'Conor family; and the silver and jewelled hilted sword of Count O'Reilly.

The second brother, Alexander O'Conor, had been many years in Spain, but at the time of his brother Thomas's death was living at a place called Creglahan, near Castlerea. Although past seventy, he was usually called "Master Sandy," but was always recognized by the people as the true "King of Connaught." I knew him well, as he afterwards resided with a relative of mine. He died at a great age, and is buried beside my ancestors, the O'Flyns, in the old churchyard of Kilkeeven, on the banks of the Suck, near Castlerea.

The Rev. Dr. Charles O'Conor (Columbanus), the celebrated antiquary, was parish priest of Kilkeeven, where I was born, and while there, it is said, collected all the Irish MSS. that could be procured in the neighborhood, as well as those belonging to his relatives whom I have already mentioned, and which he subsequently carried off to Stowe, when he became librarian to the Duke of Buckingham.

Besides Denis, Charles—the friend of Beranger in 1777—had another son, Charles, of Mount Allen, grandfather of the present Charles O'Conor, of New York.

I, of course, submitted the foregoing to the Hon. Charles O'Conor, who most courteously replied as follows:

"New York, April 10th, 1872.

"REVEREND DEAR SIR—I am very much rejoiced to learn that your work is in course of publication. . . . I feel assured that the general interests of religion will be greatly promoted by it. It is not in vain that God endows the worker in such a field with learning, talents, untiring industry, and ardent zeal.

"A minor consideration, but I hope not an unbecoming one, increases my pleasure at the event. You have spoken, kindly I am sure, of my beloved, venerated, and sainted father.

"I return the memoranda concerning certain members of my family in Ireland. It is entirely correct, I believe. I have made very slight additions: they are not corrections of any error, but simply elucidations. The propriety of publishing any such private matters must be judged of by others. Charles, of Mount Allen, with whom that narrative ends, emigrated with his whole family.

"With great esteem, I remain,
"Rev. Dear Sir,
"Yours faithfully,
"CH. O'CONOR.

"Rev. JOSEPH M. FINOTTI,
"Brookline, Mass."]

O'CONNOR, J. M.—*A Treatise on the Science of War and Fortification.* Composed for the Use of the Imperial Polytechnic School, and Military Schools; and translated for the War Department, for the Use of the Military Academy of the U. S.;

to which is added a Summary of the Principles and Maxims of Grand Tactics and Operations. By J. M. O'C., Capt. of Artillery, and late Major and Ass. Adj. Gen. in the Northern Army. "Without the rivalship of Nations, and *the practice of war*, civil society itself could scarcely have found an object or a form."—*Ferguson on Civil Society.* In two volumes, *with a volume of Plates and Maps.* New York: Printed by J. Seymour, No. 49 John-Street, 1817. F.

8vo. Vol. I., pp. iii., iv., Dedicat. to James Munroe, Pres't. U. S.; pp. v.–viii., Introd.; pp. 9–400, Text. Vol. II.: pp. 490 and six pp. contents. Vol. III., 4to, 36 plates.

[I am indebted for this copy of a rare work to the kindness of Col. Geo. Kenzel, U.S.A., and Prof. at West Point. The work, I think, was pub'd by the Government.]

O'GALLAGHER, Rev. S. F., *O. S. F. of Charleston, S. C.*—*A Brief Reply* to a Short Answer to a True Exposition of the Doctrine of the Catholic Church touching the Sacrament of Penance. —— New York: Printed for the Author, by Sherman & Pudney, No. 30 Nassau Street. . . 1815. pp. 176. 8vo. F.

[Anon. in title-page, but name signed to Dedication to the Hon. Maj. Gen. Charles Cotesworth Pinkney.—The pht. is against Dr. Wharton's Reply to Abp. Carroll, and it elicited a

Reply from W.—*v. supra* CARROLL & WHARTON. Fr. O'Gallagher, of Dublin, was sent to Charleston, S. C., by Abp. Carroll, A.D. 1793. *v.* Bp. England's Works, iii. 251.]

O'LEARY.—*A Sermon on the Festival of St. Patrick, Apostle of Ireland:* delivered in St. Patrick's Chapel, Sutton-Street, Soho. By the Revd. Arthur O'Leary. Baltimore: Printed by Wane & Murphy, No. 3, North Gay-Street. 1805. pp. 16. 8vo. ABP. B.

[Not to be found in "O'Leary's Works," Boston, P. Donahoe, 1868. When I edited the great friar's works, I did not know the existence of this pamphlet.]

—— *An Essay on Toleration;* or, Mr. O'Leary's Plea for Liberty of Conscience. Phila.: Printed and sold by Klim & Reynolds. 1785. 8vo. G. T. C.

O'NEILL, JOHN.—*A New and Easy System of Geography;* or, An Introduction to Universal Geography and Popular Astronomy. . . . The whole arranged in a Catechetical form. By John O'Neill. Illustrated with a Map of the World, a Map of North America, and a Plan of the Solar System. *Fourth edition, with considerable additions,* by Joseph Ames. Baltimore: Published by Fielding Lucas, Jun. J. Robinson, Printer. 1816. pp. 359. 12mo. F.

[I am inclined to believe that this work was adopted in the classes of St. Mary's College, Baltimore, altho' I could get no information from the Messrs. Lucas, of Balt., nor from the late lamented and good Messire, Elder of S. S.; but I remember to have seen an advert'mt by Coale, 1813, averring that 3,000 copies of the original work had been sold within a short time; also, I have an indistinct remembrance that the name of Prof. O'Neill was connected with St. Mary's College.]

ORDO *Divini Officii Recitandi, etc.*

1801. Baltimori: Typis Johannis Hayes. F.

1802. ?

1803 *to* 1809. *Ib.* Johannis W. Butler. S. S. B.

1810 *to* 1815. *Ib.* Ex Typographia Bernardi Dornin, Librorum Catholicorum Cujusvis Generis Bibliopolæ, 30 Baltimore-Str. Typis Dobbin & Murphy.

1816. ?

1817. ?

1818. *Ib.* Ex Typographia Joseph Robinson. S. S. B.

1819. *Ib.*

1820. ?

? O'SHANNESSEY.

[When and where did he live, and who was he?—In my researches only *oleum et impensa periit!* Yet I am assured he was an early Catholic writer in this country. Who will give me light on the subject?]

PARSONS, Robert.—*A Christian Directory,* Guiding Men to their Eternal Salvation. In Two

Parts. The first part thereof, etc. Now set forth with many Corrections and Additions. To this edition are prefixed the Life of the Author, and A Method for the Use of all. With two Tables. By the Rev. R. P., *Priest of the Society of Jesus.* [Quot. *Matt.* xvi. 26. *Psalm* iv. 3. *Luke* x. 42.

Two vols. 12mo, bound in one.

1st. Pp. xii. and 348. New York: John Harris, *Printer.* 1820.

2d. Pp. xxiv—260. 4 pp. unn., *Subscribers' Names.* New York: W. H. Creagh, *Printer.* 1820.

[G. Stanhope, Dean of Canterbury, pub'd in 1727, in London, "Parsons—His Christian Directory. Being a Treatise of Holy Resolution. *Put into Modern English.* And now made Publick [1st ed. Rouen: 1581]. For the Instruction of the Ignorant; The Conviction of the Unbelieving; The Awakening and Reclaiming the Vicious, and for Confirming the Religious in their Good Purposes. *The* Fifth Edition, *Corrected.*" Of course, everything *Popish* and *Romish* duly expunged. My copy, bought at the sale of Charles Carroll, of Carroll's sale of library, bears the autograph of L. M. Hawkins.

An ed. was adv'd by Dornin in 1810—was it pub'd?]

PASTORINI.—*The General History of the Christian Church*, from her Birth to her final triumphant State in Heaven, chiefly deduced from the Apocalypse of St. John, the Apostle and Evangelist. The fourth edition, with a few additional remarks and elucidations by the author, Sig. Pastorini.

(Text Apoc. ci. v. 3.) New York: Printed by Hopkins and Seymour, for Bernard Dornin, Bookseller, 136, Pearl-street. 1807. *v.* Walmesly.

J.G.S.

Title and Editor to the Pub. Introduction; Contents, xxiv.; Text 456. Subscribers' names, vii. One page headed, "For the Religious Edification of Roman Cathölics," and dated Dec., 1807, announces Bossuet's Exposition, Following of Christ, Milner's Letters, Practical Reflections, and Pious Guide.

PLIMLEY, PETER.—*Letters on the Subject of the Catholics* to my brother Abraham, who lives in the country. First American from the eleventh English edition. Baltimore: Printed for Bernard Dornin, and sold by him at his Roman Catholic Library, No. 30, Baltimore Street. 1809. F.

G. Dobbin & Murphy, Pr. pp. 83. 8vo.

[Dornin advertises the work thus: "Letters . . . in which the cruel, oppressive, and tyrannic system of Britain to degrade that great and gallant people [Irish] is examined with a candor and impartiality that reflects lustre on its enlightened and eminent author." Altho' the author of this work, Sydney Smith, was not a Catholic, yet his book is deservedly placed on our list. It is a great proof of the popularity of this work that this American edition of 1809 should be from the *eleventh English Edition,* when the work was published in England, as I have the original editions, as follows:

1807. *Two Letters on the Subject of the Catholics,* to my brother Abraham, who lives in the country. By Peter Plimley. London: Printed for J. Budd, No. 100, Pall-Mall. pp. 32 and 55. 12mo.

1808. *Two more Letters (being the Sixth and Seventh) on the Subject* . . . . London: Printed . . . . pp. 32. 12mo.

1808. *The Eighth, Ninth and Last Letter.* . . . London: pp. 68. 12mo.

PLOWDEN, Rev. Charles.—*v. supra, Account,* etc.

PLOWDEN, Francis, Esq.—*An Historical Review of the State of Ireland,* from the Invasion of that Country, under Henry II., to its Union with Great Britain on the first of January, 1801. Philadelphia: Printed and pub'd by Wm. F. McLaughlin, No. 28 North Second Street, and Bartholomew Graver, No. 40 North Seventh Street. . . . 1805–6. 5–8vo. F.

I. xxiv. and 228. App'x 231.

II. xvi. and 334. App'x 120.

III. xvi. and 306. App'x 163.

IV. xxii. and 358. App'x 121.

V. xxiii. and 324. App'x 96, one or two pages wanting. To this vol. is added "A Postliminous Preface to the Historical Review of the State of Ireland, by F. P.; containing a Statement of the author's communication with the Rt. Hon. Henry Addington, and some of his colleagues, upon the subject of that work; some strictures upon the Falsities of the British Critic; and other Anonymous Traducers of the Irish Nations; and also Observations on Lord Redesdale's Letters to the Earl of Fingal. Phila., etc. 1806." pp. 39—and 7 containing Emmet's Speech.

[F. Pl. was brother to the famous Dr. Chas. Plowden, S.J., an élève of St. Omer. Created LL.D. at Oxford, 1793. Fined £5,000 for his *Histor. Review.* Fled to France, and d. in Paris, Jan. 4, 1849.]

—— [882. *Plowden's Historical Review of the State of Ireland,* before and after the Union. 5 vols, *with large Map of Ireland, colored.* 8vo, calf, 253. Philadelphia: 1803 [?]—from J. O'Daly's Catalogue. No. 40, 1871. 9 Anglesea Str., Dublin.]

—— *A Short History of the British Empire,* from May, 1792, to the close of the year 1793. By F. P., LL.D., author of the "Native Rights of British Subjects," "Jura Anglorum," etc. *Ne quid falsi dicere audeat, ne quid veri non audeat.*—Cicero. Philadelphia: Printed for Mathew Carey, No. 118, Market Street. August 4, 1794. pp. 261. 8vo.
F.

PORTALIS.—*Speech* on the 15th Germinal, Year X., 5th April, 1802, to the Legislative Body of France, on Presenting the Convention made between the French Republic and the Holy See. Translated from the original French. New York:

Printed by Rob't Wilson, No. 71, corner of Pine and Water Streets. 1802. pp. iv. and 83. 12mo.
F.

[The Translator occupies pp. iii and iv with a neat and sensible preface.]

POTERIE, CLAUDE FLORENT BOUCHARD DE LA, was the first Catholic priest who ministered in Boston. A Frenchman, and crafty, he imposed on Dr. Carroll, Superior of the missions in the U. S., so far as to have himself appointed Missionary to Boston, where he repaired toward the close of 1788. He was not fit for the position, for he had already been suspended by the Archbishop of Paris. Shortly after his appointment to Boston he issued

A Pastoral Letter from the Apostolic Vice-Prefect, Curate of the Holy Cross at Boston:

Claudius Florent Bouchard de la Poterie, Doctor of Divinity, Prothonotary of the Holy Church of the Holy See of Rome, Apostolic Vice-Prefect and Missionary, Curate of the Catholic Church at Boston in North America, to all faithful Christians entrusted to our care, and of our spiritual jurisdiction, salvation and blessing in Jesus Christ, the Shepherd of our Souls.

But letters from Paris tore the sheep's skin from the wolf's back, and Poterie's ministrations came to a sorry and quick end, on the 29th of May, 1789, when he was suspended by Rev. W. O'Brien, of New York, sent by Dr. Carroll to examine into the charges preferred against him. John Gilmary Shea supplies me with the following title of a work apparently by the same La Poterie: (v. pp. v-vi.)

"*The Resurrection of Laurent Ricci;* or, A True and Exact History of the Jesuits. Printed in Philadelphia: 1789. Price half a dollar, 8vo, 28 pp. Dedicated "To the new Laurent Ricci in America, the Rev. Fr. John Carroll, Superior of the Jesuits *(Footing)* in the United States, also to the friar-monk-inquisitor, William O'Brien."

Cfr. *Catholic Observer*, Boston, February 27, 1847.

PRINCIPLES, *The True—of a Catholic.* By Bishop Chalenor. *v.* Challoner.

PROFESSION *of Catholic Faith.* By a Clergyman of Baltimore, and with the authority of the Rt. Rev. Bishop Carroll.

[I have not been able to find, or hear of, a copy of it. I obtain this title from a pamphlet in my possession, entitled "Observations, by a Protestant, on a Profession of Catholic Faith by a Clergyman of Baltimore, and with the authority of the Rt. Rv. Bp. Carroll. New York: pub. by David Longworth, 11 Park. Clayton & Kingsland, Printers. 1816. pp. 136. 8vo." Is it not by Dr. J. Bowden, who d. July 31, 1817, Prof. at Columbia College?]

PROOFS, *Summary—of Christian Doctrine.* Balt. 1820. J.G.S.—B.M.

PROSODY, *Latin.* Containing the Rules of Quantity and the Principles of Latin Versification. For the Use of St. Mary's College. Baltimore: Published by F. Lucas, Jr., 138, Market Street. J. Robinson, printer. 1819. pp. 72. 12mo.

Abp. B.

[Very probably written, certainly edited, by Rev. E. Damphoux, at the time President of St. Mary's College, Balt. The copy before me has his presentation to "R. R. D. D. Ambrosio Maréchal Baltimorensi Arch^{po} inscripsit ejus humillimus ac devotissimus Servus E. Damphoux, S. M. C. Praes, A.D. 1820."]

QUESTION, *The Catholic.* *v.* Sampson, *infra.*

REASONS, *Fifty.* Philadelphia. 1814. *v.* Ulrik. J.G.S.—B.M.

REEVES. *v. supra.* *Bible's History.*

REFLECTIONS, *Practical*—for Every Day of the Year. By a Father of the Society of Jesus. "With Desolation all the Land is made desolate, because there is none that considereth in his heart." Jer. ch. 12, v. 11. First Amer. ed. Published by and with the authority of the Rt. Rev. Bp. Carroll. New York: Published by Bernard Dornin at his R. C. Bookstore, 136 Pearl-st. J. Seymour, printer. 1808. pp. 440. 12mo, G.T.C.—J.G.S.

[This work was edited by Fr. Neale.]

RELIGION, *The Catholic—vindicated.* Being an Answer to a Sermon preached by the Rev. Mr. Cuyler, in Poughkeepsie, on the 30th day of July, 1812, the day set apart for fasting and prayer in the State of New York: in which sermon the Religion of the Catholics was so illiberally misrepresented as to require a Vindication. By a Roman Catholic, *And a Friend to Liberality. Text*, Rom. xvi. 17. Printed for the Author [?]. 1813. pp. 38. 12mo. F.

RICHARD, Rev. Gabriel.—"The welfare of his flock inspired him with the idea of establishing a printing-press in Detroit, and publishing a newspaper. This project he undertook in 1809, and for a time he issued a periodical in French, entitled *Essai du Michigan;* but the great distances which separated the people of the territory, and the irregularity of the mails, led to the discontinuance of his journal. His press, however, which was the first introduced into the Northwestern part of the U. S., and was for several years the only printing apparatus in Michigan, did useful service in Michigan." *v.* interesting *Notice of Very Rev. G. R.* in *The Metrop. Cath. Alm.*, etc., for 1855. Balt.: Lucas Bros. p. 43—and *The Illustrated Catholic Family Almanac*, by the N. Y. Cath. Publication Society, 1870, where, besides a notice of Fr. R., will be found his portrait, copied from the one in my collection, and extremely rare if not unique. *v. supra* Fleury and *Epistles and Gospels.*

RILEY, W. S.—*The Itinerant; or, Memoirs of*

an Actor. In two volumes. Printed and sold by J. and A. Y. Humphreys, 'Change Walk, corner of Second and Walnut-street, Philadelphia. 12mo.

[I am told that R. was born and died a Catholic.

ROBIN.—*Nouveau Voyage dans l'Amerique Septentrionale, en l'année* 1781; et Campagne de l'Armée du Comte de Rochambeau. Par M. l'Abbé Robin. A Philadelphie, et se trouve à Paris, chez Moutard, Imprimeur-Libraire de la Reine, de Madame, et de Madame Comtesse d'Artois, rue des Mathurins, Hôtel de Cluni. M.DCC.LXXXIII. pp. ix and 222. F.

[Rev. Mr. Robin officiated in Baltimore at the request of the Catholics there. His viiith Letter, *De Baltimore, ce* 14 *Septembre,* 1781, will prove interesting to Catholic readers.]

—— *New Travels through North America:* In a Series of Letters; exhibiting the History of the Victorious Campaign of the Allied Armies, under His Excellency, General Washington, and the Count de Rochambeau, in the year 1781. Interspersed with political, and philosophical observation upon the genius, temper, and customs of the Americans. Also, Narrations of the Capture of General Burgoyne, and Lord Cornwallis, with their Armies, and a Variety of interesting particulars which occurred in the course of the War in America. Translated from the Original of the Abbé Robin, one of the chaplains of the French Army in America. [Quotation from Young. *v.* following title.] Philadelphia: Printed and sold by Robert Bell, in Third Street. M,DCC,LXXXIII. *Price Two-thirds of a Dollar.* [This copy cost $15.] F.

2d p., Bp. Berkeley's poem; 2, 4, Introd.; 5–8, Contents; 9–95, Text; 96–109, App. 1, Washington's letter to de Grasse; 2, Cornwallis to Sir H. Clinton; 3, Washington's Farewell; add. p. 110, 2, Considerations on the Peace, from the *Political Magazine*, London, 1783.

—— *New Travels through North America;* in a Series of Letters; *Exhibiting the History of the Victorious Campaign of the Allied Armies, under His Excellency, General Washington, and the Count de Rochambeau, in the year* 1781. Interspersed with political and philosophical observations upon the genius, temper, and customs of the Americans: Also, Narrations of the capture of General Burgoyne, and Lord Cornwallis, with their Armies; and a variety of interesting particulars, which occurred in the course of the War in America. Translated from the original of Abbé Robin: one of the chaplains to the French Army in America.

From such events, let boast-ful Nations know,
Jove lays the pride of haughtiest Monarchs low,
And they, who kindled with American fire,
In art and arms, with most success aspire.
When turn'd to tyrants, but provoke their doom,
Grasp at their fate, and build themselves a tomb.
BUSIRIS BY YOUNG.

Boston: Printed by E. E. Powars and N. Willis, for E. Batelle, and to be sold by him, at his Book Store, State Street, M,DCC,LXXXIV. pp. 95. 8vo.
F.

P. 2, Verses on the Prospect of planting Arts and Learning in America. Written upwards of fifty years since, by the celebrated Divine and Philosopher, Dr. Berkeley, Protestant Bishop of Cloyne, in Ireland; pp. 3, 4, Introduction by the Translator; pp. 5, 6, 7, Contents; pp. 9–84, Text; pp. 85–89, Appendix. Containing, I. *General Washington's Letter to Count de Grasse.* II. *Lord Cornwallis's Letter to Sir Henry Clinton.* III. *Character of his Excellency, John Adams, Esquire.* Pp. 91–95, Character of his Excellency, John Adams, Minister Plenipotentiary from the States of North America, to their High Mightinesses the States General of the United Provinces; p. 95, Measurement of the countries ceded to America.

[*A splendid copy* (as the advertisement says) *in the most perfect order of this excessively rare first* (?) *edition, and almost impossible to duplicate, in uncut condition, with Portrait of Count Rochambeau inserted. 8vo, full polished calf, gilt back, gilt top, uncut, by Bedford,* was sold for $27 at the sale of T. H. Morrell's library, in New York, January, 1869, and since bought for $35. For one of my editions I am indebted to H. Davenport, Esq., of Boston.

A Dutch translation (*Nieuwe Reize door Nord America*) was published in Amsterdam, 1782, 8vo.]

ROLLIN, CHARLES.

[In a deeply interesting paper in *The New Hampshire Gazette*, the oldest newspaper in America, communicated by Frank W. Miller, Esq., of Portsmouth, N. H., to the *N. E. Historical and Genealogical Register*, etc., Boston, 1872, vol. xxvi., No. 2, we are told that "the history of printing in Portsmouth is mainly the record of newspapers and editors; although considerable book-work was done at one time, *about the close of the last century*, including a heavy edition of Rollin's 'Ancient History,' etc." The Press made its appearance in Portsmouth, A.D. 1756. Charles Rollin was a Catholic, and a man of unimpeachable character, but unfortunately a partisan of Paris, and it is feared did not recant at his death, although it is generally admitted that his error was only of the mind and never violated the laws of charity or reverence to ecclesiastical authority, even in defence of Jansenistical principles. *v.* Chateaubriand, *Genie du Christianisme*, L. iii. ch. 7. R. b. in Paris, Jan. 30, 1661; d. there, Sept. 14, 1741, being held in very high esteem. *Cfr.* De Feller *ad n.*]

"BOSTON, Ap. 20, 1872.

"DEAR SIR—It gave me pleasure to enquire diligently concerning that Portsmouth edition of Rollin's. . . . From the venerable Mr. Melcher, aged 83, son of the *second* Gazette printer, I learn that he has seen copies of this edition (and he is the only person I can find who has), but he thinks no specimen of it can now be found; nor could I ascertain the size (altho' he *thought* about common 8vo or a little smaller). . . . Should I at any time receive more definite information . . . I shall take great pleasure in sharing it with you.

"Yours, very truly,

"FRANK W. MILLER."

? ROUELLE, John, M.D.—*A Treatise on the Mineral Waters of Virginia,* etc. Philadelphia. 1792. 1–8vo.

[I have mislaid the reference of this author.]

RULE *of Life.* Baltimore: Printed by John W. Butler. 1807. pp. 36. 18mo. F.

The title, on the cover, represents a Cross, surmounted with I H S, and inscribed inside with the text: "My Son, . . . Fear God and depart from evil." Prov. iii.

SAMPSON, William.—*The Catholic Question in America. Quos contra statuit aequos placitosque dimisit. Cicero.* "Whether a Rom. Cath. Clergyman be in any case compellable to disclose the Secrets of Auricular Confession." Decided at the Court of Gen'l Sessions, in the City of New York. Present, the Hon. De Witt Clinton, *Mayor.* The Hon. Josiah Ogden Hoffman, *Recorder,* Richard Cunningham, Isaac S. Douglass, Esqrs., Sitting Aldermen. With the Arguments of Counsel, and the Unanimous Opinion of the Court, delivered by the Mayor, with his reasons in support of that opinion. New York: Printed by Edw. Gillespy, No. 24 William-street. 1813.

Pp. 114 comprehends the Case.

To p. 138, *Irish Penal Code Abridged.*

An App'x to pp. cxii. contains "A True Exposition of the Doctrine of the Cath. Church, touching the Sacrament of Penance, with the Ground on which this Doctrine is Founded."

To p. cxx., " Notes Referred to in the Trial."

Pp. cxxi. to cxxviii.: "A Canto on the Jesuits, taken from the Latin of J. Vanière, rendered into English by Arthur Murphy, Esq. (latest ed. printed at Middletown, Conn., for I. Riley, New York). 1–8vo. F.

[W. S., Esq., one of the counsel in the case, was a Protestant. The App'x on Confession is from the pen of Rev. A. Kohlman, S.J. Mr. Wharton, *v. supra* Carroll & Wharton, replied to it, and yet he heard the confession of a dying woman, apostate and married priest as he was. Reference to this work is made in B. Q. R., A. II., July, 1846.—James Vanière, S.J., born in Causses, diocese of Bezières, A.D. 1664, d. in Tolose in 1739. He was a very elegant Latin poet. The Georgical Poem, *Praedium Rusticum*, in 16 cantos, from which the above is taken, has secured to Fr. V. an undying admiration in the world of belles-lettres. Two interesting allusions to Fr. Vanière will be found in Vol. iii., No. 1 and 2 (June and July, 1870) of *The Nineteenth Century*, Charleston, S. C. For a notice of the distinguished Irish Catholic lawyer and poet, A. Murphy (1730–1805) see Allibone, *ad nomen.*

After the trial it was made a law in New York that a priest cannot be required to give as evidence in court what he has heard in the Confessional. Yet like attempts have been made elsewhere, as, *e.g.*, in the case of the Rev. Mr. Hickey of Baltimore; *v. Bost. Cath. Observer*, Nov. 30, 1847; in that of Rev. Mr. Teeling of Richmond; *v. Metropolitan*, iii., p. 709, and *The Cathol. Church in the U. S.*, p. 169; in that of the Rev. Mr. O'Neil of New Haven, Conn., who was fined by Judge Waldo. *v. Bost. Traveller*, Nov. 27, 1855; that of Rev. L. Young, of

Frankfort, Ky. *v. Cincinnati Telegraph*, June 10, 1868. The case of Fr. Kelly at the Durham Assizes can be learned in all its particulars from the columns of the *London Tablet*, March, 1860. Rev. Mr. McLaughlin was condemned to prison in Glasgow. *v.* an extract from the *Tablet* in the *Balt. Mirror*, Jan. 17, 1863.]

SCAPULAR—*A Short Treatise on the Antiquity, Institution, etc.*, of the Confraternity of Our Blessed Lady of Mount Carmel, Commonly Called THE ——. With a Brief Account of the Design, Rules, and Conditions thereof. To which is added, The Office of the Blessed Virgin Mary. Philadelphia: Printed for the Confraternity, by A. Fagan, No. 133 South Front Street. 1814. pp. viii, 100. 18mo.

SCUPOLI, LAURENCE.—*The Spiritual Combat*: to which is added, The Peace of the Soul, and The Happiness of the Heart, which dies to itself, in order to live to God. *The Life of Man upon Earth is a Warfare.* Job vii. 1. Baltimore: Printed for James M'Henry, by John W. Butler, South Gay Street. 1807. pp. 202. 12mo. S. S. B.

[A friend stated to have seen a copy of it, date 1808? L. S. b. in Otranto, of Naples, about 1530, d. in Naples, 1610, æt. 80, was a cleric of the order of Theatines. Some have doubted the fathership of the work, but it is generally credited to Fr. Scupoli. It may be called the *mate* of *The Imitation of Christ*, for whilst the former cleaves a road to heaven through obstacles and fights, the latter leads a soul to it by way of contemplation.

"I have carried the *Combat* in my pocket for these eighteen years past, and every day read a chapter, or, at least, one page of it," said once St. Francis de Sales to Bishop Camus. *The Spirit of St. Francis de Sales.* New York: O'Shea. 1867. pp. 92. Translated by Rev. J. M. F.]

SEMINARY, *St. Mary's*—and Catholics at large Vindicated, against the Pastoral Letter of the Ministers, Bishops, &c., of the Presbytery of Baltimore, pub'd in Sept., 1811. Thou shalt not bear False Witness against thy Neighbour. Exod. xx. 16. Baltimore: pub'd by B. Dornin, and for Sale at his Cath. Bookstore, 10, Baltimore-street. October, 1811. pp. 48. 8vo. F.

[A Reply: Defence of the Pastoral Letter of the Presb'y of Baltim. With an App'x containing Reasons from Recantation from the Errors of the Church of Rome by Mr. *James Crowley*, formerly a Student of Maynooth, &c. Balt.: Warner & Hanna. 1812. pp. 90. 12mo. B. B.

A Weed over the Fence. But James Crowley never wrote the pamphlet. *v.* pp. 55 and 56 of "Sons of St. Dominick."

In 1806 had appeared the following: "Strictures on the Establishment of Colleges; particularly that of St. Mary, in the Precincts of Baltimore, as formerly published in the *Evening Post* and *Telegraphe.*—By Different Writers.—*Nullius addictus jurare in verba magistri.*—Hor.—Baltimore . . . December . . . 1806." The "Strictures" were occasioned by an article in the *Companion* in praise of the Balt. College and its president, Mr. Du Bourg. Then a silly controversy sprang up between *Quintilian Junior* in the *Evening Post,* assailant, and Pliny the Younger, defendant, in the same paper—which controversy rambled over the *Telegraphe* also, was taken up in *Lex Talionis*, and—proved only a waste of paper, ink, and time. pp. 58. 8vo. F.

[*v*. Dubourg, *supra*, where it should be added that Bp. Dubourg is, in fact, the founder of the Association for the Propagation of Faith. *v*. *Clarke's Memoirs*, and *infra*, *Sons*, etc.

SETON.—*Memoirs of Mrs. S* * * * * *. Written by herself. A Fragment of real history. Elizabethtown, N. J.: Printed by Isaac A. Kollock, for himself and others. 1817. pp. 90. 24mo. J. G. S.

[v. Dr. White's Life of Mrs. M. E. Seton, first ed. p. 9.]

["It was publ'd by an Episcopal minister at Elizabethtown, N. J., and consisted merely of the Journal, kept by Aunt Seton on her voyage to, and residence at, Leghorn, . . . the same that you will find in the Revd. Dr. White's Life of her—with a short Preface by the above-mentioned minister. His object, as I have been told, and as in fact appears from the preface, was to weaken the effect of her Conversion to the Catholic Faith, by endeavoring to show that she was a perfect Christian before that event took place. . . . Aunt Seton and the family were very much displeased at this publication, and the minister, whose name I do not remember, was much censured for having made it from a MS. copy which had been lent to him, and without the knowledge and consent of Mother Seton."—✠ N. N. J. I have presumed on publishing this letter the more readily as Bishop Hobart (*v*. Ironside) has been charged with the authorship of the *Memoir*. The writer of the Letter once denied it emphatically. As regards the dispositions of Bishop Hobart towards the church, *cfr*. the conclusion of Mr. Ironside's *Reply to Bp. Hobart's Charge*, and *History of the Cath. Church in the U. S.*,

p. 392. The Bishop's *non-conversion* is a mysterious judgment. But his daughter, the godchild of Mother Seton, and wife of the late Dr. Ives, *did* become a Catholic.]

SHEIL, RT. REV. DR. JAMES.—*A Plain and Rational Account of the Catholic Faith;* or, The Sum of A Conference between three Brothers, a Catholic, Protestant, and Presbyterian.—To which is annexed an Appendix, Proving that the Reformed Churches are destitute of any Lawful Ministry.—"Many a time they have afflicted me from my youth," Ps. 129, v. 1. "They shall proceed no further, for their folly shall be made manifest unto men," 2 Tim. c. 3, v. 9. First American Edition, Revised and corrected from the Seventh Dublin Edition. Albany: Printed by Ryer Schermerhorn, corner of Market and Columba Streets. 1814. pp. viii. 9–314. F.

[Pub'd by subscription.]

SONS, *The—of St. Dominick:* a Dialogue between a Protestant and a Catholic, on the occasion of the late Defence of the Pastoral Letter of the Presbytery of Baltimore, against the Vindication of St. Mary's Seminary, and Catholics at large, etc. Baltimore: Printed for B. Dornin, and for Sale at his Catholic Book-Store, 29, Saratoga-st. 1812. pp. viii. 94. 8vo. F.

[*v. supra*, ST. MARY'S SEMINARY. At p. 35, we read: "The pamphlet (alluded to in the title of *St. Mary's Sem'y*) was written by a Methodist preacher of Dublin. No person of the name of James Crowley ever left Maynooth without receiving orders. The 'Sons' is attributed to the pen of Bp. Bruté, and by others to Bp. Dubourg." *v. Balt. Cath. Alm.*, 1839, p. 37, and *supra*, DUBOURG.]

SYNOD *of* '91. In the handwriting of Dr. Nagot, is preserved at St. Sulpice, Baltimore, wrapped in the Passport given to the Doctor and signed by Louis XVI.

TASSO, TORQUATO.—*Jerusalem Delivered: An Heroic Poem.* Translated from the Italian of Torquato Tasso, by John Hoole. First Am. from the Eighth London ed., with notes. Newburyport: Pub. & sold by Edward Little & Co. Exeter: printed by C. Norris & Co. and E. C. Beals. 1810. 2–8vo. F.

I. Pp. L. and 339, facing t.-p., portrait *from a medal taken after his death; p.* 8, *Angel appearing to Godfrey;* 23, *another apparition.* II. Pp. 368; p. 329, interview between Rinaldo and Armida; p. 225, Rinaldo in the enchanted wood. 1st, 2d, and 4th engravings by Hooker; 3d, Stothard del. P. Maverick, sc. Newark, N. J.

TAYLOR, REV. WILLIAM.—*The Christian's Monitor; or, Practical Guide to Future Happiness:*

A New Rom. Cath. Prayer Book, Adapted to all Ranks and Conditions; under the Patronage of the Rt. Rev. Bp. Connolly. By the Rev. William Taylor of St. Patrick's Cathedral. First Edition. New York: W. H. Creagh, 70 William-Street. 1819. pp. 386. 18mo. F.

Facing the title-page an engraving represents Cain and Abel offering their sacrifices, the former looking daggers and doubling his fists at his brother.

—— —— *Sermon, on the Festival of St. Patrick, the Apostle of Ireland;* Delivered in the Roman Catholic Cathedral, of New York, on Sunday, the 21st day of March, 1819. By the Rev. Wm. Taylor, one of the Officiating Clergymen of said Church. New York: Printed by McDuffee & Tarrand, No. 1 Murray Street. 1819. pp. 20. 8vo. Abp. B.

[In the pref. to the Monitor Mr. T. promises a N. Y. edition of the Douay Bible, but it was not published, as far as I know. Mr. Taylor afterwards removed to Boston in the spring of 1821. He was a very eloquent man and a good controversialist, as I judge from his correspondence with the Hon. H. B. C. Green, M.D. (whom he baptized Nov., 1824), a copy of which I possess through the kindness of Mrs. Dr. Leprohon (Dr. Green's daughter), of Portland, Me. Bp. Cheverus is said to have entertained the project of nominating Mr. T. for his coadjutor. From an autograph letter of Dr. Cheverus before me, dated *Montauban, April* 10, 1826, I clip the following: "You know that our friend Mr. Taylor did not bring your esteemed favor of December 9th, but he forwarded it. . . . I wish myself that our dear Mr. Taylor would have remained some time with him (Bp. Fenwick). . . . By Mr. Taylor's letters I expect him soon. I shall do my best to make him comfortable and happy, but here his preaching will lose much of its charms. I have explained to him what he may expect, so that he may be enabled to determine what is best for him. As for me I shall be happy to welcome him, and his constant attentions to yourself and family since my departure have endeared him more and more to me. . . . *To Mr. Walley, Brookline.*"—When Bishop Cheverus left Boston, September, 1825, Mr. Taylor remained Administrator of the Diocese until the Sunday after December 3, 1825, when Bishop Fenwick arrived and took possession, on which occasion Mr. T. delivered a very interesting sermon, giving an account of the state of the diocese, but at its conclusion he announced that he would sail for Europe. The following Sunday Rev. Mr. Taylor left Boston for New York, where he sojourned for a while, but finally sailed for France, and, fixing himself at Bordeaux, was made honorary canon by his friend Archbp. Cheverus. When the Archbishop, who had been raised to the peerage, went to Paris, Rev. Mr. Taylor accompanied him. He was there taken sick and died in the Irish College, in August, 1828. Mr. Taylor's name appears among the subscribers to M. Carey's Essays, 1822.—*Cfr. History of the Cath. Church in the U. S.* Courcy & Shea. p. 391, in text, and *ad calcem*, and the *Catholic Observer*, Boston: 1847. June 5 and 12.]

THAYER, Rev. John—*Controversy between the Rev. John Thayer, Catholic Missionary of Boston, and the Rev. George Leslie, Pastor of a Church in*

Washington, N. H. Boston. 1793. pp. iv.–167. 8vo. F.

[To a public invitation, rather a challenge to debate, given by Mr. Thayer, on his return from Europe (Nov. 24, 1790), where he had become a Catholic, the following acceptance was returned: "As the gauntlet is thrown down by Mr. Thayer, it is taken up by George Leslie." The controversy between Mr. Th. and Mr. L. began in a public paper, Oct. 5, 1793; in this copy it ends at p. 74. Then follow some desultory pieces, rather small Tracts by Mr. Thayer, with Rejoinders by others, *i.e., A Sincere and Unbiassed Reader of the Holy Bible—A Searcher after Truth—Simplex—Answer—Barebones*—etc., etc., etc., whom Father Thayer keeps all at bay like a noble stag attacked by hounds. One John Gardner, a celebrated lawyer and a great speaker in the House of Representatives, enters the lists repeatedly, but at p. 115 we find the following: "Mr. Gardner disbelieves all miracles. But is there not something miraculous in his being struck with the palsy, in his right hand, at the very time he was writing all his blasphemies against God and his saints? (This is a positive fact.) If he will believe, perhaps he may be made whole." The remaining pieces, partly Catholic and partly Protestant, are most interesting. Mr. Thayer d. in Limerick, Feb. 5, 1815, in the arms of Mr. Ryan, whose two daughters afterward came to Boston to found an Ursuline convent. They opened a school near the Cathedral in Franklin St. From *The Family Memorial.* Hingham: J. Farmer, Printer. 1835, Part II. (the only vol. I have been able to secure, at the moderate price of $11), p. 119, "The Family of Thayer," I copy:

No. 1. *Richard Thayer* [spelt also *Thaire, Theyar, Thair, Theyer,* some of them betraying Huguenot origin,] the first of the name appearing in N. E. was admitted freeman in 1640, d. in Braintree, Aug. 27, 1695.

No. 74. *Cornelius Thayer*, married Lydia, and settled in Boston. Their children were:

1. Lydia, b. March 6, 1707.
2. Nathaniel, b. July 17, 1710.
3. Samuel, b. Dec. 30, 1712.
4. Deborah, b. Jan. 27, 1714.
5. Cornelius, b.
6. Juzell, b. March 13, 1725. (Boston Records.)

No. 77. "*Rev. John Thayer*, a son of Cornelius Thayer, and grandson of Cornelius Thayer and Lydia Thayer (No. 74), a native of Boston, converted to the Catholic faith 1783, and who received Priest's orders in Rome, began his Mission here (in a small brick church in School Street, Boston, built by some French Protestants, and afterwards sold to one or more individuals who had separated from other churches), June 10, 1790.—(*Hist Coll.*, 9, 196)."

"Rev. Dr. Thayer, of Lancaster, Mass., says he died at Rome [no, he d. at Limerick,] and bequeathed his estate to the propagation of the faith he had embraced." Attached to my copy I have the original "Probate Certificate—John Cheverus, D.D., Adm'r on Estate of John Thayer, Oct. 20, 1818." In it is said, "John Thayer late of Boston deceased testate," *signed:* "John Heard, Jun." Cfr. Abp. Spalding's *Sketches of the Early Missions of Kentucky*, ch. v., and Campbell's "Memoirs of Abp. Carroll and his Times," in the *Balt. Catholic Magazine.*]

—— *An Account of the Conversion of the Rev. Mr. John Thayer*, lately a Protestant Minister, at Boston in North America, who embraced the Roman Catholic Religion at Rome, on the 25th of May, 1783; written by himself. To which are annexed Several Extracts from a Letter written to his brother, in answer to some Objections. Also A Letter from a Young Lady lately received by him into the church, written after making her first Communion. *Misericordias Domini in æternum cantabo.* I will sing the mercies of the Lord for ever. Ps. lxxxix. 1. The fifth edition. Baltimore: Reprinted (from the London Edition) and sold by William Goddard. M.DCC.LXXXVIII. pp. 28. Small 12mo. F.

[This is called a *fifth American* edition, and my copy of another edition—"Kilkenny: Printed and sold by John Reynolds, High Street, 1805"—with precisely the same title as the above of Balt., is also qualified "The Fifth Edition," *i.e.*, both Goddard of Balt. and Reynolds of Kilkenny meant that they had printed the 5th after the 4th London ed. The Kilkenny ed. is in 8vo, pp. 32.]

[*Relation de la Conversion del Sr. Juan Thayer*, antes Ministro Protestante en Boston en la America Septentrional, y convertido à la Religion Catolica en Roma el dia 25 de Mayo de 1783. Escrita por el mismo: Se añaden dos cartas, la una à un hermano suyo en la que responde à los argumentos que le hace sobre la resolucion tomada; y la otra de una Señorita Inglesa que abjuró sus errores, y le dà cuenta del estado de su alma en el dia siguiente à su primera Comunion. *Traducido del Frances. Misericordias Domini in æternum cantabo.* Publicaré siempre las misericordias del Señor, Psalm 88, vers. 1. Con superior permiso, En Valencia en la oficina de D. Benito Monfort, Año 1788. pp. 77, small 12mo. F.

As mentioned, this is a transl. from the French translation.

The only other American edition I have seen is that pub. by Rev. Jas. Fitton:

"An Account of the Conversion of Rev. J. Thayer, formerly a Protestant Minister of Boston. Written by himself. To which is added, A Letter to his Brother, and his controversial writings. By the editors of the *U. S. Catholic Press*, Hartford, Conn. MDCCXXXII. pp. 38, 12mo. F.

In this ed. no *Controversial Writings.* But the Letters (there are two) should both bear the date London, August 24, 1787, as in the Balt. ed. In the Spanish ed., the 2d Letter is dated "Paris, 1 de Mayo de 1787. *En el Seminario de S. Sulpicio.*" Whilst tarrying in Paris, before his way back to the U. S., Mr. T. issued an appeal, in the French language (coincidence of the Times!) to secure prayers for the conversion of America. The hon. Fr. Spencer took the hint from him, many years after, and both learned the practice from Holy Writ. The prayer for the Knowledge of the True Faith ascribed in the *Golden Manual*, p. 764, to Mr. Thayer, was copied by him from a Spanish Book.]

—— *Controversy between the Rev. John Thayer, Catholic Missionary, of Boston, and the Rev. George Leslie, Pastor of a church in Washington, New Hampshire.* Philadelphia: Printed by Richard Folwell, No. 33, Arch Street. 1795. pp. 32. 12mo. F.

—— *A Discourse, Delivered, At the Rom. Cath. Church in Boston, on the 9th of May,* 1798, Recommended by the President, for Humiliation and Prayer throughout the United States. Printed at the pressing Solicitation of those who heard it.

Printed by Samuel Hall, No. 53, Cornhill, Boston. 1798. pp. 31. 8vo. J. G. S.

—— Same (Title as above, with words "*Second Edition*"). F.

[Title of a Dublin edition of the Controversy: "The Catholic Controversy, maintained in the Periodical Publications of Boston, New Salem, and other Towns of the U. S. of America, against the calumnious objections and false imputations of the Rev. George Leslie, Pastor of a church in Warrington (*sic*), N. H.; J. Gardner, Esq., Barrister, and other writers, under the fictitious appellations of A Searcher after Truth, Simplex, etc., etc. To which are added a full Refutation of the Charges adduced against Catholicity, by Mr. Belknap in his History of New Hampshire, with an Answer to Dr. Lathrop's Lecture on the Errors of Popery. And a Letter from Mons. Allegre, son of a French Protestant Clergyman, to the Author, with an Account of his Conversion, translated by a Scotch Lady, a Convert to the Catholic Communion; also, A Letter from a Young Gentleman in France to his Friends in America, respecting his conversion, effected by an Irish gentleman, who lately abjured the errors of Protestantism, and a specimen of Bostonian toleration at a Catholic convert's interment. By the Rev. John Thayer, formerly a Puritan Minister, of Boston, and afterwards converted to the Holy Catholic Religion, at Rome, in 1783. Printed by R. Coyne, Capel-street, Dublin, 1809. pp. 121. 8vo. F.

"To the Irish ed. of this work Mr. Gideon Ouseley replied in 1812, in a pamphlet of 40 or 50 pages, reissued in 1813 as 'The Inquiries of Mr. Ouseley, Irish Missionary, addressed to Rev. John Thayer, Rom. Cath. Missionary, in consequence of his public challenge in his Cath. Controv'y to all Protestants, Ministers especially,' p. 140.

"To this an answer in '18 or '20 pp. appeared, signed 'Layman.' Ouseley published a 3d ed. in 1814, a 4th in '21, and a 5th some years after; all enlarged. The latter was reprinted in the United States under the following title 'Old Christianity against Papal Novelties; including a Review of Dr. Milner's "End of Controversy." By Gideon Ouseley. . . . "And a mighty angel took up a stone like a great millstone, and cast it into the sea, saying, Thus with violence shall that great city Babylon be thrown down and shall be found no more at all," Rev. xviii. 21. No falsehood can endure—Touch of celestial temper, but returns—Of force to its own likeness. Milton. Fifth Am. from the fifth Dublin edition.—A cut of the Bible.—Philadelphia: Sorin & Ball, 42 North 4th Str. Stereotyped by L. Johnson. 1847.'"

The French edition appeared evidently in 1788. Mr. Nagot reprints it in 1791 in a *Recueil de Conversions Remarquables, nouvellement operees dans quelques Protestants.* 12mo, Paris: Crapart, 1791. pp. 532; in which it occupies pp. 1–188. In the preface (p. iv.) Mr. Nagot says: "La Relation de la Conversion de M. Thayer est connue depuis trois ans. On l'a jugée si edifiante qu'elle a été imprimée en anglais, en français, en italien et en espagnol. In the *Tableau General des Principales Conversions,* 12mo, Paris, 1827, Mr. Thayer's account is given without the other papers, pp. 68–103. Allibone never heard of Thayer.

I am indebted to Dr. J. G. Shea for some of the above items. G. W. Richards, of Phila., had a nicely-preserved copy of the Dublin edition.

In 1797, J. Boyce, b. Inn's-quay, London, published a Fourth Edition of "An Account of the Conversion of the Rev. Mr. John Thayer, lately a Protestant Minister at Boston in North America, who embraced the Roman Catholic Religion at Rome, on the 25th May, 1783. Written by Himself." To which are annexed Several Extracts from a Letter written to his brother in answer to some objections. Also a Letter from a Young Lady lately received by him into the Church, written after making her first communion. *Misericordias Domini in æternum cantabo*—"I will sing the mercies of the Lord for ever." Ps. lxxxix. 1. pp. 53. 12mo. Abp. B.

After I had finished this chapter on Thayer, I received the following from the very kind librarian of Georgetown College: "Controversy between the Rev. John Thayer, Catholic Missionary of Boston, and the Rev. George Leslie, Pastor of a Church in Washington, N. H. Georgetown ('Potomack'): Printed by Alex. Doyle. 1791:

"In the end of the book in which this pamphlet is bound up is a MS. account of the conversion of Adam Livingston, of Jefferson Co., Va., and some description of the events at Wizard's Clip, his place of residence."—A collection of documents relating to these extraordinary occurrences, which took place about the beginning of this century, has been prepared for the *Boston Pilot Press* by the writer, and will be published during the winter.

At p. 232 of the "Life of St. Angela Merici," edited by J. G Shea; Phila.: Cunningham, 1858, see an interesting account of Rev. J. Thayer, and especially of his connection with the foundation of a convent of Ursulines, in Boston, Mass.]

THOMAS, Fr.—of Jesus.—*The Sufferings of Our Lord Jesus Christ;* written originally in Portuguese, by F. Thomas, of H. Jesus, of the Order of the Hermits of St. Augustin, and newly translated into English. To which is added, The third and last part, never before published in English. In two volumes. Philadelphia: Published by Bernard Dornin, North West Corner of Walnut & Third Streets. Lydia R. Bailey, Printer. 1818. 2–12mo. F.

I. Pp. iii, iv, *Contents;* vi–viii, *Preface to Translation* [professing to be an improvement on Dr. Welton's; by the bye, Mr. O'Shea of N. Y. reprinted, 1866, an ed. *from the last Lond. ed.*, far different from the one before me; it seems to be Dr. Welton's, qualified as *pompous*, *frothy*, *improper*, etc., by the Dornin edr.]; 9–13, Life of Fr. Thomas; 15–346, Text.—II. Pp. iii, iv, *Contents;* 5–330, Text; 9 unnum. pp. Subscribers; 3 do. List of Books. [The original text is Portuguese, and the work was written while the holy man was languishing in a Morocco dungeon, 1578–1582; within a very short time after its appearing in Lisbon, it was translated into Spanish, Italian, Latin, and French. In the fly-leaf of a copy in the Library of Holy Cross, near Worcester, is entered the following memo.:

"Ex libris Francisci Rogati Fromm Francis. Recoll. prov. Germ. sup. Presbyteri Nunc Missionarii Cathol. pro America fœderata in Comitatu Westmorelandiæ et Statu Pensilvaniæ 1791."]

TURBEVILLE, H.—*A Manual of Controversies:* clearly demonstrating the Truth of a Catholic Religion, by Texts of Holy Scriptures, Councils of All Ages, Fathers for 500 Years, Common Sense and Reason, and fully answering the principal Objections of Protestants and all other Sectaries. By H. T., a Clergyman. The 1st Am. from the 5th London ed. corrected. Philadelphia: Printed by B. Graves, for David Doyle. 1806. F.

12mo. pp. i, *verso*, and ii *contents*; blank, unn. dedication to Sir C. F. by H. T.: do. "To the Reader," H. T.: do. 2, *approbatio*; 5–302, Text; 3 pp. Subscribers.

[An ed. by J. Doyle, 1833, presents the following title: "*An Abridgment of Christ. Doctrine:* with proofs of Scripture on points controverted. By way of Questions and Answers. Composed in 1649, by Rev. Henry Tuberville, D.D., of the English College of Douay: now approved and recommended for his Diocess, by the Rt. Rev. Benedict, Bishop of Boston. 'This is the way, walk ye in it,' Isaiah xxx. 21. New York: Published by John Doyle, No. 12, Liberty Street. Stereotyped by A. Chandler. 1833. pp. 151. 18mo." Wm. Jones, of Dublin, published an edition in 1794. pp. 179. 18mo.]

VADE MECUM, *The Devout Christian's*—April 23, M.DCC.XCII. "There was, however, an earlier edition." Lately published (October 12, 1789), by M. Carey, The Devout Christian's Vade Mecum: Being a Summary of Select and Necessary Devotions, Containing, among other articles, the *hymns and psalms, as sung in English, in the Roman Catholic Chapels of Philadelphia.* [Carey's advertisement *ad calcem* of Challoner's *Garden of the Soul*, a. 1792.]

—— —— *Roman Catholic Prayer Book, or Devout Christian's Vade Mecum*, being a Summary of Select and Necessary Devotions. "And I went unto the Angel, and said unto him, give me the little book; and he said unto me, take it." Rev. c. x. v. 9. Baltimore: Printed by Warner & Hanna, No. 37, Market Street, corner of South Gay-street. 1801.

Pp. 235—32mo, and 2 pp. Contents.

["W. & H. were not Catholics, but printed Prayer-books for Cath. Booksellers," wrote to me the venerable and lamented Messire A. Elder, of Baltimore.]

—— —— Balt.: Warner. 1812. G. T. C.

—— —— New York: Kimmersley? 1813. *ib.?*

[It has since been repub. by Kelly & Piet, Baltim., and previously (1840) by Owen Phelan, 36 Chatham Str., New York, Eugene Cummiskey, Philadelphia, and in 1871 by the Catholic Publication Society, New York.]

VALINIERE, Rev. Pierre Huet de la.—*Vraie Histoire;* ou, Simple Précis des infortunes, pour ne pas dire des Persécutions qu'a souffert et souffre encore le Rev. P. H. de la V., mis en vers par lui-même en Juillet, 1792. A Albany, imprimé aux dépens de Auteur.

[It is a "Poem narrating the misfortunes, nay, Persecutions of an excellent but eccentric Priest"; for an interesting Biography of him, see *The Cath. Ch. in the U. S.*, by De Courcy & Shea. pp. 460, *seqq. et alibi.*]

ULRIK, A.—*Fifty Reasons, or Motives, why the Roman Catholick, Apostolick Religion ought to be preferr'd to all the Sects this day in Christendom.* And which induc'd His Most Serene Highness A. U., Duke of Brunswick and Lunenburg, &c., to abjure Lutheranism. To which are added, *Three Valuable Papers:* Phila.: Printed and Sold by A. S. Blocquerst, N. 130 South 5th St. 1814. pp. 144. 24mo. On the back of the title, 'Three valuable papers, annexed to these Motives, I. The Decision of the Prot. University of Helmstadt, in favor of the Rom. Cath. Rel. II. Copies of Two Papers written by the late Charles II., of Blessed Memory. III. A copy of a Paper written by the late Duchess of York. J. G. S.

VANIERE. *v. Murphy & Simpson.*

VOYAGES AND TRAVELS, *A Collection of*—containing the Voyage of P. Kolben to the Cape of Good Hope; a Voyage to China by Lewis

Le Compte; Anecdotes of the Elephant from Wolfe's Travels. Philadelphia: 1787. 12mo.

[Fr. Louis Le Compte belonged to the Company of Jesus.—Other volumes of collections of societies, voyages, etc., have appeared before 1820. They were in part, at least, Catholic.—J. G. S.]

WALLACE, REV. JAMES.—*A new treatise on the use of the Globes and practical Astronomy;* or, a comprehensive view of the System of the World. In four parts. 1. An extensive collection of Astronomical and other definitions. 2. Problems performed by the Terrestrial Globe, including those relative to Geography, Navigation, Dialling, &c., with many new and important problems and investigations, particularly useful to the Navigator and practical Astronomer. 3. Problems performed by the Celestial Globe, including those of finding the longitude at sea, new methods of finding the latitude with only one altitude of the Sun, or a star, at any given time, with the method of representing the spherical triangles on the globe, &c. 4. A comprehensive account of the Solar System, with the elementary principles and most valuable modern discoveries in Astronomy to the present time. The nature and motion of comets, of the fixed stars, eclipses, the theory of the tides, laws of motion, gravity, &c., with diagrams elucidating the demonstrations. The whole serving as an introduction to the higher Astronomy and Natural Philosophy, is illustrated with a variety of important notes, useful remarks, &c., and each problem with several examples. The necessary astronomical instruments are pointed out and the most useful tables are inserted in the work. Designed for the instruction of youth, and particularly adapted to the U. S. By J. Wallace, Member of the New York Literary Institute, &c. Quid munus Republicæ majus aut melius afferre possimus, quam si Iuventutem bene erudiamus? Cicero. New York: Printed and published by Smith & Forman, at the Franklin Juvenile Bookstores, 195 and 213 Greenwich Street. 1812. pp. viii. and 512. O. A. M. D. G. F.

[J. Wallace, formerly Professor of Mathematics in Columbia College, N. Y., became a Jesuit, and taught Mathematics at Georgetown College: left the Company and became a Professor at Columbia College, S. C. Did he not travel to Egypt in a U. S. frigate, whilst he was attached to G. T. College? B. in Ireland about 1783, ordained priest in Balt. A.D. 1814, d. Jan. 15, 1851, at his residence, Lexington District, S. C. In 1817 or '18 he accompanied (*v.* Dr. England's works, iii., 253) Rev. B. Fenwick on a mission of peace to Charleston, S. C. That mission is aptly described.]

WALMESLEY. *v.* Pastorini and Bibles ad an. 1807.

WALSH, Michael.

[He belonged to Newburyport, and published a work on Book-keeping. According to the information I have received from Salem (where his son John, a lawyer, kept a highly-esteemed private school, but left it in 1824, and removed to the West, where he died about 1835 or '36), he is thought to have been an Irishman and a Catholic. The late Nathan Bowditch, in his memoir of his illustrious father, at p. 25, writes: "Excepting a few lessons which he took in book-keeping from Mr. Michael Walsh, etc." This was about 1791 or '92.]

WALSH, Robert, LL.D.

[B. Balt. 1784 of an Irish father of same name; educated at St. Mary's, Balt., and Georgetown College (where, when about 12 years old, he delivered a poetical address before Gen. Washington). After visiting England, France, and other parts of Europe, he settled in Phila., æt. 25, admitted to the Bar, which he soon deserted (it is said on account of deafness) for the more congenial pursuit of letters. In 1837 he removed to Paris, where for many years he was U. S. Consul, and there resided until his decease, Feb. 7, 1859, æt. 75. He published:]

1810. *Letter on the Genius and Disposition of the French Government;* including a view of the Taxation of the French Empire. Addressed to a Friend. By an American recently returned from Europe. (*Quotations.*) Baltimore: Published by P. H. Nicklin & Co.; also by Hopkins & Earle, Philadelphia; Farrand, Mallory & Co., Boston; E.

F. Backus, Albany; Williams & Whiting, New York; J. Parker, Pittsburgh; and E. Monford, Wellington & Co., Charleston, S. C. 1810. F.

Preface iii, iv, dated Philadelphia, Dec. 2, 1809. pp. 253, 8vo.

["In it he reviewed with ability and severity the policy of Napoleon. It made a profound sensation, passed through four eds. in England, and was reviewed with great favor by the Edinburgh Review." *Appl. Am. Cycl. ad n.*—a 2d ed. Boston. 1810. B. P. L.]

1811–12. *The American Review of History and Politics*, and general Repository of Literature and State Papers. "*Neque enim levia aut ludicra petuntur Præmia.*"—Virgil, Lib. xii. Vol. I. Philadelphia: Printed for Farran & Nicholas. Sold by D. Mallory & Co., Boston; Lyman, Hall & Co., Portland; Swift & Chipman, Middlebury, Vt.; D. W. Farrand & Green, Albany; Philip H. Nicklin & Co., Baltimore; J. W. Campbell, Petersburgh; Maccoun, Tilford & Co., Lexington, Ky.; Morford, Willington & Co., Charleston, S. C.; Patterson & Hopkins, Pittsburgh; and by the Booksellers generally. Fry & Kammerer, Printers. 1811. F.

Small 8vo. I. January, No. I.; February, No. II. 1811. pp. xvi, 408. Appendixes pp. 112.

[It was the *first* Quarterly Review established in America. Dear me! these papists are such *obscurantists!* Mathew Carey is the first to report proceedings of Congress, to establish a well-conducted magazine, to give the idea of book trade sales, to organize Sunday-schools, societies, etc., etc., and Robert Walsh to undertake a Quarterly!

Two vols., eight quarterly numbers (solid papers) were published, but died for want of support. I have not been able to procure the other three vols. The *Review* was republished in Lond., different types.]

1813. *Correspondence respecting Russia between Robert Goodloe Harper and Robert Walsh, Jr.* Phila. 8vo.

[Robert Goodloe Harper, in whose office Mr. Walsh studied law, married a daughter of Charles Carroll of Carrollton, and was the grandfather (?) of the accomplished Miss Emily Harper of Baltimore, a household name with the Catholics of the U. S. At a dinner given at Georgetown, June 5, 1813, he eulogized "Alexander the Deliverer" in a speech of much praise of that monarch and of his rule, etc. On the publication of his address Mr. Walsh replied to it, pointing to the dangerous assertions of Harper's. The latter made an elaborate reply, and Walsh responded with a second letter, after which the speech with the correspondence were published in a volume.—*v.* Duyckink, *Cyclopædia of American Literature*, i. 638, 9.]

1813. *Essay on the future State of Europe.* 8vo.

1817. *The American Register;* or, Summary Review of History, Politics, and Literature. Phila.: Thomas Dobson & Son, at the Stone-House, No.

41, South Second Street. William Fry, Printer. 1817. F.

8vo. I. Pp. xl, and 450. II. Pp. xxxvi, and 464.

1821–37. He edited the *Philadelphia National Gazette.*

1822. *The Museum of Foreign Literature and Science.*

1827–37. *The American Quarterly Review.* 22 vols.

1835. *The Select Speeches of George Canning.* Am. ed. Phila.

1841. *The Select Speeches of William Windham and W. Huskisson.* 8vo. Both last works enriched with biographical sketches.

1819. *An Appeal from the Judgments of Great Britain Respecting the U. S. of America.* Part First, Containing an Historical Outline of their Merits and Wrongs as Colonies; and Strictures upon the Calumnies of the English Writers. "Quod quisque fecit, patitur: auctorem scelus Repetit, suoque premitur exemplo nocens."—*Senec.* Second edition. Philadelphia: Published by Mitchell, Ames & White. William Brown, Printer. 1819. F.

Pp. lvi, and 512–8vo [p. II was never published (?)].

[Allibone informs us that "it was pub'd in the same year both in Phila. and Lond. 8vo—512. 2d ed. 1819. Phila. 2d Lond. ed. 1820, 8vo. Reviewed in N. Am. Review, x. 334, by Edw. Everett; Edinb. Rev., xxxiii., 395, by Lord Jeffrey; and repub. in his contrib. to Edinb. Rev. 1853, 799. Lond. Mon. Rev., xciii., 297. See also Analec. Mag., xiv., 472; xv., 67; xvi., 302, 355; Blackw. Mag., xvi., 634, by John Neal. Marshall, John, LL.D., p. 1227.—For this work he received the thanks of the Legislature of Pennsylvania, by which copies were purchased for the use of the members. 1st ed. is similar to 2d in every respect, except the word *first*, and the errata not printed with it.]

1836. *Didactics: Social, Literary, and Political.* By Robert Walsh. "Endeavor, without intermission, and with good aid soever, to think justly, act uprightly, and live usefully. For the accomplishments of those great ends of rational being—which constitute, in fact, the main securities of worldly happiness—are indispensable a religious conscience, an enlightened judgment, a firm character, an active spirit, and the habit of conscious determination." In two Volumes. Philadelphia: Carey, Lea & Blanchard. 1836. F.

12mo. I. Pp. xii–258. II. iv–268.

Says the author: These materials . . . date since 1810 to the present time. R. W., Philadelphia, February 2d, 1836. *Vide* N. Amer. Rev. xliii, 260, 1. E. A. Poe, in his Literati: Rob. Walsh.—South Lib, Mess, ii, 399.

[He was also a contributor to the *Port-folio*, to *Delaplaine's Repository*, to the *Encyclopædia Americana*, and was for many years Paris correspondent of the *National Intelligencer* and the *Journal of Commerce*. On the death of Ezechiel Sanford (1822), Mr. Walsh completed his publication of the expurgated edition of English poets, with biogr. prefaces, to be completed in 50 vols. 18mo (Phila.: Lea & Blanchard. $25). Mr. S. had only reached vol. 22d.

I am indebted for all these valuable items to Mr. Allibone (*ad n.*), by whom also we are referred to Griswold's "Prose Writers of America"; Duyckinck's "Cyc. of Am. Lit.," i. 6, 38; ii. 37, where Walsh's portrait is given; *Blackwood's Mag.*, xvii., 203 (by John Neal); *N. Am. Rev.*, xliii., 258 (by J. C. Palfrey); *Hist. Mag.*, 1859 (obituary); "The Philadelphia Book," 1836, 72; "Works of T. Jefferson," 1854; "Corresp. of St. John Sinclair," ii., 55; "Mem. Rev. Sidney Smith," 1855, 2 vols. 8vo; Proceed. Mass. Hist. Soc., 1858-60, 231.—The N. Y. Corresp. of the *Bost. Transcript*, March 7, '59, wrote an interesting letter on the demise of R. W., whose last words were: "I die in the faith of my ancestors—in the faith of the Holy Roman Catholic Church."—From a letter of "Laffan" (M. Hennessy, *N. Y. Times*), in the *Bost. Pilot*, we learn that R. W. married a daughter of Jasper Moylan, Esq., a lawyer of Phila., brother to Gen. Stephen Moylan (*v. supra Æd. Burke*), and of the Rt. Rev. Francis Moylan, Bp. of Cork.]

[*v. supra ad n.* Cheverus.]

WARD. *v.* England's Conversion, and *Errata*.

WEEK, *The Office of the Holy*—according to the *Roman Missal* and *Breviary*. Containing the Morning and Evening Service, from Palm-Sunday, to Tuesday in Easter Week; in Latin and English. With a Preface to the Service of Each Day, explaining the Mysteries Represented in the Office and Ceremonies of the Holy Week. The First American Edition. Baltimore: Printed for Bernard Dornin, and sold at his Rom. Cath. Library, 30 Balt. St. G. Dobbin & Murphy, Printers. . . . 1810. pp. 480. 12mo. F.

The text ends 471. Subscribers' names and advertisement form 473-80. At p. 479—adv'd No. 14th, as "printed and published": "*Le Office de la Semaine Sainte*, selon le *Messel* et le *Breviaire* Romain contenant les Office du Matin, les Vepres, etc. Depuis le Dimanche des Rameaux, jusqu'au mardi de Paques, inclusivement. En Latin et en François. Avec des prefaces, placees avant l'office de chaque jour pour en expliquer les mysteries et les ceremonies. Price 150 cents. Premiere edition d'Amerique."

WHITE, *Authentic Documents relative to the Miraculous Cure of Winefrid*—of Wolverhampton, at St. Winefrid's Well, alias, Holy-Well, in Flintshire, on the 28th day of June, 1805. With Observations thereon. By the Rt. Rev. John Milner, D.D., Bp. of Castabala, V.A., F.S.A. Lond. and Cath. Acad. Rome. It is good to hide the secrets of the King; but it is honourable to reveal and confess the works of God.—*Tobias* cxii, v. 7. First

Am. from the 3d Lond. ed. Baltim.: Printed for B. Dornin, and sold at his Rom. Cath. Library, 30, Baltimore-Street. G. Dobbin & Murphy. . . . . . Print. . . . . 1810. pp. 42. 8vo. F.

WHITE, Calvin.

[I am indebted to the courtesy of Richard Grant White, the distinguished writer, for the following only too brief notice:

"Dear Sir: . . . Calvin White was my grandfather. He became a Roman Catholic; but although he was an accomplished scholar, and a writer of clearness and force, he published no books that I heard of: nothing more than sermons, if that, and certainly nothing after he left the Prot. Episcopal Church, which, if I remember rightly what I have been told, was about 1818. I saw in my college days a manuscript of his, in which he set forth the steps by which he went from the Church of England to that of Rome; and it seems to me that, granting his premises, his conclusions could not be denied. This book is unfortunately lost. You will find something about him in Sabine's "Loyalists of the Revolution"; for, although a mere boy then, he was a stout Tory. His was a perfectly pure, honest, and kindly heart. He had both dignity and humor, and was the courtliest gentleman I ever saw, although he was only the parson of a country parish, and had but a small farm besides his little salary. . . .

"I am, Rev'd Sir, yours very respectfully,

"Rich'd Grant White."

I have given this letter to settle the question as to Rev. Mr. White's claim to be reckoned among Catholic writers previous to 1820, as some of my respected correspondents have insisted upon. It is *unfortunate* indeed that his manuscript should have been lost.]

XAVIER, SAINT FRANCIS—

1795. *The Life of Francis Xavier, Apostle of the Indies*—"'Tis not the business of a wise man to dispute about living well, but to live well without dispute." Phila.: Hogan & McEvoy, No. 1, North 3d St.; for Alex. Brodie, 241 South 2d St., January, 1798. pp. 192. 12mo. J. G. S.?

1814. *The Life and Missionary Labours of that Holy Man, Francis Xavier, commonly called The Apostle of the Indies.* "In Labours more abundant." New York: Published by Thomas Bakewell. Paul & Thomas, Printers. 1814. With portrait. pp. vi–180. F.

[A Protestant work.]

APPENDIX.

APPENDIX.

A.

GRASSI.—Rev. John Grassi, an Italian Jesuit, arrived in the U. S. A. D. 1810; was Superior at Georgetown until 1817, when he returned to Italy, and occupied important places; was Rector of the College of Propaganda, and died Dec. 12, 1849, Assistant of Italy. He published:

NOTIZIE *Varie* sullo Stato Presente della Republica degli Stati Uniti dell' America Settentrionale scritte al principio del 1818. Dal P. Giovanni Grassi della Compagnia di Gesù.

> Tempo verrà che fian d' Ercole i segni
> Favola vile a naviganti industri,
> E i mar riposti, or senza nome, e i regni
> Ignoti ancor tra voi saranno illustri.
>
> TASSO, canto XV., st. XXX.

In Roma, 1818. Presso Luigi Perego Salvioni. Col Permesso. pp. viii and 120. 12mo. F.

It has a "Table of the most Remarkable things in the Geography of the United States in Northern America."

—— edizione seconda. Milano. Per Giovanni Silvestri. M.DCCC.XIX. pp. iv and 147. 12mo.

A new Preface, iii, iv, by 'Il Tipografo.'

—— A third edition, accresciuta di recenti Memorie dello stesso Autore. Torino: Chirio e Mina. 1822. pp. 140.

F.

B.

VIEL, Rev. Etienne Bernard Alexandre—S. J.

"Born in New Orleans, Oct. 31, 1736, d. in the College of Juilly, in France, Dec. 16, 1821. He resided many years in Attapacas. He translated Fénelon's *Telemacus* in Latin verse, and in 1816 he published the *Miscellanea Latino-Gallica*, also a French translation of the *Ars Poetica* of Horace, and two of his *Epistles*." Gayarre's Hist'y of Louisiana, Spanish Domination, p. 626, Feller, Biographie Univ. (Ed. 1844).

C.

FAGAN.— Since part of the work was in the printer's hand, I have become indebted to Mr. G. R. Fagan, of J. Fagan & Son, Stereotype Founders, Philadelphia, for the following items: "My father's grandfather, a Catholic, was Capt. John Walsh, of Dublin, who came to Philadelphia about 1750, and settled here. He commanded one of the ships of the Hon. Thomas Fitzsimmons, a Catholic of this city, who afterwards became a member of the U. S. House of Representatives. During the revolution Capt. Walsh commanded a Letter of Marque sailing from this port, called 'The Black Prince," and made a number of captures of British merchantmen. His only daughter married John Fagan (my father's father). He was the builder of the old church of St. Augustine, in this city, destroyed by a mob in 1844."

To this valuable information, I am happy to add some interesting items more closely connected with the name of Augustine Fagan, furnished me by Mr. John Fagan, senior partner of the firm above alluded to: ". . . . Nearly 60 years ago I went as a store-boy to attend in the book-store of Augustine Fagan,

133 South Front Street, in this city. I was no relative. . . . I was with him four years, partly in his store, and some time setting up type in his composing-room above. I remember well the Catholic books you have specified, also *The Key to Paradise*, and *Milner's End to Controversy* . . . After continuing in Front Street, up to 1817, Mr. Fagan gave up the printing business and turned grocer. I left him . . . I think he died in 1823 or '24. He was a Catholic, and a prominent Trustee in St. Mary's Church at the time of the Harold [Hogan] controversy. . . . Fagan and his co-trustees sided with the rebelling clergyman, and he it was who wrote their circular and pamphlets [not all], for he was a man of literary ability. I suppose he came young from Ireland, perhaps in 1803 or '4, for I think he learned the business here.

"I merely remember that two or three of those books were issued by Mr. Dougherty. . . . I cannot recall whether he had a store or not, and suppose he did nothing further in that way. . . . When I finished my printing education, it may interest you to know that I became compositor, proof-reader, and, finally, proprietor of the Stereotype Foundry, established here by J. Howe in 1823. . . ."

The above is a pretty interesting record by a gentleman writing in 1871, Sept. 26, and was an apprentice boy sixty years ago, one who says, "I retired from business eight years ago, relinquishing it to my son Geo. R. Fagan." Oh! for the old gentlemen of the olden style!

D.

WHITE, ANDREW, of the Society of Jesus, came to America with Leonard Calvert, second son of Lord George Baltimore, and wrote a *Relatio Itineris sub finem Aprilis*, 1634, the original is in the Archives of the Domus Professa in Rome. It has been published in Force's Tracts. Also in "*A Relation of the Colony of the Lord Baron of Baltimore*, in Maryland, near Virginia; a Narrative of the First Voyage to Maryland, by the Rev. Father Andrew White, and sundry reports from Rev. Fathers Andrew White, John Altham, John Brock, and other Jesuit Fathers of the colony to their Superior General at Rome. Copied from the archives of the Jesuits' College [Domus Professa] at Rome, by the late Rev. William M'Sherry, of Georgetown College, and presented by the College to the Maryland Historical Society. Translated by N. C. Brooks, A.M., Member of the Society, Baltimore. 1847." pp. 47. 8vo. F.

My copy bears corrections at the hand of Mr. Brantz Meyer. I had made arrangements to have a facsimile of the original taken in Rome: but the fear of the troubles which have since taken place forced the owners of the MS. to bury it with their archives. Part of Fr. White's *Relation* has been embodied in Burnap's *Life of Calvert.* A good Memoir of Fr. White, by Richard H. Clarke, will be found, with a note of several references, in the Baltimore *Metropolitan*, iv. p. 73. *v.* also *Balt. Cath. Almanac*, 1840, '41.

It was my intention to give in an appendix a List of Titles, like the above, of old writers, chiefly missionaries, whose works have either been published lately, or republished; but my list lacks yet half a score titles: Yet I thought to give Fr. White's, as a sample of a feature of the second part of the Bibliography.

E.

MATHEW CAREY

is a household name in the United States as a printer, a bookseller, a poet, a writer, a publicist, an editor, a philanthropist, and a patriot. I do not purpose to give an extensive biography of him. I limit myself to a catalogue of *his* works as far as I have been able to ascertain their titles.

But it is high time that a society were established of such Catholics as take an interest in our Catholic history, and have an inclination for such pursuits, and a regular biographical series of American Catholic writers and men of note, clergy and laity, in a uniform style, was undertaken. The extensive Catholic library of the writer would be at their disposal, and with such men as J. G. Shea, E. B. O'Callaghan, R. H. Clarke, and others, whom I know to be eminently qualified for the purpose, although leading secluded lives in colleges and convents, a work of intense interest could be produced. And it will not only preserve the monuments of Catholic history in the United States, but it would shed much light even on the secular history. For it is a fact that no justice has yet been done to the Catholic literary, political, and religious elements in the history of our beloved country. And in connection with this, I would suggest that an "American Catholic Historical Society" should be established in some city, with a *library* and proper officers. Non-Catholic denominations have such institutions, and they are earnestly encouraged.

As for Mathew Carey's history, he was born in Dublin, Ireland, January 28, 1760, died in Philadelphia September 16, 1839. His last moments were attended by his intimate friend, the Very Rev. Dr. Moriarty, O.S.A., and the Rt. Rev. Dr. Gartland. His father, a wealthy baker, was opposed to Mathew becoming a printer (the great mistake of parents interfering with their sons' honorable inclinations), yet he yielded, and Mathew entered a printing office at the age of fifteen. For *A Letter to the Catholics in Ireland* he was persecuted, and fled to Paris, where he was befriended by Dr. Franklin. He returned after one year, and conducted the *Freeman's Journal.* In October, 1783, with his father's aid, he started the *Volunteer's Journal* with great success, but by his bold writings he drew upon himself the persecution of the government, and, after enduring imprisonment and many vexations, he at last fled, in female disguise, and landed at Philadelphia November 1, 1784. In 1785, January 25, he started the *Pennsylvania Herald* with much success, but it involved him in a difficulty with Colonel Oswald (not *Osborn*, as *Appleton's Cyclopædia* has it). They fought a duel January 1, 1786, and became good friends. The occasion of this duel is interesting. Oswald may be considered the *first Know-Nothing* in America. Being shot through the thigh bone, Carey was laid up for about fourteen months.

In 1791, M. C. married Miss B. Flahavan. He was on the Committee of Health during the prevalence of the yellow fever in 1793. In the same year he founded the Hibernian Society in behalf of Irish emigrants; he took part in forming the Sunday-School Society in the United States in aid of Bishop White; he came in collision with the famous *hybrid*, William Cobbett, but conquered him; he promoted the Printers' Association under the presidency of the veteran Hugh Gaine, the meeting for its foundation took place in New York, the association lasted but a few years, and the trade sales afterwards took its place.

In 1806, a member of the Select Council of Philadelphia, he published a pamphlet in favor of subjecting personal property to taxation as well as real estate. From 1819 to 1833 he published no less than *fifty-nine* separate pamphlets on the subject of the protective tariff *alone*, and some passed through many editions. It is well-nigh an impossibility to give a list of all Carey has published.

Sam. Drake, Esq., has told me that a gentleman wrote to M.

C., asking for a list of the titles of *his* pamphlets, at the same time sending him the list he had already made. Carey answered, with a list of additional titles, remarking at the same time that in his correspondent's list there were titles of pamphlets which he had entirely forgotten! And yet he always wrote in a cogent, clear style; his mind was encyclopædic; he was endowed with a wonderful power of grasping subjects, and an extraordinary logical mind.

Mr. Joseph Reed, son of President Reed, said of him: "Mr. Carey, a man to whom we are all a great deal more indebted than we are aware of, and who is entitled to respect and regard for the generosity of his nature, the extent and variety of his knowledge, and his devoted and disinterested exertions in the public service. He has given more time, money, and labor to the public than any man I am acquainted with, and, in truth, he founded in Philadelphia a school of public spirit. This is bare justice to an excellent citizen."

He was upright, sincere, and charitable. This much for his private character: "For a long series of years he had a charity list," writes Mr. Hunt, "on which were enrolled the names of hundreds to whom he regularly gave, once each fortnight, a donation of groceries and other necessaries of life."

He was indefatigable, for with him *time* was not money, but *merit.*

At the College of Holy Cross, near Worcester, Mass., is preserved an autograph letter of George Washington to Mathew Carey. It was found in Paris by the lamented Rev. George Goodwin, and by him presented to the College. The copy which I here transcribe was kindly furnished me by the Rev. Alexius Jamison, S.J.:

"MOUNT VERNON, 15th Mar., 1785.

"SIR: I purposed so soon as I understood you intended to become the publisher of a News Paper in Philadelphia to request that a copy of your weekly production might be sent to me.—I was the more pleased with this determination when by a letter by my friend the Marquis de la Fayette. I found he has interested himself in your behalf.

"It has so happened, that my Gazettes from Philadelphia, whether from inattention at the Printing or Post offices, or other causes, come very irregularly to my hands. Let me pray you therefore to address those you send me, in the appearance of a letter.—The common paper, usually applied, will do equally well for the cover.—It has sometimes occurred to me, that there are persons who, wishing to read News Papers without being at the expense of paying for them, make free with those which are sent to others; under the garb of a letter it is not presumeable this liberty would be taken.

I am—sir,

Yr. most obedt. servt.,

GO. WASHINGTON.

MR. MATHEW CAREY, Printer of the *Eveng. Herald.*"

For notices of Mathew Carey, *cfr. Our American Merchants*, edited by Freeman Hunt, p. 307. Boston: Crosby & Nichols. 1864. An eloquent and practical notice of its kind; the best I have read.—*Cyclopædia of American Literature.* . . . By E. A. and G. L. Duyckinck. New York: C. Scribner. 1855. Vol. I., pp. 640–2. With Carey's portrait, a striking countenance, the countenance of a *solid* man.—*The New American Cyclopædia.* By G. Ripley and C. A. Dana. New York: D. Appleton. Vol. iv., pp. 431–3, ad n.—*A Critical Dictionary of English Literature.*

By S. A. Allibone. Philadelphia: Childs & Peterson. 1858. Vol. i., p. 340, ad n.—*Dictionary of American Biography*. By F. S. Drake. Boston: Osgood & Co. 1782. P. 161, ad n.—*Carey's Autobiography* in the *New England Magazine*, 1833–34.

1777. M. Carey's first essay was written when he was about seventeen: *On the Subject of Duelling*. Inserted in the *Hibernian Gazette.*

—— In the *American Museum*, Oct., 1789, v. vi. p. 281, Carey published his *Thoughts on Duelling*, and again *Cursory Thoughts on Duelling*, Jan., 1791, v. viii. p. 20. F.

1785. *On the Entrance of Dr. Franklin into the State House of Philadelphia, the day* [Sept. 14, 1785] *of his being appointed President of the Commonwealth of Pennsylvania*, an ode, v. *Am. Museum*, v. i., Feb., 1787. F.

1785, Nov. 9. A paper in reply to Col. Oswald, v. *seq.*

1786, Jan. 16. *The Plagi-scurriliad:* A Hudibrastic Poem. Dedicated to Col. Eleazer Oswald. [Quotations.] By Mathew Carey. Printed and sold by the Author. January 16, M.DCC.LXXXVI. Pp. 30 [4 pp. torn in my copy], 12mo. F.

The interesting history of this splendid satire can be summed up by a few paragraphs from the preface: "Our disputes originated from some illiberal remarks written in his paper [the *Gazetteer*, No. 218] against new-comers. As a new-comer, I thought myself called upon to answer them, which I did in Nov. 9, 1785, under the signature of A CITIZEN OF THE WORLD." The preface plainly hints also at the probability of a personal encounter [v. *supra*, p. 270].

1786, April 20. *Debates and Proceedings of the General Assembly of Pennsylvania.* No t.-p. but, "To his E. Benj. Franklin, President of the Commonwealth of Pennsylvania, LL.D. etc., etc. Honored sir, permit me to dedicate to you these *primitiæ*, or first-fruits of the eloquence of a Commonwealth, etc." *Verso*, Preface. Text, pp. 1–132. 8vo. From Session March 3 to Ap. 1, 1786.—Finis. F.

—— October. "He commenced with several partners the *Columbian Magazine*, but withdrew from it in December."—*Duyckinck*.

1787, January. *The American Museum*, or Repository of Ancient and Modern Fugitive Pieces, etc., Prose and Poetical. Vol. i. No. 1. *The Second Edition*. Philadelphia: Printed by Mathew Carey.—I., from Jan. to June. After t.-p. an address, by M. C., dated June 30, 1787, a blunder of the binder; pp. v–xvi, Subscribers' names, alphabetically, headed by G. Washington, 506 in all. Text, pp. 570, uniform paging. 1st and 2d nos, *Sec. ed.*, pp. 571–6, Contents.—II. July to Dec., t.-p. same; pp. 3–11, Subscribers, *double* column; 13, Dedic. to Lafayette; 15, 16, Preface; pp. 17–598, Text; pp. 1–15, Chronicle; 16–22, Index.

In the Oct. No., "The Prayer of an American Citizen," poetry, by M. C.

1788. III. Jan. to June, t.-p. *same*, iii–xiv, Subscr., double col., arranged by States; xv–xvi, Preface; Text, 27–394. With this No. a regular chronicle of foreign and Amer. events is faithfully given at the end of each No. Index very inaccurate.—IV. July to Dec. Copy of Letter from Gen. Washington, and others; t.-p. same; Dedic. to Gen. Washington; Preface; Subscribers; Text, 17–387; Index.

1789. V. Jan.–June, t.-p. same; Dedic. to Pres. Mifflin; Preface; Subscribers, ever increasing; Text, 18–609; Index, 610–20; Proceedings of Congress; Index.—VI. July–Dec., t.-p. same; Dedic. to Senate and Congress; Preface; Subscribers, 1,596 in all! alphab'y; Text, 23–492, and 1–46; Proceedings of C.; Index.

1790. VII. Jan.–June. *The American Museum*, or, Universal Magazine. Containing Essays on Agriculture, Commerce, Manufacture, Politics, Morals, and Manners; Sketches of National Characters, Natural and Civil History, and Biography; Law Information, Public Papers, Proceedings of Congress, Intelligence; Moral Tales, Ancient and Modern Poetry, etc., etc. Philadelphia: Carey, Stewart & Co. M.DCC.XC." Dedic. to Dr. Carroll, Bishop elect of the Catholic Church, etc., by *The Printers*. Text; 6–34, App. I. Poetry, 1–40; II. Public Papers, 1–44; III. Proceedings of C., 1–44; IV. Foreign Intell., 1–40.—VIII. July–Dec., t.-p. same; diff. type; Text, 4–28; App. I. Poetry, 1–40; II. Public Papers, 1–80; III. Proceedings C., 1–20; VI. Intelligence, 1–48; Index.

1791. IX. Jan.–June, pp. 4–344. App. I. Poetry; II. Public Papers; III. The Gazette, *i.e.*, Intelligence.—X. July–Dec., pp. 5–344; App. I., II., III., as above.—X. July–Dec., 5–308. App. *ut ante*.

1792. XI. Jan.–June, pp. 5–308. App. as before.—XII. July–Dec., iii–iv. Preface signed July 31. It complains of negligent payers, although in the minority, yet a great loss to the printer, and several times a danger of shipwreck. pp. 7–372. App as above. On t.-p. of Dec. No., a notice, dated Dec. 31, announces a discontinuance of the *Museum*, because the ed'r cannot give his attention to it, and of the construction put on the P. O. law by the Phila. P. M., who refused to take the *Museum* into his office. Last page. *End of the American Museum.*

12—8vo. F.

M. Carey was the inspiring soul of the periodical and a copious contributor to it. Every No. had its page of *contents*, each vol.

its index. Marriages and deaths are monthly recorded from all parts of the U. S.

1790. *First Catholic Bible published in the U. S.*, v. *supra*, p. 32. Copies of this Bible are preserved by J. G. S., the Abp. B. (A portion of it was in the lib'y of the late Rev. M. Gallagher, of Springfield, Mass.) F.

1792, Feb. 8. *The Christian Economy.* Translated from the Original Greek of an old manuscript [fiction], found in the Island of Patmos, where St. John wrote his Book of Revelation. Philadelphia: From the press of Mathew Carey, No. 118, Market Street, Feb. 8, M.DCC.XCII. pp. 44. 12mo. [Carey's ?] F.

1793. C. published an *imperfect* account of the fever which ravaged Philadelphia that year. This ppht. seems to be a distinct production (the work was entered in the Clerk's Office Nov. 2, 1792) from the four editions of the *account*, for in

1st ed., 1793, Nov. 14, the preface says: "The imperfect account of the fever I lately published. . . ." Again: "I have printed a small number of copies of this edition. . . ."

2d ed., Nov. 23. *A Short Account of the Malignant Fever lately prevalent in Philadelphia:* with the statement of the proceedings that took place on the subject in different parts of the United States. By M. C. *Second Edition.* Phila.: Printed by the Author. Ded. to the Am. Phil. Socy. pp. viii–112. 8vo. F.

C. begins the preface headed *November* 23, 1793, thus: "When I published the first edition of this pamphlet. . . ."

—— do in French. 8vo. Phila. W. A. A. S. (*a*)

(*a*) In the lib'y of the Worcester Am. Antiquarian Society.

—— *November* 30. *A Short Account*, etc. *Third Edition, Improved.* Phila.: Printed for the Author. pp. 122. 12mo, and 16 pp. List of buried. F.

—— *December* 14. *Observations on Dr. Rush's Enquiry into the Origin of the Late Epidemic Fever of Philadelphia.* Phila.: From the Press of the Author. pp. 23. 12mo. F.

[*An Account of the Bilious Remittent Yellow Fever, etc.* By Benj. Rush, M.D. *Second Edition.* Philadelphia: Dobson. 1794. F.

No allusion made to Carey's remarks.]

1794. Jan. 16. *A Short Account of the Malignant Fever* . . . to word *States.* To which are added, Accounts of the Plague in London and Marseilles, and a List of the Dead. From August to the middle of December, 1793. By M. C. *Fourth Edition,* Improved. Philadelphia: Printed by the Author. pp. viii–160. 8vo. F.

[Uniformly bound with it are the works of Dr. *Jean Deveze,* both in English and French, 145, 8vo; Dr. *W. Currie,* 85, 8vo, on the same subject; and pamphlets on the plague of 1797–98.]

—— —— Translated into German by Carl Erdmann. Lancaster: Jacob Bailey. 1794. pp. 1796. 8vo. F.

1794, Jan. 8. *A Short Account of Algiers,* . . . With a Concise View of the Origin of the Rupture between Algiers and the United States [Lat. quot. from Buchanan]. Phila: Printed by J. Parker, for M. Carey, No. 18, Market Street. pp. 46 [?]. 12mo. F.

—— *The Columbian Muse:* A Selection of American Poetry from various Authors of Established Reputation. New York: Printed by J. Carey, for Mathew Carey. Philadelphia. 1794. pp. 234. 12mo. F.

1795. *Features of Mr. Jay's Treaty.* To which is annexed a View of the Commerce of the United States, as it stands at Present, and as it is fixed by Mr. Jay's Treaty. Phila.: Printed for Mathew Carey by Lang & Ustick. pp. 51. 12mo. F.

—— Nov. 2. *Treaty of Amity, Commerce, and Navigation,* between His Britannic Majesty and the United States of America, conditionally ratified by the Senate of the U. S. at Philadelphia, June 24, 1795. To which is annexed a Copious Appendix. *Second Edition.* Phila.: Printed by Lang & Ustick, for Mathew Carey, No. 118, Market-street. pp. 190. 12mo. F.

1796. *Address to House of Representatives of the United States on Lord Grenville's Treaty.* Phila.: Printed by Sam. Harrison Smith, for Mathew Carey. [By Carey?] pp. 48. 12mo. F.

—— *Miscellaneous Trifles in Prose.* Phila: 18mo. W. A. A. S.

—— *Porcupine's Political Censor.* Phila. [Carey's?]

1799. *January* 16. *A Plum Pudding for the Humane, Chaste, Valiant, Enlightened Peter Porcupine* [William Cobbett]. By his obliged friend, Mathew Carey. Phila.: Printed for the Author. pp. 48. 8vo. F.

—— April 15. *The Porcupiniad.* A Hudibrastic Poem in three Cantos. Addressed to William Cobbett by Mathew Carey. Canto II. and III. Phila.: Printed for and sold by the Author. pp. iv–44. 12mo. F.

1800. *The School of Wisdom;* or, American Monitor. Containing a Copious Collection of Sublime and Elegant Extracts from the most Eminent Writers on Morals, Religion, and Government. [Quot. from Rambler.] Philadelphia: Printed for Mathew Carey, No. 118, Market-street. 1800. (*Copyright* secured.) F.

Preface begins *verso* of t.-p., signed "M. C., December 1, 1800." Preface, pp. ii–iv; Contents, v–xii; Subscribers, 1–4; Text, 5–304. 12mo.

1801. *Carey's American Pocket Atlas.* Containing Nineteen

Maps, viz.: 1, A Map of the United States; 2, Vermont; 3, New Hampshire; 4, Maine; 5, Massachusetts; 6, Rhode Island; 7, Connecticut; 8, New York; 9, New Jersey; 10, Pennsylvania; 11, Delaware; 12, N. W. Territory; 13, Maryland; 14, Virginia; 15, Kentucky; 16, North Carolina; 17, Tennessee; 18, South Carolina: 19, Georgia. With a brief description of each State. Second edition, greatly improved and enlarged, Philadelphia: Printed by H. Sweitzer, for Mathew Carey. No. 118 Market Street. 1801. (*Price Two Dollars.*) Text, pp. 114. 12mo. F.

1802. *Desultory Reflections*, Excited by the Calamitous fate of John Fullerton. Addressed to those who frequent the Theatre and to the Dramatic Critics. *Fourth edition.* New York: Printed and sold by G. F. Hopkins, at Washington's Head. pp. 18. 12mo. F.

1804. *Second Catholic Bible.*

1806. *American Minor Atlas.* Containing twenty maps. B. P. L.

? 1806. *Debates and Proceedings of the General Assembly of Pennsylvania on the Memorial Praying a Repeal or Suspension of the Law Annulling the Charter of the Bank.* Mathew Carey, Editor. Phila.: Carey & Co. pp. 132. 8vo. F.

1808, Nov. 25. Proposal for publishing by subscription a new work, entitled *Persecution not Peculiar to Catholics.* Cath. Lib.—Abp. N. Y.

1810. *Desultory Reflections upon the Ruinous Consequences of the Non-Renewal of the Charter of the U. S. Bank.* 2d ed. Phila.: Fry & Kammerer. 8vo. W. A. A. S.

—— 3d ed. W. A. A. S.

1811. *Carey's Franklin Almanac for the Year* 1811. Being

the third after Leap Year. Philadelphia: Printed for Mathew Carey. F.

—— *Letters to Adam Seybert on the Renewal of the Charter of the U. S. Bank.* 2d ed. Phila.: 8vo. W. A. A. S.

—— *Calm Address to the People of the Eastern States on the Subject of the Representation of Slavery, the Representation in the Senate, and the Hostility to Commerce Ascribed to the Southern States.* Boston. 12mo. W. A. A. S.

1814, Nov. 8. *The Olive Branch;* or, Faults on Both Sides, Federal and Democratic. Philadelphia: Pub. by M. Carey. pp. 252. 12mo. F.

[First ed. it is entered Nov. 8, 1814.]

1815, Jan. 4. Second ed. F.

—— Feb. — Third ed., greatly enlarged and improved. By M. Carey. Phila. and Boston: Rowe & Hooper. pp. xxiii. & 13–336. F.

—— April. *Olive Branch, etc.* Fourth edition, enlarged. Phila.: Printed for the Author. 2 vols. 12mo. pp. 241 and 276. F.

—— September. *The Olive Branch, etc.* Sixth edition, enlarged. Philadelphia: Printed by the Author. pp. 458. 8vo. F.

1816, January. *The Olive Branch, etc.* Seventh edition, enlarged. Middlebury, Vt.: Printed and Published by William Slade, Jun. pp. 468. 12mo. F.

—— [There appeared this year *An Answer to certain parts of a work published by Mathew Carey, entitled The Olive Branch; or, Faults on Both Sides.* By A Federalist. pp. v–232. 12mo. n. d. F.

The work was entered in the Clerk's Office, New York, by

Wm. McKean, February 17, 1816. The preface is dated "United States, December, 1816."]

There is also an eighth edition of the *Olive Branch*, and a ninth was in the press of Jonathan Foster, Winchester, Va., July 4, 1817, under which date Mr. C. published an *Appendix to the Eighth Edition of the Olive Branch.* Philadelphia: M. Carey & Son. pp. 48. 8vo. *v.* 1821. F.

1816. *The Criminal Recorder;* or, An Awful Beacon to the Rising Generation of both Sexes, erected by the Arm of Justice to persuade them from the Dreadful Miseries of Guilt. Collected from Authentic Documents. By A Friend of Man. With six engravings. 1 dollar. [Carey's ?]

—— *Essays on Banking.* By M. Carey. 12mo. 1 dollar.

—— Advt. *Carey's American Pocket Atlas.* 23 Maps. Fourth edition, greatly improved and enlarged. Price $2. v. *supra.*

—— —— *American Minor Atlas.* 4to. Same Maps as previous. Price $1 50.

—— —— *Scripture Altas.* 10 4to Maps. Price $1 50.

—— —— Sheet Maps of the U. S., States and Territories, South America. Price 75 cents.

—— —— —— —— Europe, Asia, Africa. Price 50 cents.

—— —— *Atlas Minimum;* or, A New Set of Pocket Maps of Various Empires, etc. Drawn and engraved by J. Gibson. 18mo. Price $1.

——Advt. (as already printed for Mr. Carey, Philadelphia) *Carey's General Atlas, Improved.* Being a selection of Maps of the World and Quarters. 58 fol. maps handsomely colored. Price $15.

—— do. 4to. Price $5.

1817. Proposals for publishing by subscription the *Religious Olive Branch;* or, Faults on nearly All Sides, establishing by uncontrovertible evidence that the hideous crime of religious persecution has been perpetrated by nearly all denominations of Christians when possessed of power. February 24, 1817, to October, 1834. Abp. N. Y.

R. H. C.

1819, March 6. *Vindiciæ Hibernicæ.*

Says an industrious biographer: "In 1817, the agitation of Catholic emancipation in Ireland urged Carey to the prosecution of a design which he had long had in contemplation. He was still further excited by the publication of William Godwin's novel of *Mandeville* (*Mandeville: a Tale of the 17th Century.* Edinburgh. 1817. 3 vols. 12mo), presenting in powerful [exaggerated] colors a view which Carey considered unjust of the Irish insurrection of 1641. In consequence of this he set to work to prepare an account of his native country which should expose the errors and misstatements of English historians. He made a large collection of materials, and planned his work with great deliberation, but sent his manuscript, as fast as each day's work was completed, to the printer, so that it was in type almost as soon as written. It appeared under the title of *Vindiciæ Hibernicæ* in 1818 (1819 ?), with such success that four editions were called for."

Vindiciæ Hibernicæ; or, Ireland Vindicated: An Attempt to Develop and Expose a few of the Multifarious Errors and Misrepresentations Respecting Ireland in the Histories of May, Temple, Whitelock, Borlase, Rushworth, Clarendon, Cox, Carte, Leland, Warner, Macaulay, Hume, and others, particularly in the Legendary Tales of the Pretended Conspiracy and Massacre of 1641. By M. Carey, Member of the American Philosophical Society and of the American Antiquarian Society, Author of the

Olive Branch, etc., etc. Philadelphia: Published by M. Carey & Son. 1819. pp. xxxvi, and 17–504. 8vo. [v. 1823.] F.

—— *Report on American Manufactures.* Philadelphia. 8vo. W. A. A. S.

—— *Addresses of the Philadelphia Society for the Promotion of National Industry.* Adv. in *New Olive Branch.*

1820. M. C. takes part in the Hogan (St. Mary's) schism, and writes pro-Hogan pamphlets. But he became disgusted and left the apostate to his fate. v. *supra* Hoganiana.

—— *The New Olive Branch;* or, An Attempt to establish an Identity of Interest between Agriculture, Manufactures, and Commerce, and to prove that a large portion of the Manufacturing Industry of this Nation has been sacrificed to commerce, and that Commerce has suffered by this policy nearly as much as Manufactures. Philadelphia: M. Carey & Son. 1820. pp. x–248. 8vo. F.

["This work may be considered as a second edition, much enlarged and improved, of the *Three Letters to Mr. Garnett.*"—*Introd.*

In the last quoted edition we read *verso* of title-place the following note characteristic of the man:

"As this book has been written, and is now published, merely from public motives, no copyright is secured. Should any printer or bookseller in any part of the Union, either from the importance of the subject, the desire of doing good, or the hope of making profit, feel disposed to republish it, he has not only permission, but is invited to carry his views into operation. The writer requests, however, to be consulted, and have two weeks from this day to make corrections, should any be found necessary. March 17, 1820."]

—— *Three Letters to Mr. Garnett on the Present Calamitous State of Affairs.* pp. 238. Adv'd in above.

—— *Address to Congress.* Ruinous Consequences of a Dependence on Foreign Markets for the sale of Flour, Cotton, and Tobacco. Phila.: 1828. pp. 40. 8vo. F.

—— Second edition. 8vo. W. A. A. S.

1821. *Address to W. Tudor, Esq.*, author of the *Letters on the Eastern States,* intended to prove the Calumny and Slander of his Remarks on the *Olive Branch.* Phila. 12mo. W. A. A. S.

—— The *New Olive Branch, etc.* Second edition [?]. Phil: M. Carey & Sons. pp. 346. 8vo.

—— *Memorial to Congress of the Pennsylvania Society for the Encouragement of American Manufactures.* Phila. 8vo. W. A. A. S.

—— [?] *Sketches of Contemporary History.* 8vo. W. A. A. S.

—— *Address to the Farmers of the U. S. on the Ruinous Consequences to their Vital Interests of the existing Policy of this Country.* Second edition. Phila. 8vo. W. A. A. S.

1822. *The Prospect before Us.* Fourth edition. Phila. 12mo. W. A. A. S.

—— *Appeal to Common Sense, Common Justice;* or, Irrefragable Facts opposed to Plausible Theories. Second edition. Phila. 8vo. *Ib.*

—— *Essays on Political Economy, etc., etc., etc.* Phila.: H. C. Carey & J. Lea, Chesnut Street. Sixth edition. pp. x–251. F.

1823, October 26. *Vindiciæ Hibernicæ, etc.* Second edition, enlarged and improved. Phila.: H. C. Carey & J. Lea, Chesnut Street. pp. xx and 21–512. 8vo. F.

[Of 458 subscribers' names, 301 hail from Boston and 53 from the rest of Boston Diocese, *i.e.*, the New England States.]

—— *View of the very great Natural Advantages of Ireland, and the cruel Policy pursued for Centuries towards that Island.* Phila. 8vo. W. A. A. S.

1824. *Political Economist.* From Jan. 24 to May 1. Phila. Vol. I. 8vo. *Ib.*

—— *Examination of a Tract on the Alteration of the Tariff written by Thomas Cooper.* Third edition. Phila. 12mo. *Ib.*

—— *Address before the Philadelphia Society for Promoting Agriculture,* July 20. Phila. 8vo. *Ib.*

—— Fourth edition. 12mo. *Ib.*

—— Fifth edition. 8vo. 1827. *Ib.*

1825. *Canal Policy.* Second edition. Phila. 8vo. *Ib.*

—— *Letters Relating to the Chesapeake and Delaware Canal.* Phila. 8vo. *Ib.*

—— *Exhibit of the Shocking Oppression and Injustice Suffered for* 16 *months by John Randall,* Contractor for the Eastern Section of the Chesapeake and Delaware Canal. Third edition. Phila. 8vo. *Ib.*

—— *Appeal to the Justice and Humanity of the Stockholders of the Chesapeake and Delaware Canal.* Phila. 8vo. *Ib.*

—— *Last Appeal on the same Subject.* Second edition. Phila. 8vo. *Ib.*

—— do. Third edition. *Ib.*

—— *Essays tending to prove the Ruinous Effects of the Policy of the U. S. on the Three Classes, Farmers, Planters, and Merchants.* Addressed to Edward Livingstone, Esq. Phila. 8vo. *Ib.*

—— *Reflections on the Proposed Plan of a College in Philadelphia.* Phila. 8vo. *Ib.*

—— Address to the Public on the same Subject. Phila. 8vo. *Ib.*

—— *Reflections on the Subject of Emigration from Europe with a View of Settlement in the U. S.* Phila. Third edition. 8vo. *Ib.*

—— *Internal Improvement.* Phila. 8vo. *Ib.*

—— *Cursory Views of the Liberal and Restrictive Systems of Political Economy.* Phila. Fourth edition. 8vo. *Ib.*

—— *Political Economy.* Being an Examination of the Treasurer's Report. Phila. 8vo. *Ib.*

1827. *Address of the Pennsylvania Society for the Promotion of Manufactures and the Mechanic Arts to the Public.* Phila. 8vo. *Ib.*

—— *Examination of the Charleston (S. C.) Memorial.* Phila. 8vo. *Ib.*

—— *Memorial of the Citizens of Philadelphia to Congress.* Phila. 12mo. *Ib.*

—— *Preface to Alexander Hamilton's Report on Manufactures, with the Report.* Sixth edition. Phila. 8vo. *Ib.*

—— *Universal Emancipation.* Phila. 8vo. *Ib.*

—— *Address of the Greek Committee to the Citizens of Pennsylvania.* Phila. 8vo. *Ib.*

—— *Letters on Religious Persecution.* Fourth edition. Phila. 8vo. *Ib.*

1828. *Emigration from Ireland and Immigration to the U. S.* Phila. 8vo. *Ib.*

—— *Matter of Fact vs. Messrs. Huskington and Peel.* Phila. 8vo. *Ib.*

—— *Examination of the Boston Report on Free Trade.* Phila. 8vo. *Ib.*

—— or about 1826. *Reflections on the Renewal of the Charter of the Bank of Pennsylvania.* Fourth edition. Phila. 8vo. *Ib.*

—— *To the Friends of Ireland,* assembled at the Court House, Phila., Dec. 1, 1828. Abp. N. Y.—R. H. C.

—— November 7. *A Brief View of the Policy of the Founding of the Colonies of Massachusetts, Rhode Island, West Jersey, Pennsylvania, Maryland, Virginia, and Carolina, as Regards Liberty of Conscience.* Abp. N. Y.—R. H. C.

1829. *Internal Improvement.* Phila. 8vo. W. A. A. S.

—— *Protecting Systems.* Phila. 8vo. *Ib.*

—— *African Colonization.* Phila. 8vo. *Ib.*

—— *Common Sense Addresses to the Citizens of the Southern States.* Fourth edition. Phila. *Ib.*

—— *Autobiographical Sketches in a Series of Letters.* Phila. 12mo. *Ib.*

1830. *Essays on Rail Roads.* Second edition. Phila. 8vo. *Ib.*

—— *Miscellaneous Essays.* Phila. 8vo. *Ib.*

—— *New Olive Branch.* Second edition. Phila. 8vo. *Ib.*

—— March. *Letter to the Editor of the N. Y. Daily Sentinel on Female Wages.* 8vo. *Ib.*

—— *Prospects on and Beyond the Rubicon.* Phila. 8vo. *Ib.*

—— *Review of the Evidence of the Pretended General Conspiracy of the Roman Catholics in Ireland to Massacre all the Protestants that would not join them on the 22d of Oct., 1641.* Third edition. Phila. 8vo. *Ib.*

—— *Essays on the Public Charities of Philadelphia.* Fifth edition. 8vo. *Ib.*

—— *Infant Schools.* Phila. 8vo. *Ib.*

—— *Essay on the Protecting System.* Phila. 8vo. *Ib.*

—— *Annals of Liberality, Generosity, etc.* Third Ser. No. 3. 8vo. *Ib.*

—— *Connected View of the whole Internal Navigation of the U. S.*, with a Map and Statistical Details. Second edition. Phila. 8vo.

—— (?) *A Short Account of the Yellow Fever*, etc. Phila.: 1830. Fifth edition. 8vo. *Ib.*

1831. *Brief View of the System of Internal Improvement of Pennsylvania.* Phila. 8vo. *Ib.*

—— *New Olive Branch.* Address to the Citizens of South Carolina. Phila. 8vo. *Ib.*

1832. *Prospects on the Rubicon.* Part Second. Being Letter on the Prevailing Excitement in South Carolina. Third edition. Phila. 8vo. *Ib.*

—— *The Tocsin.* A Solemn Warning against the Dangerous Doctrine of Nullification. Third edition. Phila. 8vo. *Ib.*

—— *Essay on the Dissolution of the Union*, threatened by the Nullifiers of South Carolina. Second Part. Third edition. Phila. 8vo. *Ib.*

—— *Address to the Liberal and Humane.* Phila. 8vo. *Ib.*

—— *Dissolution of the Union.* Phila. 8vo. *Ib.*

—— *Olive Branch No.* 3; or, An Enquiry Whether an Arrangement is Practicable between the Friends and Opposers of the Protecting System. Phila. 8vo. *Ib.*

—— *The Crisis.* An Appeal to the Good Sense of the Nation against the Spirit of Resistance and Dissolution of the Union. Third edition. Phila. 8vo. *Ib.*

—— *Defence of a Liberal Construction of the Powers of Congress as regards Internal Improvement.* Second edition. Phila. 8vo. *Ib.*

—— *Looking-Glass for the Nullifiers.* Phila. 8vo. *Ib.*

—— *Signs of the Times:* South Carolina Toasts. Phila. 8vo. *Ib.*

—— June 19. *Autograph Letter to Wm. Dunlop, Esq., of New York.* Phila. p. 1. 4to.

—— *Reflections on the Causes that led to the Formation of the Colonization Society*, with a View of its probable Results, etc., etc. Phila. By W. F. Geddes (gratuitous). pp. 19. 12mo. [Section plate of Slave Ship.] F.

—— *May* 29. *Letters on the Colonization Society, etc., etc.*, to the Hon. Charles F. Mercer, M.H.R.U.S. Third edition, enlarged and improved. Phila. Young, Printer. pp. 32. 12mo. [Same plate, and map of Monrovia.] F.

1833. *Seventh ed.* Phila. 8vo. W. A. A. S.

—— *March* 25. *Review of the Evidence, etc.* v. an. 1830. Abp. N. Y.—R. H. C.

—— *Prospects beyond the Rubicon.* Phila. 8vo. W. A. A. S.

—— Same subject continued. 2d series. Phila. 8vo. *Ib.*

—— *Appeal to the Wealthy of the Land*, Ladies as well as Gentlemen, on the Character, Conduct, Situation, and Prospects of those, whose sole Dependence for Subsistence is on the Labor of their Hands. 2d ed. Phila. 8vo. *Ib.*

—— ? *Strictures on Mr. Lee's Exposition of Evidence on the Sugar Duty*, in behalf of the Committee appointed by the Free Trade Convention. 8vo. *Ib.*

—— *Feb.* 19. "*Look out before you Leap.*" Addresses to the Citizens of the Southern States, etc. 2d ed., improved. Phila. Printed by Haswell & Harrington (gratuitous). pp. 24. 8vo. F.

1835. *March* 20. *Letters on the Colonization Society, etc., etc.* Tenth edition. For sale by Carey & Hart, Phila. Price five dollars per hundred. Stereotyped by L. Johnson. pp. 32. 12mo. [Map and plate as above, and view of Monrovia.] F.

1836. *Sept.* 8. *Vindication of the Small Farmers, the Peasantry and the Laborers of Ireland.* Abp. N. Y.—R. H. C.

1837. *A Plea for the Poor.*

—— *Vindiciæ Hibernicæ.* Another edition, perhaps the *third*, published in that year by R. P. Desilver, 255 Market Street, was found in the library of the late Rev. W. O'Reilly, of Newport, R. I.

1838, *Aug.* 20. *Letter on Irish Immigrants*, addressed to Rt. Rev. Bp. Hughes. Abp. N. Y.—R. H. C.

—— *Philosophy and Common Sense.* Practical Rules for the Promotion of Domestic Happiness. Phila. 8vo.

1839. *A Vindication of the Separate System of Prison Discipline.* Abp. N. Y.—R. H. C.

[Is not this by H. Carey, the son ?]

☞ *Thoughts on Penitentiaries and Prison Discipline.*

[A defence of the *Auburn Prison Discipline.* Hassard's *Life of Abp. Hughes*, p. 329. "On the fly-leaf the Abp. wrote: I have read this pamphlet through, and whatever theory may be adopted, it seems to me that the well-known principles of human nature will be its soundest *basis.* Facts here quoted are far from sufficient to prove the great superiority of modern improvement in prison discipline. It seems to me that the fear of punishment is the strongest restraint on the depraved; and this barrier will be entirely broken down if prisons be changed from places of punishment to houses of correction, where the wolf and the tiger, after having preyed upon humanity, are to be wheedled out of their ferocity and soothed into kindness by the influence of an ill-timed, sickly affectation of humanity. The difference of punishment between murder and robbery has saved many a life, when otherwise the life and purse would be taken together." *Ib.*]

CAREY, James, "was a brother of Mathew (one *t*, if you please —so his descendants demand), and should have been, if he were not, a Catholic. In my notes for Mathew Carey's biography I have a mass of unpublished matter about him and his family. Another brother of M. C. was

—— JOHN, who edited in London the official Letters of Washington, 2 vols. 8vo, 1795—the 1st ed. ever published. He edited also many classical works for London publishers, including Ainsworth's Quarto Latin Dictionary." Laffan: M. H.

Peter Pennyless, a Fragment, by J. C., was published in the *Am. Mus.*, viii, 207.

[About *the one t* my friend is mistaken. Mathew's descendants were not yet born when the great publisher spelled his name with only *one t.* "A Letter from G. Nicholas, of Kentucky, to his friend in Va.," etc. Lexington: Printed. Philadelphia: Reprinted, By James Carey, No. 16, Chesnut-street. 1799. F. J. Thomas does not mention him nor his brother either.]

Henry C. Carey, Esq., so well known for his works on social science, of American economists *facile princeps*, in a very courteous letter (Feb. 25, 1867) writes: "My uncle John was great as an editor, but not at all known as an author, and in his day the tendency here to classical republications was very small indeed [his illustrious brother *did create* a tendency]. . . . He has a grand-daughter in this country who is quite a remarkable woman, although known only as the author of a condensation of my large work, 'A Manual of Social Science.' My uncle William was quite an author, and of his works I have seen large volumes. . . . . . Of many of my father's works I have no copy. . . . My uncle John was never in this country. My uncle William was here for about a year.]

CAREY, W. Paulett, "1768–1839, brother of John and Mathew C., took part in the struggle of 1798, and, subsequently removing to England, distinguished himself as an eloquent advocate of art, artists, and political reform, and as the author of many critical contributions to the periodicals of the day. Among those in whose behalf his pen was early enlisted may be mentioned Chartrey, Hogan, Gibson, and James Montgomery." *Allibone.* At p. 383, *American Museum,* in vol. iv., Oct., 1788, will be found a poem on *Indian Incantation.* In vol. v., p. 335 (Ap., 1789) and fol., we have an *extract from a periodical entitled "The Miscellanist," written in Dublin, by W. P. Carey.* In said periodical edited by his brother we have (viii., App. I., p. 26) *Song, to Absent Laura;* ib., p. 29, *Elegy to Laura.* Scene, *A Churchyard,* and a sumptuous monument of a deceased patriot in view.—ix., p. 16. App. I., *Verses on a Lady singing in an adjoining arbour;* ib., p. 19. Elegiac Sonnet, *On the indisposition of a young lady who caught cold coming from the play;* xi., 1792, App. I., 17. *The Orphan;* xii., 1792, App. II. *Damon's Farewell.*

—— ? (Wm.) *Memoirs of the Patronage and Progress of the Fine Arts in England and Ireland,* with Anecdotes of Patrons and Artists. Port. of Lord de Tabley, and inscription in author's handwriting. 8vo, half-calf, 5s. 1826.

[Adv. in a Dublin catalogue.]

—— At the foot of "*Love in a Village,* by Bickerstaff, *as per-*

formed at the New Theatre, in Philadelphia, from the Press of M. Carey, March 1, M.DCCC.XCIV." [F.], we read an adv't of "BOOKS printed by MATHEW CAREY, and for sale, at his store, No. 118, Market-Street, Philadelphia": there are 35 titles, of which the following, I believe, belong to works *edited* if not *composed* by himself:

The Romp, a Musical Entertainment. Price 1s.

The Farmer, a Comic Opera. Price 1s.

Don Juan, a Pantomimical Ballet. Price 1s.

No Song, no Supper. Price 1s.

The Misses Magazine. Price, bound in two volumes, 11s. 3d.

A brief Examination of the Observations of Lord Sheffield on the Commerce of the United States. Price 5-8ths of a dollar.

American Jest Book, in two parts, with very neat engravings. Price, bound, 3-8ths of a dollar.

History of Charles Grandison, abridged. Price, a fifth of a dollar.

Select Poems. Price, a sixth of a dollar.

Charms of Melody, a choice collection of valuable Songs, 2s. 10^{1}d.

Beauties of Fielding. 3s.

Beauties of Blair. 3s. 9d.

The Ladies' Library. 6s. 6d.

[The other titles are of works only printed by M. C., or such as I have given elsewhere.]

ADDENDA ET FRAGMENTA.

Whilst the work was in press, and chance there was not to alter the forms, I came across items, whereof some were titles in full, some only fragmentary hints, and again some complements of titles already given *in corpore*. I give them here, and I know that this little gathering of *Memos* will be acceptable to the Bibliophilos.

ARISPE, D. Miguel Ramos de—

In 1814 (Philadelphia ?), I am told, was published a translation of the following Spanish work on Mexico:

Memoria, que el Doctor D. [*Don*] *Miguel Ramos de Aríspe, Cura de Borbon, y Diputado en las presentes Cortes Generales y Extraordinarias de España por la provincia de Coahuila, una de las cuatro internas del Oriente en el Reyno de México*, presénta a el Augusto Congreso, sobre el Estado Natural, Politico, y Civil de su dicha Provincia, y las del Nuevo Reyno de Leon, nuevo Santander, y los Texas, con exposition de los defectos del systema general, y particular de sus goviernos, y de las Reformas, y nuevos establecimientos que necessitan para su prosperidad. Cadiz: En la imprenta de D. José Maria Guerrero, calle de el Emperador numero 191: año de 1812. pp. 60. 4to. F.

My researches to secure the U. S. edition have proved fruitless: hence I give the title of the original Spanish, of which I lately came in possession.

BANDOLE, Abbe—November, 1781. *Address delivered to Congress, the Supreme Executive Council, and the Assembly of Pennsylvania, etc., etc.*, who were invited by His Excellency the Minister of France, to attend in the Roman Catholic Church of Philadelphia, during the celebration of Divine Service, and thanksgiving for the capture of Lord Cornwallis. Carey's *American Museum*, Vol. IV., July, 1788, pp. 28 and 30, and the *Catholic Church in the U. S.*, p. 217, where the name is spelt *Bandale.*

BROSIUS. *Reply of a Roman Catholic Priest to a Peace-loving Preacher of the Lutheran Church.* Lancaster: Printed by John Albrecht & Co. 1796. pp. 196. 16mo. G. T. C.

[v. *ante*, p. 54. "From the signatures it appears that the disputants were F. B. Melscheiner and F. X. Brosius, priest." Rev. J. S. Sumner, S.J.]

BURKE, Aedanus—*Letter to the Governor of South Carolina*, giving an Account of the Execution of a man named Love, at Ninety-six, in November, 1784." *The American Museum*, by Mathew Carey, Vol. I., Numb. II. The second edition. February, 1787.

CALMET'S works were sold, April, 1872, in N. Y., by Bangs Merwin & Co., with an additional Vol. V., and the following title:

Sacred Geography; or, A Companion to the Holy Bible, etc., originally composed by Edward Wells, D.D., now verified and corrected, also augmented by a series of geographical excursions, etc., etc., etc. Published under the direction of the editor of Calmet's *Dictionary of the Holy Bible,* intended as a *fifth volume* to that work. With maps and plates. Charlestown, 1817. *v. ante*, p. 73.

CAREY, MATHEW.—To titles at Appendix C, add—

1821. *The New Olive Branch*, etc., etc. Second edition. Philadelphia: M. Carey & Sons. F.

This edition is connected with *Essays on Political Economy* (pub. 1822), and connects the paging from 252 to 408. A Dedication to the "Citizens of the U. S." is signed March 17, 1820.

—— *Address to the Farmers of the U. S.*, etc. Second edition. F.

It hitches on the *Essays* at p. 409 to 463. Then *The Farmer's and Planter's Friend*, pp. 466–546. An Index is given embracing the three words.

1822. *Essays on Political Economy.* F.

Flying leaves i., ii., do.; Subscriber's name, *different* from previous 2 pp.; *Preface* same; *Addresses*, etc. Sixth edition, text 7–251. *The New Olive Branch*, etc., as above, 253–382.

Continuous with it: *Address to Congress; being a View of the Ruinous Consequence on the Dependence on Foreign Markets*, etc., Second edition. First published, May 10, 1820. pp. 383–463.

The Farmer's and Planter's Friend. pp. 466–546.

An index to the whole volume. F.

—— *Essays on Political Economy*, etc., etc. By M. Carey, Member, etc. | Quotations. | Philadelphia: H. C. Carey & I. Lea, Chesnut Street. 1822. F.

Blank i., ii.; *Approbations:* 2 unnumb. pp.; Tables of National Industry; t.-p.; Subscribers' Names; Preface, vii.–x.; another t.-p.; *Addresses of the Philadelphia Societies for the Promotion of National Industry.* | Quotation. | *Sixth Edition.* Philadelphia: 1822. Text, 7–251.

1823, Oct. 20. *Vindiciæ Hibernicæ:* or, Ireland Vindicated, etc., etc., etc. By M. Carey, etc. Second edition, enlarged and improved. | Quotation. | Philadelphia: H. C. Carey & I. Lea, Chesnut Street. F.

Flying leaf, *Recommendations:* t.-p.; 2 pp. Dedication, signed *Philadelphia: March* 6, 1819; pp. v.–viii., *Subscribers' Names* [300 in Boston and 33 in N. E., whilst only 93 in N. Y., in Philadelphia 9]; 2 pp. Key to References; Prefaces, ix.–xxiv.; Text, 21–306; Index.

1829, Sept. 18. *Letters on Religious Persecution* proving that that most heinous crime has not been peculiar to Roman Catholics, etc., etc., etc. In Reply to a libellous attack on the Roman Catholics, in an Address delivered to a Society of *Irish Orange Men*, styling themselves The Gideonite Society. With an Appendix, containing an Address to a Number of Respectable Citizens, principally Clergymen, who had recommended Blanco White's "Evidences against Catholicism." By a Catholic Layman. Fifth Edition, improved. | Quotation. | Philadelphia: Printed by Griggs and Dickinson. pp. 50, 8vo. F.

1832, *January*. *Reflections on the Causes that led to the formation of the Colonization Society.* With a view of the probable Results, etc., etc., etc. By M. Carey. Philadelphia: Printed by Wm. F. Geddes (gratuitous). pp. 19, 8vo. F.

With *a Section of A Slave Ship*, and a *View* of Monrovia.

—— April 26. *Letters on the Colonization Society*, etc., etc., etc., addressed to the Hon. C. F. Mercer, etc. By M. Carey. Second Edition, enlarged and improved. Young, Printer, Philadelphia. F.

pp. 32. 8vo.

—— May 29. Same as above. Third Edition, enlarged and improved. pp. 32. 8vo. F.

Maps, etc.

1833. July. *Appeal to the Wealthy of the Land,* . . . on the Character, Conduct, Situation, and Prospects of Those whose sole Dependence for Subsistence is on the Labour of their Hands. By M. Carey. | Quotations. | *Second Edition, Improved.* Philadelphia: Stereotyped by L. Johnson, No. 6 George Street. (*For gratuitous distribution.*)

8vo. My copy, *imperfect*, ends at p. 36. F.

1834. May 16. *Review of the Evidence on the Legendary Tale of a General Conspiracy of the Roman Catholics of Ireland "to Massacre all the Protestants that would not join with Them," on the Twenty-third of October*, 1641. Extracted from the *Vindiciæ Hibernæ.* | Quotation. | By M. Carey, M.A.P.S., author of the *Olive Branch*, etc. Seventh Edition. Philadelphia: Stereotyped and printed by L. Johnson. For sale in *Philadelphia*, by Eugene Cummiskey; *New York*, by John Doyle; *Baltimore*, by John Myres; *Charleston*, by S. Dease; *Hartford*, by the Editors of the *Catholic Press* [then conducted by the Rev. James Fitton, I believe]. pp. 24. 8vo. F.

1835. February 19. "*Look before you Leap.*" Addresses to the Citizens of the Southern States: being a Solemn Warning against the Destructive Doctrine of a Separation of the Union, advocated in the late Message of H. E., George McDuffie, Gov. of S. C., as leading inevitably to Civil War, with all its awful consequences. | Quotation. | Second Edition, Improved. By the author of *The Olive Branch.* Philadelphia: Printed by Haswell & Harrington. (Gratuitous.)

pp. 24. 8vo. v. *supra*, p. 290. F.

—— March 20. *Letters on the Colonization Society*, etc., etc., etc. Tenth Edition [a new edition, with many additions, and different types]. For sale by Carey & Hart, Philadelphia. Price Five Dollars per Hundred. Stereotyped by L. Johnson.

pp. 32, double col. 8vo. F.

—— Same as above. Eleventh Edition. F.

1836. Sept. 8. *Vindication of the Small Farmers, the Peasantry, and the Laborers of Ireland*, etc., etc., etc. | Quotations. | By M. Carey, M.A.P.S., M.A.A.S., etc. Dedicated to Daniel O'Connell, M.P. Philadelphia: For sale at the stores of Carey & Hart, Robert Desilver & Co., and Eugene Cummiskey. *No copyright is secured for this pamphlet; whoever chooses, may republish it, provided the edition be handsome.*

pp. 20. 8vo. F.

1837. Jan. 24. *A Plea for the Poor:* An Enquiry How far the charges against them of Improvidence, Idleness, and Dissipation are founded in Truth. | Quotations. | By a Citizen of Philadelphia. (*Fifth Edition.*) Philadelphia: GRATUITOUS. N.B. Three editions of this pamphlet (1,250 copies) have been published and distributed gratuitously at the expense of the author. The fourth, 250 copies, was published at the expense of a benevolent citizen of Philadelphia; the present edition, the 5th, also 250 copies, is published at the expense of a respectable Catholic clergyman of Baltimore.

pp. 16. 8vo. F.

CAREY'S ?—*A Vindication of the Early History of Ireland.* This pamphlet in my possession has no title-page, ends with p. 24, at the bottom whereof it is written "121 pages missing."

CAREY, WILLIAM—

The Dying Peasant. *v.* Appendix to M. Carey's *Vindication of the Small Farmers*, p. 19, where W. C. is also quoted as the "author of the *Critique on the Painting of Death on the Pale Horse*," and as "Honorary Correspondent of the Royal Institute of France, etc., etc." v. *supra*, p. 292.

CARROLL, BISHOP—"*Liberality.* At the annual artillery election dinner in Boston, the 6th inst. [June, 1791], the blessing was asked by the rev. dr. Parker, a Protestant Episcopalian, and thanks returned by the right rev. Bishop Carroll, a Roman Catholic." Carey's *Am. Mus.*, 1791, Vol. IX., App. iii., p. 43.

CASA, MONSIG. G. DE LA—Abp. of Benevento. *Galateo;* or, A Treatise on Politeness and Delicacy of Manners; from the Italian of Monsig., etc. Also, The Honor of the Table, with the whole art of carving; illustrated with a variety of cuts. | Quot. from Chesterfield. | Baltimore: Printed for George Hill. B. Edes, Printer. 1811. 24mo. Translator's pref. xiii. Casa's Text, 183. Additions, 185–274. F.

CHALLONER. *Pensez-y-Bien;* ou, Reflexions sur les Quatre Fins Dernieres. Nouvelle edition, augmentée d'un Chapitre sur la Devotion à la Sainte Vierge, de plusieures histoires édifiantes, de paroles [*sic*], de prières dévant la sainte Messe, et d'une table des matières très étendue. *Tolle et Lege.* Prenez et Lisez. A New York: De l'Imprimerie de J. Desnoues, No. 7, Murray Street. Permissu Superiorum. An 1814. pp. 336. 14mo. G. T. C.

At p. 87, I have doubtingly ascribed to Bp. Challoner. *The Grounds, etc.* Since I have come across "Grounds of the Old Religion; or, General Arguments in favour . . . Controvertists, modestly proposed to the Consideration of his countrymen. By the Ven. and R. R. Richard Challoner, D.D., Bishop of Debra, V. A. L. *Thus sayeth* . . . . The Fifth edition. London : Printed by J. P. Coughlan, Duke-Street, Governor-Square. M,DCC,XCVIII. pp. 50. Brief Account of the Life of Dr. R. Ch., by Rev. J. Milner, F.S.A. p. iv. Preface. Text 1–230, and Contents.

—— At p. 109, note to *England's Conversion*—Is not this the work of Bp. Challoner? Milner in his Life mentions that C. was the author of *The Young Gentleman instructed in the Grounds of the Christian Religion.* If this is the work mentioned above, the query in the note is herewith answered in the negative, of course.

O'CONOR (p. 212): *Impartial History.* . . . Belfast: Reprinted by Joseph Smyth. 1815.

CUNNINGHAM, LETITIA.—"*The Case of the Whigs, who loaned their money on the Public Faith, Fairly stated,*" including a Memento for Congress to review their engagements, and to establish the Honour and Honesty of the United States of America. Phila.: Francis Bailey. 1783. pp. 51. 12mo.

[Some not only suggest but maintain that L. C. was a Catholic, but I can find no records. A well-instructed non-Catholic bookseller in New York informs me that for a time she entered a convent in Europe.]

FAIRCLOUGH.—An address delivered before the Hibernian Society of Alexandria, D. C., in St. Mary's Church, on St. Patrick's Day, the 17th March, 1825, by the Rev. Jos. W. F., A.M. (Chaplain). *Join with your piety brotherly love, and with brotherly love charity.* 2 Epis. Peter, 1 chap., v. 5–7. Published by order of the Society. Alexandria: Printed by Henry Pittman. 1825. p. 16. 12mo. F.

[In 1817 was published in London the following: "On the Rule of Faith : in Reply to Mr. Joseph Fletcher, Minister of the

Independents at Blackburn, and Author of the Lectures on the Roman Catholic Religion. By Joseph Fairclough, 'Si ignoras, disce: si nosti, erubesce.' *Optatus Melivetanus bib. sec. contra Parmenianum.* London: Sold by Keating & Co., Duke-street, Grosvenor Square, etc. pp. 31, 8vo. F.

On the last page, unnumb'd, we read: "On the Infallibility of the Church, *by the same Author*, in Reply to Mr. Fletcher's Lectures, *will be published toward the end of June, or early in July.* It is said that this is the same Mr. F. who came to this country with R. Baxter, S.J. (v. *supra*), only a deacon. Mr. Fairclough, after being ordained, was stationed in Alexandria, Va., where his name is still honored. He remained there until 1831 (?), when his successor, taking charge of the place, submitted the late incumbent to very ignominious treatment. I think Mr. F. subsequently returned to England. v. Baxter, p. 29.

FIELD, M.—Oakey Hall, in his Manhattaner in New Orleans, has some items, I am told, relating to M. Field.

GASTON, Judge, vindicated from the charge of perjury in taking office under the Constitution of N. C. Bp. England's *Works*, IV. 103, *seqq.* The charge was preferred by Rev. Rob. Breckenridge, of Baltimore.

GOTHER.—P. 133. Bishop Challoner published an Abridgment of the *Papist*, etc. Gother was Chaplain to R. Holman, Esq., at Warkworth, in Northamptonshire, and there the boy Milner lived also with him.

HAROLD, Rev. W. V.—

The concluding remarks of Dr. Harold's sermon (*v. supra*, p. 136) have been transcribed by Rev. James Fitton into his *Sketches of the Establishment of the Churches in New England.* Boston: *P. Donahoe.* 1872. pp. 111–116.

HAY. *An Abridgment of Christian Doctrine.* By the Rt. Rev. Bp.—With some alterations in the language. Published with the approbation of the Right Rev. Bp. Carroll. Printed for B. Dornin, and sold by him at his Roman Catholic Library, No. 30, Baltimore Street, Baltimore. Geo. Dobbin & Murphy, Printers. 1809. pp. 108. 24mo. G. T. C.

Hoganiana. p. 173. The titles of pamphlets published on the Hogan schism and given in the Text amount to one hundred and forty-two.

Imitation, The, of the Bl. Virgin. *supra,* p. 176. In the *Catholic World* for July, 1872, at p. 569, this work is credited to Fr. Francis Arias, a holy and learned Spanish Jesuit.

KEWLEY, JOHN.—

An Enquiry into the Validity of Methodist Episcopacy, with an Appendix containing two original Documents never before published. By an Episcopalian of the State of Maryland. Wilmington: Printed by Joseph Jones, for the Author. 1807.

Title, verso blank. Epistle dedicatory, 4 pp. to iv. Text, 5–68. Appendix, 10 pp. without folios.

[While Rector of St. George's Church, N. Y., Mr. Kewley became a Catholic, went to Europe and entered a religious order. J. G. Shea. *v. Sketches of the Church in N. E.,* by Rev. J. Fitton. Boston: P. Donahoe. 1872. pp. 283, where the name is spelt KEELY.]

LARZELIERE [?], I.—[A Catholic Priest at Mount Holly, near Philadelphia, about A.D. 1800—said to have published something. My inquiries from a Rev. official in Phila. resulted in the information that "no records go back as far as 1800. Mount Holly was in the Diocese of Philadelphia." *v. Houdet,* p. 174.]

O THELOS !

And now I lay down my pen. The rack on which my mind has been since I issued the circular (July 31, 1871!) can be imagined only by inspecting the heap of letters received—some encouraging, others discouraging—some even charging me with treading on the corns of the writers who "had intended," and actually "planned," aye,—had "collected materials," etc., etc.

I PARVE LIBER.

☞ PLEASE, kind readers, brothers, bookworms, and all of that ilk, send me corrections, and castigations, that I may publish them all (with proper acknowledgments) in the *Second* Part, so continuously paged in Arabic numbers as to make them of easy binding with this volume.

The Lord help us! but by-and-by we shall yet get a (sublunary) perfect Bibliography that will stand a monument to the fact that no other converted nation can exhibit such a noble record of earnest endeavors to publish works calculated to create a healthy Christian spirit. The Catholic literature in the United States previous to 1820, scanty as it may appear, must be allowed to have been in advance of the money-making, sickly, riding-on-both-sides-of-the-fence efforts of more recent dates. Mathew Carey was wrong in publishing all kinds of works—albeit, there are allowances to be made in his favor; and it would be unjust to look upon him as the prototype of wishy-washy modern Catholic publishers or book-sellers. *Bernard Dornin* was the prototype of the true and honest Catholic publisher. Had Dornin lived *hisce temporibus*, he'd die of starvation—he was too honest.

The reader is at perfect liberty to agree or not to agree with these remarks. Yet

"To be or not to be; that's the question,"

AND,

FINIS CORONAT OPUS!

VALETE!

INDEX.

ERRATA.

Page	Line
14	12. *For* Témuquana, *read* Timuquana.
15	18. *For* (Frambach ?), *read* (Schneider).
	[Dr. J. G. Shea has a MS. copy of Coleny's England and the other Northern Reformed Countries reconciled to Rome, made by his great-grandfather in 1767.]
20	24. *For* 64 68, *read* 64–68.
26	ult. *For* MDCCXXIV., *read* MDCCXCIV.
40	16. *For* composed, *read* prepared.
42	7. *Cancel* words, "This puzzle is rendered more intricate by the following title:" *and read*, "Thus we have:"
42	15. For *justicatives*, read *justificatives*.
65	ult. *For* most, *read* more.
74	7. *For* O'Callaghan, *read* O'Gallagher.
87	23. [In connection with authorship of *Grounds*, see *Addenda* infra.]
73	15. *Dele* posthumous.
107	9. For *infra*, read *supra*.
105	1. *Read* "DOCTRINE, CATHOLIC—and Principles explained; with a brief Account of the *Conversion of the Duchess of York* (one of the Royal Family of England) as written by herself: also, a Sketch of the Life and an Account of the Conversion of Sir Michael Ramsay to the Catholic Church by Archbishop Fénelon, as given by Ramsay himself. *Highly interesting*. New York: William Higgins, No. 16 Barclay Street. 1817. A. Spooner, Printer, Brooklyn. Pp. 92. 24mo. J. G. S."
114	21. *Read* "Pious Reflections for every Day in the Month. Newburyport. 24mo. J. G. S."
132	ult. *For* the work, *read* this last edition.
164	12. *For* De, *read* the.
169	13. *For* J. J., *read* T. J.
208	21. *For* reverend, *read* revered.

NOTE.—I cannot allow this last page to go to press without expressing my sentiments of deep gratitude to Dr. J. G. Shea for his gratuitous and unwearied kindness in giving me all the aid with which his extended knowledge on kindred subjects has so bounteously strengthened my efforts.

www.ingramcontent.com/pod-product-compliance
Lightning Source LLC
LaVergne TN
LVHW020223110826
845151LV00003B/814

* 9 7 8 1 4 2 5 5 3 2 0 7 9 *